THE HIDDEN

THE HEART OF ENGLAND

By Peter Long

© Travel Publishing Ltd.

Regional Hidden Places

Cambs & Lincolnshire
Chilterns
Cornwall
Derbyshire
Devon
Dorset, Hants & Isle of Wight
East Anglia
Gloucs, Wiltshire & Somerset
Heart of England
Hereford, Worcs & Shropshire
Kent
Lake District & Cumbria
Lancashire & Cheshire
Lincolnshire & Nottinghamshire
Northumberland & Durham
Sussex
Thames Valley
Yorkshire

National Hidden Places

England
Ireland
Scotland
Wales

Hidden Inns

East Anglia
Heart of England
Lancashire & Cheshire
North of England
South
South East
South and Central Scotland
Wales
Welsh Borders
West Country
Yorkshire
Wales

Country Living Rural Guides

East Anglia
Heart of England
Ireland
North East of England
North West of England
Scotland
South
South East
Wales
West Country

Published by: Travel Publishing Ltd, 7a Apollo House, Calleva Park, Aldermaston, Berks, RG7 8TN

ISBN 1-904-43404-5

© Travel Publishing Ltd

First published 2001, second edition 2003,

Printing by: Ashford Colour Press, Gosport

Maps by: © Maps in Minutes ™ (2003)
© Crown Copyright, Ordnance Survey 2003

Editor: Peter Long

Cover Design: Lines & Words, Aldermaston

Cover Photograph: The Crown Inn, Old Dalby, Melton Mowbray, Leicestershire

Text Photographs: © www.britainonview.com

FOREWORD

The **Hidden Inns** series originates from the enthusiastic suggestions of readers of the popular **Hidden Places** guides. They want to be directed to traditional inns "off the beaten track" with atmosphere and character which are so much a part of our British heritage. But they also want information on the many places of interest and activities to be found in the vicinity of the inn.

The inns or pubs reviewed in the **Hidden Inns** may have been coaching inns but have invariably been a part of the history of the village or town in which they are located. All the inns included in this guide serve food and drink and some offer the visitor overnight accommodation. A full page is devoted to each inn which contains a coloured photograph, full name, address and telephone number, directions on how to get there, a full description of the inn and its facilities and a wide range of useful information such as opening hours, food served, accommodation provided, credit cards taken and details of entertainment. **Hidden Inns** guides however are not simply pub guides. They provide the reader with helpful information on the many places of interest to visit and activities to pursue in the area in which the inn is based. This ensures that your visit to the area will not only allow you to enjoy the atmosphere of the inn but also to take in the beautiful countryside which surrounds it.

The **Hidden Inns** guides have been expertly designed for ease of use and are printed in full colour. **The Hidden Inns of the Heart of England** is divided into seven chapters each of which is laid out in the same way. To identify your preferred geographical region refer to the contents page overleaf. To find a pub or inn and details of facilities they offer simply use the index to the rear of the guide or locator map at the beginning of each chapter which refers you, via a page number reference, to a full page dedicated to the specific establishment. To find a place of interest, again use the index to the rear of the book or list found at the beginning of each chapter which will guide you to a descriptive summary of the area that includes details of each place of interest.

We do hope that you will get plenty of enjoyment from visiting the inns, pubs and places of interest contained in this guide. We are always interested in what our readers think of the inns or places covered (or not covered) in our guides so please do not hesitate to write to or e-mail us. This is a vital way of helping us ensure that we maintain a high standard of entry and that we are providing the right sort of information for our readers. Finally if you are planning to visit any other corner of the British Isles we would like to refer you to the list of Travel Publishing guides to be found at the rear of the book.

Travel Publishing

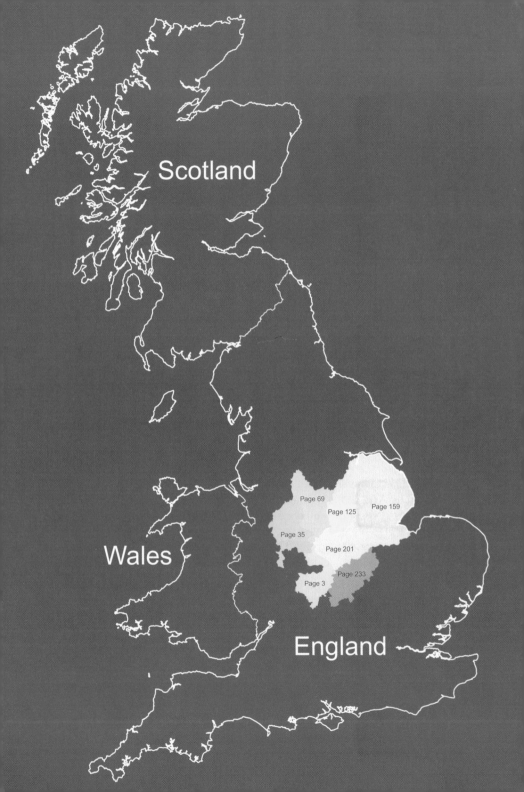

Scotland

Wales

England

CONTENTS

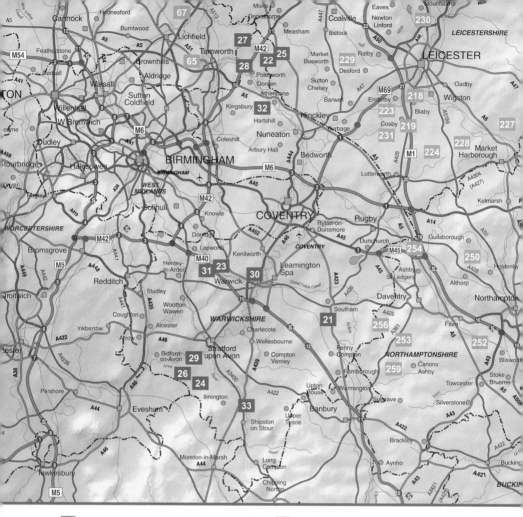

Please note all cross references refer to page numbers

WARWICKSHIRE

A rich vein of medieval and Tudor history runs through Warwickshire and the romantic ruins of Kenilworth Castle, the grandeur of Warwick Castle and

Bridge over Avon, Stratford

the elegance of Royal Leamington Spa set the tone for this most delightful of counties. However, it is Stratford-upon-Avon that is most visitors' focal point and, known throughout the world as the birthplace of William Shakespeare, the old part of the town is completely dominated by this exceptional man, who lived from 1564 to 1616. Along with the various timber-framed houses that are linked with the Bard, Stratford is also the home of the Royal Shakespeare Company.

Another town that has found fame through one of its citizens is Rugby, as it was a pupil who, in the early 19th century, broke the rules of football during a match and in so doing founded the game that bears the name of the town. Close by is the ancient village of Dunchurch, often dubbed the 'Gunpowder Plot Village' as it was here that the conspirators waited to hear if they had succeeded.

While Stratford is the obvious focal point for most visitors to Warwickshire, the region boasts any number of attractive and peaceful villages and hamlets well off the beaten tourist track.

Warwickshire's waterways form an important and extensive part of the 2,000 miles of Britain's inland network, boasting as it does long stretches of the Oxford Canal, as well as restored lengths of the Stratford Canal and the upper Avon.

Village after village along the Rivers Avon, Arrow or Alne, many relatively untouched since Tudor

Warwick Castle

times, reflect some of the best traditional architecture and scenery to be found in the region, and the hilltops revealing breathtaking views of the surrounding countryside.

Dusk over Stratford upon Avon

The West Midlands and the extreme north of the county of Warwickshire is dominated by the major cities of Birmingham and Coventry. It often gets overlooked by visitors but repays a closer look. It is an area rich in natural beauty, with a wealth of beautiful gardens, some excellent museums and historic buildings, and a long and distinguished industrial and cultural heritage.

ARBURY HALL

George Eliot was born on the Arbury Hall estate, where her father was land agent; in Mr Gifgil's Love Story she portrays Arbury as Cheverel Manor, and gives detailed descriptions of many of the rooms in the house, including the Saloon and the Dining Room – comparing the latter, unsurprisingly given its grandeur, to a cathedral. The Hall's grounds include a delightful 10-acre garden with a real air of tranquillity.

ARROW

The village of Arrow is interesting to stroll around (despite some development) - as is the pretty stream that divides Arrow and Alcester. Though fruit farming around here is much rarer than it used to be, there are still to be found delicious fresh dessert plums for sale in the late summer and early autumn.

Nearby **Ragley Hall** is a genuine 17th century treasure. The Warwickshire home of the Marquess and Marchioness of Hertford, it is a perfectly symmetrical Palladian house set in 400 acres of parkland and gardens landscaped by Capability Brown. One of England's great Palladian country houses, it was inherited by the eighth Marquess in 1940 when he was only nine. During the Second World War the house was used as a hospital, and thereafter became almost completely derelict. In 1956 the Marquess married, and he and his wife set about making the Hall their home. All the main rooms have been redecorated in colours similar to the original ones that would have been used, and the process of restoring and improving continues. This magnificent stately home boasts James Gibb's elegant Baroque plasterwork in the Great Hall, as well as Graham Rust's stunning 20th century mural, The Temptation. A tour takes in Ragley Hall's fabulous collection of treasures from a bygone age, featuring paintings (including some modern art), china, furniture and a goodly assortment of Victorian and Edwardian dolls and toys. The Stables house an impressive carriage collection.

The main formal garden, to the west of the Hall, descends in a series of wide terraces, now entirely occupied by roses.

Ragley Hall

The rest of the garden, covering 24 acres, consists of shrubs and trees interspersed with spacious lawns providing vistas across the 400 acre park. The lake, created in 1625, is now used for fishing, sailing, swimming and water skiing; there is also a lakeside picnic area. The cricket pitch is in regular use. A country trail of about two miles wends its way through the park and the woods, to end at a very popular adventure playground. The Hall also boasts licensed terrace tea rooms. Special events such as craft fairs, gardeners' weekends, dog trials and outdoor concerts are held throughout the year.

BEDWORTH

This small town was once part of the North Warwickshire coalfield established at the end of the 1600s. Local people were largely responsible for the building of the **Coventry Canal**, running from Coventry to Fradley near Lichfield and completed in 1790, 22 years after work on it began. It was constructed to connect the fast-growing town with the great new trade route, the Grand Trunk – and to provide Coventry with cheap coal from the Bedworth coal field.

French Protestant families fleeing persecution sought refuge here, bringing with them their skill in silk and ribbon weaving. The **Parish Church**, completed in 1890, is a good example of Gothic Revival. Its grounds include a scented garden. The open air market and main shopping precinct share the town's central All Saints Square with the splendid Chamberlaine almshouses, founded by a 17th century rector of Bedworth, the Rev Nicholas Chamberlaine. Close by, the Old Meeting church dates from 1726 and is one of the earliest nonconformist chapels in the region. Bedworth's award-winning **Miners' Welfare Park** contains some of the finest spring and summer bedding layouts in the region, as well as areas devoted to tennis, bowls, pitch and putt, roller skating and cricket.

CHARLECOTE

The National Trust's **Charlecote Park** is a magnificent stately home occupying extensive grounds overlooking the River Avon. Home of the Lucy family since 1247, the present house was built in the mid-1500s. Thomas Lucy was knighted here by Robert Dudley, Earl of Leicester, deputising for Elizabeth I, who spent two

Charlecote Park

nights here in 1572. The house was comprehensively modernised during the 1700s, but when George Hamilton Lucy inherited it in 1823 he took the decision to 'turn the clock back' and create interiors according to rich Victorian

'Romantic' ideals of the Elizabethan era.

The house, apart from the family wing which is still used by descendants of these early Lucys, has not been changed since. The lavish furnishings of the house include important pieces from William Beckford's Fonthill Abbey sale in 1823. A treasure-trove of historic works of sculpture and painting, no visitor can fail to be impressed by the house's sheer magnitude, grace and beauty.

The park was landscaped by Capability Brown and reflects his use of natural and man-made features complementing each other. The park supports herds of red and fallow deer (in about 1583 the young William Shakespeare is alleged to have been caught poaching Sir Thomas' deer; years later he is said to have taken his revenge by using Sir Thomas as his inspiration for the fussy Justice Shallow in *The Merry Wives of Windsor*), as well as a flock of Jacob sheep first introduced here in 1756.

Charlecote Mill is situated on the site of an earlier mill mentioned in the Domesday Book, at which time it was valued at six shillings, eight pence (33p). In 1978 this 18th century building was restored with the help of volunteers from Birmingham, and the west waterwheel was repaired at the expense of the BBC for their film of George Eliot's novel, *The Mill on the Floss*.

COMPTON VERNEY

Before crossing the Fosse Way, the Roman road that runs from Exeter to Lincoln passes **Compton Verney Manor House**. For many years closed to the public, this magnificent manor has been renovated and is now open to visitors. An exquisite collection of works of art has been assembled, including British portraiture, European Old Masters and modern works, along with a unique collection of British Folk Art. Workshops, evening talks, lectures and special events bring to life the processes and inspiration behind some of these great works. The manor house stands in 40 acres of parkland landscaped by Capability Brown and rich in flora and fauna, with a lake, arbour, stirring stone obelisk, Victorian watercress bed, Cedar of Lebanon, and Adam Bridge. The handsome avenue of Wellingtonias lines what was once the entrance to the estate.

COUGHTON

The **Parish Church** of this very pretty village was built by Sir Robert Throckmorton between 1486 and 1518. It has six bells which were restored in 1976 but are still carried in their original wooden frame. Inside there are some interesting oddments: a faceless clock, fish weather vanes and a dole cupboard from which wheaten loaves were distributed to the needy.

The crowning glory of the village is one of the great Tudor houses, **Coughton Court**, home of the Throckmorton family since 1409. The family were very prominent in Tudor times and were instigators of Catholic emancipation, playing a part in the Gunpowder Plot – the wives of some of the Gunpowder Plotters awaited the outcome of the Plot in the imposing central gatehouse. This, and the half-timbered courtyard, are particularly noteworthy, while inside there are important collections of paintings, furniture, porcelain and other family items from Tudor times to the present day.

This National Trust property has

Coughton Court

extensive gardens and grounds, a lake, a riverside walk and two churches to add to the interest. The fountain pool in the courtyard leads out to formal paths of lime trees. Spring heralds a magnificent display of over 100,000 daffodils and other spring blooms. Also on site are the Tudor Restaurant serving coffee, lunches and teas, an attractive gift shop and a plant centre.

A little way east of Coughton, at **Kinwarton** just south of the B4089, there stands another National Trust property in the shape of **Kinwarton**

Dovecote. This circular 14th century dovecote still houses doves and retains its 'potence', a pivoted ladder by which access is possible to the nesting boxes. Visitors can home in every day from April to October.

DUNCHURCH

'The gunpowder plot village': on November 5th, 1605, the Gunpowder Plot conspirators met at the Red Lion Inn, Dunchurch, to await the news of Guy Fawkes' attempt to blow up the English Houses of Parliament. The Red Lion still exists today, as a private residence known as **Guy Fawkes House**. This attractive village with its rows of thatched cottages has a 14th century church built by the monks of Pipewell Abbey, with one of the oldest parish registers in England.

Such was the considerable trade in looking after travellers who stopped over in Dunchurch during the great coaching days (up to 40 coaches a day stopped here), it is said that every property in the centre of the village was at some time an inn or ale house. For centuries Dunchurch has been a popular stopover point for travellers on the main Holyhead-London road. A coaching stop to take on fresh horses, Dunchurch was also the staging post for pupils, masters, parents and visitors travelling to Rugby

School. Many famous and important people have stayed in the village over the centuries, including Princess Victoria, Longfellow, the Duke of Wellington and William Webb Ellis of Rugby Football fame. Today, the village is in a designated conservation area with a lovely village green complete with village stocks and maypole, charming 16th, 17th and 18th century buildings, many of which retain the traditional Warwickshire thatched roofs. In 1996 the village won the prestigious Best Kept Large Village in Warwickshire award.

The Old Smithy on the Rugby Road is believed to have been the inspiration for Henry Wadsworth Longfellow's poem *Under the Spreading Chestnut Tree*.

FARNBOROUGH

The National Trust's **Farnborough Hall** is a lovely honey-coloured stone house built in the mid-1700s and the home of the Holbech family for over 300 years. The interior features some superb plasterwork, and the delightful grounds include a terrace walk, 18th century temples and an obelisk.

FENNY COMPTON

This charming village close to **Burton Dassett Hills Country Park** and just half a mile from the **Oxford Canal** provides endless opportunities for scenic walks along the edge of the **Cotswold Scarp**.

Burton Dassett Park itself is distinguished by rugged open hilltops topped by a 14th-century beacon with marvellous views in all directions.

HENLEY-IN-ARDEN

Perhaps the finest old market town in Warwickshire, its mile-long High Street brimming with examples of almost every kind of English architecture from the 15th century onwards. Many old timber-framed houses were built with Arden oak, but little remains today of the **Forest of Arden**, the setting for Shakespeare's *As You Like It*. The forest's stocks were greatly diminished in the 1700s by the navy's demand for timber. Among the many sights of interest are the 15th century **Church of St John the Baptist** and the ruins of **Beaudesert Castle**, home of the de Montfort family.

Henley-in-Arden

ILMINGTON

Along the northeastern Cotswolds, at the foot of the Wilmington Downs, lies the village of Ilmington. This eye-catching place has several lovely old houses. Its part-Norman church, which features oak furnishings by Robert Thompson of Yorkshire, is approached through a Norman arch. This is truly a hidden place and one of the most picturesque one could hope to find. Lying in the valley between the Campden and Foxcote hills, it is surrounded by green fields and Cotswold countryside. Here there are fine old stone cottages with roses round the doors, and gardens full of The village's name means 'the elm grown hill'. It was made famous on Christmas Day 1934, when the first radio broadcast by George V was introduced by Walton Handy, the village shepherd, and relayed to the world from **Ilmington Manor**, the fine Elizabethan house once owned by the de Montfort family. The remains of a tramway, once the main form of transport to the village, can still be seen.

The nearby **Ilmington Downs** are, at 850 feet, the highest point in the county, commanding fine views of the surrounding country. Across the B4632 you will pass **Meon Hill**, where an Iron Age fort stood dominating the valley.

KENILWORTH

Although the town was here before the Domesday Book was compiled, Kenilworth's name is invariably linked with its castle. Today the remains of this castle stand as England's finest and most extensive castle ruins, dramatically ensconced at the western edge of the town.

Kenilworth Castle's red sandstone towers, keep and wall glow with an impressive richness in the sun, particularly at sunrise and sunset. Here you can learn about the great building's links with Henry V (who retired to Kenilworth after the Battle of Agincourt), King John, Edward II and John of Gaunt. The tales of this great fortress, immortalised (if enhanced) in Sir Walter Scott's novel *Kenilworth* written in 1821, are many and varied. The marvellous Norman keep,

Kenilworth Catsle

the oldest part of the ruins, was built between 1150 and 1175. John of Gaunt's Great Hall once rivalled London's Westminster Hall in palatial grandeur. After Simon de Montfort's death at the Battle of Evesham in 1265, Kenilworth was held by his son. At that time the castle was surrounded by the Kenilworth Great Pool, a lake covering about 120 acres.

An audio tour takes visitors on a revealing journey around the Castle, recounting stories of Kenilworth's turbulent past. There are fine views from the top of Saintlowe Tower, and lovely grounds for exploring and picnicking, as well as beautifully reconstructed Tudor gardens. Special events throughout the year include a festival of Tudor Music, Saxon and Viking exhibitions, medieval pageantry, various re-enactments, plays and operas in the grounds and much more. The remains of **Kenilworth Abbey** can be seen in the churchyard of the Norman parish church of St Nicholas in the High Street. Much of interest was discovered during excavations and there are many relics on display in the church, including a 'pig' of lead. It is said that this formed part of the roof at the time of the Dissolution but was then melted down and stamped by the Commissioners of Henry VIII.

KINGSBURY

Kingsbury Water Park boasts over 600 acres of country park, with loads to see and do, including birdwatching, picnic sites, nature trails, fishing and good information centre. There is also a cosy café and special unit housing the park's shop and exhibition hall. Also with the park, **Broomey Croft Children's Farm** makes for an enjoyable and educational day out for all the family, with a wealth of animals housed in renovated early 19th century farm buildings.

LAPWORTH

Here where the Grand Union and Stratford Canals meet, handsome Lapworth boasts some characterful old buildings. At Chadwick End, a mile west of the A4141, **Baddesley Clinton** is a romantic, medieval moated manor house which has changed little since 1633. Set against the backdrop of the Forest of Arden, this National Trust-owned property has had strong Catholic connections throughout its history. There is a tiny chapel in the house, and secret priests' holes, used to hide holy fathers during the fiercely anti-Catholic times during the reign of Charles I. The grounds feature a lovely walled garden and herbaceous borders, natural areas and lakeside walks. More modern additions to the site include the second largest ice rink in the country. Lunches and teas are available.

LONG COMPTON

Just a short distance from the Oxfordshire border, this handsome village lies close to the local beauty spot known as **Whichford Wood**. It is a pleasant Cotswold village of thatched stone houses and some antique shops. A mile or so to the south of Long Compton, straddling the Oxfordshire border, are the **Rollright Stones**, made up of the King Stone on one side of the lane, with the other two stone groupings – known as the King's Men and the Whispering Knights – on the other. Legend has it that this well-preserved stone circle is a king and his men, tricked by a sorceress into falling under her spell, and then petrified.

NUNEATON

Originally a Saxon town known at Etone, Nuneaton is mentioned in the Domesday Book of 1086. The 'Nun' was added when a wealthy Benedictine priory was founded here in 1290. The Priory ruins left standing are adjacent to the church of St Nicholas, a Victorian edifice occupying a Norman site which has a beautiful carved ceiling dating back to 1485.

The town has a history as a centre for coal-mining, which began in Nuneaton as early as the 14th century. Other industries for which the town has been famous include brick and tile manufacture and ribbon-making on hand looms. As the textile and hatting industries boomed, the town began to prosper. Today's Nuneaton is a centre of precision engineering, printing, car components and other important trades.

Nuneaton Museum and Art Gallery, located in Riversley Park, features displays of archaeological interest ranging from prehistoric to medieval

times, and items from the local earthenware industry. There is also a permanent exhibition of the town's most illustrious daughter, the novelist and thinker George Eliot.

Born to a prosperous land agent at Arbury Hall in 1819, Eliot (whose real name was Mary Ann Evans) was an intellectual giant and free thinker. She left Warwickshire for London in adulthood, and met George Henry Lewes, a writer and actor who was to become her lifelong companion. Lewes, married with three children, left his family so that he and Eliot, very bravely for the time, could set up house together. Eliot's novels return again and again to the scenes and social conventions of her youth, and are among the best written works of English literature.

ROYAL LEAMINGTON SPA

This attractive town boasts a handsome mixture of smart shops and Regency buildings. **The Parade** is undoubtedly one of the finest streets in Warwickshire. It starts at the railway bridge, dives between a double row of shops and comes up again at the place marked with a small stone temple announcing 'The Original Spring Recorded by Camden in 1586'.

In 1801 very few people knew of the existence of Leamington, but by 1838 all this had changed. By this time the famous waters were cascading expensively over the many 'patients' and the increasingly fashionable spa was given the title 'Royal' by permission of the new Queen, Victoria. **The Pump Rooms** were opened in 1814 by Henry Jephson, a local doctor who was largely

Royal Leamington Spa

responsible for promoting the Spa's medicinal properties. This elegant spa resort was soon popularised by the rich, who came to take the waters in the 18th and 19th centuries. Immediately opposite the Spa itself are **Jephson's Gardens** containing a Corinthian temple which houses a statue of him. The town's supply of saline waters is inexhaustible, and a wide range of 'cures' is available, under supervision, to this day.

Warwick District Council Art Gallery and Museum in Avenue Road boasts collections of pottery, ceramics and glass, as well as some excellent Flemish, Dutch and British paintings from the 1500s to the present.

RUGBY

The only town of any great size in north-eastern Warwickshire. Rugby has a **Market Place** surrounded by handsome buildings and the striking Church of St

Andrew that was built by the Rokeby family after their castle had been destroyed by Henry II. The old tower dates from the 1400s. With its fireplace and 3 foot-thick walls, it looks more like a fortress and was, indeed, a place of refuge.

Rugby is probably most famous for its **School**, founded in 1567. Originally situated near the Clock Tower in the town, it moved to its present site in 1750. There are many fine buildings, splendid examples of their period, the highlight being the school chapel, designed by William Butterfield. These buildings house treasures such as stained glass believed to be the work of Albrecht Durer, the 15th century German artist and engraver.

There are few places in the world where you can gaze with any certainty over the birthplace of a sport that gives pleasure to millions. The game of Rugby originated here at the school when William Webb Ellis broke the rules during a football match in 1823 by picking up and running with the ball. The **James Gilbert Rugby Museum** is housed in the original building where, since 1842, the Gilberts have been making their world-famous rugby footballs. This Museum is crammed with memorabilia of the game and its development.

Rugby Town Trail is a two-hour walk that brings to life the town's history from its Saxon beginnings to the present day.

The walk begins and ends at the **Clock Tower** in Market Place. This edifice was intended to commemorate the Golden Jubilee of Queen Victoria in 1887, yet it was not completed until 1889 because over-indulgent citizens had dipped too deep into the Tower funds to feast and drink at the Jubilee. The Trail takes in many of the town's main tourist attractions, including the house where Rupert Brooke was born, and his statue in Regent Place. Caldecott Park in the centre of town has beautiful floral displays, trees and a herb garden. Picnicking areas and a play area are two more of the highlights of this lovely park, and there are also facilities for bowls, putting, tennis and boules.

Rugby is bounded by two of the greatest Roman roads, Fosse Way and Watling Street, which meet just northwest of Rugby, at **High Cross**, one of the landmarks of the area.

The town is as far inland as it is possible to get in the British Isles, yet Rugby is an excellent centre for all kinds of water sports and aquatic activities. The Oxford Canal winds its way through the borough, and the Rivers Avon, Leam and Swift provide good angling, pleasant walks and places to picnic.

Cock Robin Wood is a nature reserve on Dunchurch Road, near the junction with Ashlawn Road. Here the visitor will find extensive areas of oak, ash, rowan, cherry and field maples, as well as grassy areas and a central pond, a haven for insects, frogs and butterflies.

The **Great Central Walk** is a four-mile ramble through Rugby. Along the way visitors will encounter an abundance of wildlife, plants and shrubs, as well as conservation areas and picnic sites.

RYTON-ON-DUNSMORE

This village is home to the **Henry Doubleday Research Association** at Ryton Gardens. This organic farming and gardening organisation leads the way in research and advances in horticulture. The grounds are landscaped with thousands of plants and trees, all organically grown. Also on site are a herb garden, rose garden, garden for the blind, shrub borders and free-roaming animals. **Ryton Pools Country Park** is a 100-acre country park opened in 1996. The 10-acre Ryton Pool is home to great crested grebes, swans, moorhens and Canada geese. There is also an attractive meadow area for strolling or picnicking, a Visitor Centre, shop and exhibition area. **Pagets Pool** near the north-eastern end of the park is one of the most important sites in Warwickshire for dragonflies, with 17 species including the common blue, emperor dragonfly and black-tailed skimmer. Other highlights include guided walks and a model railway run by Coventry Model Engineering Society.

STRATFORD-UPON-AVON

After London, many visitors to England put Stratford-upon-Avon next on the itinerary, and all because of one man. William Shakespeare was born here in 1564, found fame in London and then retired here, dying in 1616. Needless to say, the places connected with his life and work have become meccas for anyone interested in the cultural history, not just of these islands, but of the entire world.

Each of the houses associated with the Bard has its own fascinating story to tell, and staff at the houses are happy to guide visitors on a journey encompassing what life might have been like in Stratford-upon-Avon during Shakespeare's day.

With the help of a £300,000 grant, the half-timbered house that is **Shakespeare's Birthplace** has been returned to the way it would have looked in his day. Household inventories, books and pictures have been assembled, and a room thought to have been his father John's workshop was been re-created with the help of the Worshipful Company of Glovers.

Further along, on Chapel Street, stands **Nash's House**. This half-timbered building was inherited by Shakespeare's granddaughter, Elizabeth Hall, from her first husband, Thomas Nash. It now contains an exceptional collection of Elizabethan furniture and tapestries, as well as displays, upstairs, on the history of Stratford. The spectacular Elizabethan-style knot garden is an added attraction. Next door, in New Place, Shakespeare bought a house where he spent his retirement years, from 1611

to 1616. Today all that can be seen are the gardens and foundations of where the house once stood. An exhibit in Nash's House explains why this, Shakespeare's final home in Stratford, was destroyed in

Royal Shakespeare Theatre

the 18th century. Opposite New Place is the **Guild Chapel**, and beyond this is the Grammar School, where it is believed that Shakespeare was educated.

Hall's Croft in Old Town is one of the best examples of a half-timbered gabled house in Stratford. It was named after Dr John Hall, who married Shakespeare's daughter Susanna in 1607. This impressive house contains outstanding 16th and 17th century furniture and paintings. There is also a reconstruction of Dr Hall's 'consulting room', accompanied by an exhibition detailing medical practices during Shakespeare's time. Outside, the beautiful walled garden features a large herb bed; visitors can take tea near the 200-year-old mulberry tree or have lunch in the restaurant here.

Hall's Croft is near **Holy Trinity Church**, an inspiration for many poets and artists because of its beautiful setting beside the River Avon. It is here that Shakespeare is buried. Dating partly from the 13th century, it is approached down an attractive avenue of limes. The north door has a sanctuary knocker, used in the past to ensure any fugitive who reached it 37 days' grace. Shakespeare's wife Anne Hathaway and their daughter Susanna and her husband John Hall are also buried here.

Shakespeare is not the only illustrious name to have associations with the town. **Harvard House** in the High Street, dating from 1596, was the childhood home of Katherine Rogers. Her son, John Harvard, went to the American Colonies in the early 1600s and founded the university named after him in 1636. In 1909 Harvard House was restored and presented to Harvard University. It boasts the most ornately carved timbered frontage in the town. Cared for by the Shakespeare Birthplace Trust, it houses the nationally important Neish Collection of Pewter.

There are many other fascinating old buildings in Stratford. The old market site in Rother Street has a history dating from 1196, when a weekly market was granted by King John. In the square is an ornate fountain-cum-clock tower, a gift from GW Childs of Philadelphia in the jubilee year of Queen Victoria. It was unveiled by the actor Sir Henry Irving, who in 1895 became the first Knight of the Stage.

Stratford has become a mecca for theatre-lovers, who flock to enjoy an evening at one of the town's three theatres. The first commemoration of Shakespeare's passing was organised by the actor David Garrick (of Garrick Theatre and the Garrick Club fame), 150 years after the Bard's death. People have been celebrating this illustrious poet and playwright's life and times ever since. The **Royal Shakespeare Company** has an unrivalled reputation both in the UK and worldwide, and wherever the RSC perform, the audiences are certain of witnessing performances of the highest standard. The **Royal Shakespeare Theatre** opened in 1879 with a performance of *Much Ado About Nothing* starring Ellen Terry and Beerbohm Tree. The season was limited to one week as part of a summer festival. It was so successful that, under the direction of FR Benson, it grew to spring and summer seasons, touring the nation in between. In 1925, because of the excellence of the performances and direction, the company was granted a Royal Charter. Sadly, a year later the theatre was destroyed by fire. At the time, playwright George Bernard Shaw sent a one-word telegram: Congratulations! Apparently the building was a bit of an eyesore, but there are few such buildings in today's Stratford. The company, undeterred, continued by giving performances in cinemas while a worldwide fundraising campaign was launched to build a new theatre, which was opened on 23rd

Anne Hathaway's Cottage

April, 1932, the 368th anniversary of the Bard's birth. A tour of the RSC theatre gives visitors the opportunity to discover what goes on behind the scenes and to see the RSC collection of over 1,000 items.

Quite apart from the industry that has grown around Shakespeare and his life and times, Stratford boasts a number of other world-class attractions. Stratford's **Butterfly Farm** provides a specially designed and constructed habitat for Europe's largest collection of butterflies. There is also an area devoted to Insect City and, for the brave of heart, Arachnoland where the world's largest spider, rain forest scorpion colonies and other 'spinners' can be seen in perfect safety.

The Royal Shakespeare Theatre Summer House on Avonbank Gardens is home to the **Stratford Brass Rubbing Centre**, which contains a large collection of exact replicas of brasses of knights and ladies, scholars, merchants and priests of the past.

A mile west of Stratford is the village of Shottery, the birthplace of Anne Hathaway, Shakespeare's wife. Here visitors will find the Elizabethan farmhouse now known as **Anne Hathaway's Cottage**, and can retrace the steps which the courting couple, who married in 1582, might have taken.

UPPER TYSOE

From Upper Tysoe there is a lovely walk south over **Windmill Hill** (which actually has a windmill on it), leading to the church on the edge of **Compton Wynyates Park**, with views of the attractive Tudor manor below – a refreshing bit of brick building in this Cotswold-edge stone country.

UPTON HOUSE

Here on the border with Oxfordshire, Upton House is a late 17th century National Trust property built of the mellow local stone. The house was remodelled in 1927-9 for the second Viscount Bearsted to house his growing art collection and also to modernise the premises. The collections in the house are the chief attractions, featuring paintings by English and Continental Old Masters including El Greco,

Brueghel, Bosch, Hogarth and Stubbs. Brussels tapestries, Sèvres porcelain, Chelsea figures and 18th century furnishings are also on display. In the fine gardens, in summer there can be seen the typically English scene of white-clad cricketers; in winter, the Warwickshire Hunt hold their meet here.

WARMINGTON

The **National Herb Centre** enjoys a great location on the northern edge of the Cotswolds on the B4100 close to the Warwickshire-Oxfordshire border. A centre for research and development work for the UK herb industry, the site has been developed with an eye towards providing visitors with a fascinating range of activities and sights. The Plant Centre has one of the widest selections of plants, trees and shrubs with herbal uses in the country. The Herb Shop stocks a range of herbs, health foods and gifts, many produced on site.

WARWICK

Over the past ten centuries **Warwick Castle** has witnessed some of the most turbulent times in English history. From the era of William the Conqueror to the grand reign of Queen Victoria, the Castle has left us a fascinating legacy to enjoy today. Dominating the town, it is surely everyone's ideal of a medieval building, one of the country's most splendid castles and certainly one of the most visited. It still serves as a home as

well as retaining the greater part of its original masonry. Standing by the River Avon, Warwick is in a good defensive position and became part of Crown lands as recorded in the Domesday Book in 1086.

A tour of this palatial mansion takes you from the grim austerity of the original dungeons with their gruesome torture chambers to the gloomy but sumptuous opulence of rooms later adapted for comfortable living. The castle's magnificent State Rooms, once used to entertain the highest members of the nobility, house some superb art treasures including works by Holbein, Rubens and Velasquez. As the castle is owned by Madame Tussaud's, striking waxworks play their part in the displays. In the castle's Ghost Tower, visitors can learn of the dark and sinister secrets surrounding the fatal stabbing of Sir Fulke Greville who is said to haunt the premises to this day. In the Great Hall visitors come face to face with Oliver Cromwell's death mask. And the armoury houses one of the best private collections in the country.

The castle exterior is best viewed from **Castle Bridge**, where the 14th century walls can be seen reflected in the waters of the River Avon. There is a walk along the ramparts, and much to explore within 60 acres of grounds, including a re-created Victorian formal rose garden, the Peacock Gardens and an expanse of open parkland designed by Capability Brown. Events throughout the year include **Medieval Tournaments**, open-air

Warwick Castle

on Jury Street houses the **Warwickshire Yeomanry Museum**, with displays of uniforms, arms, swords, sabres and selected silver, and Warwick Town Museum, which features changing exhibitions.

Warwickshire Museum (free) in Market Place occupies an imposing 17th century market hall housing collections that illustrate the geology, wildlife and history of the county. Notable exhibits include giant fossils, live bees, ancient jewellery and the historic Sheldon Tapestry map of Warwickshire.

Changing programmes in the ground floor galleries offer exciting exhibitions of acclaimed local and national artists' work.

History of a different kind can be seen at picturesque **Oken's House**, an ancient building once owned by Thomas Oken, a self-made businessman who died childless in 1573 and left his fortune to found almshouses for the poor. This carefully restored Elizabethan house is now home to **The Doll Museum,** displaying hundreds of dolls, teddies and toys from days gone by. Visitors can have a go at hopscotch or spinning tops, or hunt for Teddy's friends, while video bring the exhibits to life, demonstrating how all the mechanical toys on display work.

One of the most important buildings in Warwick is St John's House, dating from 1666 and considered a very good example of the period. Today the building houses a museum where visitors

firework concerts and special entertainment days.

A strong link with the castle is found in the **Collegiate Church of St Mary** in Old Square, a splendid medieval church on the town's highest point. Of pre-Conquest origin, the church contains the magnificent fan-vaulted Beauchamp Chapel, built to house the monuments of Richard Beauchamp, Earl of Warwick, and his family. The chapel contains an outstanding collection of Warwickshire tombs, a chapter house and a Norman crypt. In summer visitors can ascend the tower to enjoy the excellent views.

The centre of Warwick was rebuilt after a fire in 1694, and though many older buildings survived, the centre is dominated by elegant Queen Anne buildings. A walk around High Street and Northgate Street takes in some of the finest buildings, including **Court House** and **Landor House**. Court House can find out how people lived in the past. Upstairs is the **Museum of the Royal Warwickshire Regiment**.

Two of Warwick's medieval town gateways survive, complete with chapels. Of these, Westgate Chapel forms part of **Lord Leycester's Hospital**, a spectacularly tottering and beautiful collection of 15th century half-timbered buildings enclosing a pretty galleried courtyard. Inside, the main interest is provided by the **Queen's Own Hussars Regimental Museum**. This 600-year-old medieval treasure has a unique chantry Chapel dating back to 1123, a magnificent Great Hall and Guildhall together with other timber-framed buildings, first established by the Earl of Leicester as an old soldiers' home in 1571. The historic Master's Garden, featuring a Norman arch and 2,000 year-old vase from the Nile, is a spectacular summer attraction.

Warwick Racecourse in Hampton Street offers flat and National Hunt racing throughout the year. This picturesque racecourse makes a good day out for all the family, with a regular programme of 25 meetings throughout the year. The central grandstand incorporates the first stand built in 1809, among the oldest surviving in the country.

WELLESBOURNE

Wellesbourne Wartime Museum is located on the site of a wartime airfield. On display are tools, ration books and an exhibit in the style of a contemporary battle operations control room. The **Wellesbourne Watermill** is a genuine brick-built working flour mill dating back to 1834. This restored mill on the River Dene is one of few in the country to be seen working as it once did.

WOOTTON WAWEN

Handy for walks on nearby **Stratford Canal**, Wootton Wawen also contains some fine timber-framed buildings and Warwickshire's oldest church – **St Peter's,** an impressive structure that still has its Saxon tower, now more than a thousand years old. The main building is actually three churches in one; with three separate chapels tacked on to each other with a refreshing disregard for architectural design which does not in any way detract from the church's charm. One of these chapels, the barn-roofed Lady Chapel, is now **The Saxon Sanctuary**, a colourful exhibition that traces the history of 'Wagen's' woodland village in the Forest of Arden. It reveals how this small village conceals a Roman road, two monasteries, an ancient fort, mysterious underground passages, a river that changes with fashion, a disappearing pond and an aqueduct!

St Peter's stands within a picturesque churchyard which has won the Diocesan 'Best Kept' award several times and next to it stands **Wotton Hall**, dating from 1637. Maria Fitzherbert, wife of George IV, spent her childhood here and is thought to return in ghostly form as the 'Grey Lady' seen wandering the Hall.

THE BELL INN

BANBURY ROAD, LADBROKE, WARWICKSHIRE CV47 2BY
TEL: 01926 813562

Directions: Leaving the M40 at junction 12, head north on the B4451. From the centre of the village of Bishops's Itchington take the turning on the right signposted for Ladbroke.

The Bell Inn is a pretty whitewashed country pub tucked away amongst the thatched cottages that make up the small village of Ladbroke. Dating back to the 16th century it is not surprising to learn that this is a listed building and many original features have been retained, including the exposed beamed ceilings, and enhance the traditional atmosphere within.

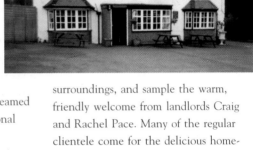

The lounge and restaurant areas have been tastefully carpeted and furnished, and the open fires keep the chill off the air in cooler weather. Here you can enjoy a relaxed drink in friendly, cosy surroundings, and sample the warm, friendly welcome from landlords Craig and Rachel Pace. Many of the regular clientele come for the delicious home-cooked food, with a menu of classic English favourites available most lunchtime and evenings. The house specialities are the steaks and fish dishes, while vegetarians are also well catered for.

There is a small children's selection and a sensibly priced OAP's lunchtime menu too. The bar serves real ales from the cask together with a popular selection of draught beers and lagers. The restaurant can seat up to 72, so it is usually possible to find a table. Otherwise, meals can be taken in the beer garden when weather permits. Other facilities include a large car park, dart board and there are regular games evenings too.

- 🕐 Mon-Sat 11.30-14.30, 19.00-23.00; Sun 12.00-14.30, 19.00-22.30
- 🍴 Restaurant serving wide ranging menu
- 💷 Visa, Mastercard, Delta, Switch
- 🅿 Beer garden, BBQ area
- 🎵 Regular games evenings, darts
- @ craig.pace@btopenworld.com
- ❓ Heritage Motor Museum 6 miles, Leamington Spa 9 miles, Warwick Castle 11 miles, Warwick Racecourse 11 miles, Charlecote Park 12 miles, Draycote Water Country Park 9 miles

THE BOOT INN

CHURCH ROAD, WARTON, NR. TAMWORTH, STAFFORDSHIRE B79 0JN
TEL: 01827 893863

Directions: From the M42 take the A5 east from junction 10 turning left at Dordon towards Polesworth. The village of Warton is then signposted just a mile further on

Since arriving as leaseholders in April 2003, Paul and Karen Lockwood have given a new lease of life to the **Boot Inn**. The premises may be over 130 years-old but behind the eye-catching frontage the interior is fresh and contemporary. There is no sign of dingy dark carpets or all the clutter that you find in a traditional pub. Here the paintwork is fresh and light, with feature walls picked out in trendy aubergine while the floors are either light coloured wood or, upstairs in the restaurant, laid with a geometric designed carpet. The whole place has a contemporary style while retaining a friendly, welcoming atmosphere.

Popular with the locals, though many may find it hard to recognise in its newly refurbished state, this really is the place for the whole family. There is some great food to be sampled and the friendly service includes orders taken at the table. You can choose from the regular printed menu, which incorporates a 'Young Adults' selection for teenagers, or from the daily specials board with everything freshly prepared using mainly local produce. Younger children are also welcome. You can eat in the dining area or the superb non-smoking restaurant which is located upstairs. Food is served lunchtime and evening Tuesday to Saturday, 12-12.30 and 6-9.30, and lunchtime on Sunday, with bookings recommended for Friday, Saturday and Sunday. Two real ales head a long list of beers, lagers and ciders.

🕐 Mon-Sat 12.00-23.00; Sun 12.00-22.30

🍴 Menu of tasty pub favourites

💷 Visa, Mastercard, Delta, Switch

🅿 Beer garden, car park

❓ Twycross Zoo 3 miles, Snowdome 6 miles, Drayton Manor Park 10 miles, Hartshill Hayes Country Park 7 miles, Arbury Hall 12 miles, The Belfry 9 miles

THE COCK HORSE INN

OLD WARWICK ROAD, ROWINGTON, WARWICKSHIRE CV37 7AA
TEL: 01926 842183

Directions: From the M40, take the exit at junction 15 following the A46 towards Warwick. After a couple of miles turn left onto the A4177. After another 2 miles bear left onto the B4439 and the village of Rowington is then just a further 3 miles.

Built of warm red brick, **The Cock Horse** Inn is the epitome of traditional English inns. It dates back to the 18th century, with many interesting features, and up until the 1930s was called simply The Cock. The picturesque outside is echoed in its interior - low ceilings, an inglenook fireplace and flag stone floors vie to catch your attention in this charming hostelry. Your hosts are David and Wendy Preston and in their two years here, the couple have created a fine establishment that enjoys a far reaching reputation for serving excellent real ales and superb quality food.

Available at lunchtimes and in the evenings, you can choose from a varied bar menu, which offers a great value two course lunch through the week together with other popular dishes. The non-smoking restaurant seats 30 and here they serve an a la carte menu of fine starters, fillet steak Rossini, barbary duck and much more. The place gets so popular, bookings are advisable for the restaurant, especially at weekends, and here you are welcome to bring children too. Members of CAMRA, and featuring in the Good Beer Guide, it is not surprising to find extensive range of real ales at the bar. Flowers, Hook Norton, Adnams Broadside and Fullers London Pride are permanent features with two regularly changing guest ales. The enthusiasm for real ales extends to an annual beer festival, held at the August Bank Holiday, when there is also a lively programme of music.

- Mon-Sat 12.00-23.00; Sun 12.00-22.30
- Bar and a la carte menu
- Visa, Mastercard, Delta, Switch
- Car park, beer garden, children's play area
- Live music every Friday, monthly jazz and folk nights, regular jam sessions, annual Beer Festival
- Warwick Castle 5 miles, Warwick Racecourse 5 miles, Stratford-upon-Avon 12 miles, Packwood House 3 miles, Baddesley Clinton 2 miles, Grand Union Canal 1 mile, Hatton Country World 3 miles

THE COLLEGE ARMS

LOWER QUINTON, NR. STRATFORD-UPON-AVON,
WARWICKSHIRE CV37 8SG
TEL: 01789 720342 FAX: 01789 721903

Directions: Leaving the M40 at junction 15, take the A46 then the A439 into
Stratford. Following the ring road around the town, take the A3400 towards
Shipston-on-Stour quickly turning right onto B4632 towards Chipping Campden.
After about 5 miles along this road, Lower Quinton is signposted to the left

Lower Quinton is a delightful village on the very edge of the Cotswolds. **The College Arms** has origins in the early-16th century when it was a farm owned by Henry VIII, not becoming a hostelry until 1897. It was purchased by Magdalene College and has been in their continued ownership for between 400 and 500 years. Because of this connection it is the only public house in England legally permitted to display the college coat of arms.

Today, you will find a charming country inn that provides comfortable relaxed surroundings in which to enjoy superb food and fine ales. You will find a wealth of original features including the exposed beams, stone floors and open fires, all creating a traditional, cosy atmosphere. Food is served every lunchtime and weekday evenings. The menus are superb, offering an excellent selection of classic dishes, all home-cooked using the freshest of ingredients, and seasonally updated. Vegetarians are well catered for and there are usually fish dishes too. Meanwhile, the bar keeps Hook Norton real ale on tap together with a guest ale, Boddingtons, and other popular draught beers and lager.

Your hosts Tony and Lynn Smith also provide comfortable bed and breakfast accommodation in four superb en-suite rooms, equipped with TV and tea and coffee making facilities.

- 🕐 Mon-Fri 12.00-15.00, 19.00-23.00; Sat 12.00-23.00; Sun 12.00-23.00
- 🍴 Classic home-cooked food with a superb menu (last food orders taken 14.00 Sat & Sun)
- 💷 Visa, Mastercard, Delta, Switch
- 🛏 4 en-suite rooms
- Ⓟ Car park, patio garden
- 🎵 Occasional Medieval and Irish music, darts, pool
- @ email: collegarms@easicom.com website: www.thecollegearms.co.uk
- ❓ Hidcote Manor Gardens 4 miles, Stratford-upon-Avon 6 miles, Warwick Castle 17 miles, Broadway 10 miles, Upton House 13 miles, Cotswold Falconry Centre 12 miles

THE FOX AND DOGS

ORTON ROAD, WARTON, NR. TAMWORTH, STAFFORDSHIRE B79 0HT

TEL: 01827 892448

> **Directions:** From junction 10 of the M42 head east along the A5. At the roundabout at Dordon turn left and continue straight along this road, crossing the B5000 to Polesworth. Just after the railway station turn right and then Warton will be signposted to the left

The Fox and Dogs is a handsome whitewashed English inn with a well proportioned front and two large bay windows looking out onto the road. The building originally housed a blacksmith's shop but has been welcoming customers for food and ale for over 200 years. The inside is a delight - think olde worlde, and you've got the picture. Gnarled oak beams grace the ceilings, there is a wealth of shining brass and copper, the feature walls are bare brick, and an open fire offers a warm welcome in the winter months. Your host is Sylvia Allbrighton and she worked in the Fox and Dogs for over a number of years before taking over the running of the place three years ago.

The food is first class with the inn specialising in home made dishes, such as steak pie which is always a favourite, all prepared on the premises. Sylvia's daughter Julie runs the kitchens and takes great pride in serving freshly prepared, tasty dishes. You can choose from the printed menu or a daily specials board with everything served in ample portions. Children are welcome if you're dining and you can eat throughout the inn or, in the summer months, in the huge beer garden at the rear. Food is available most lunchtimes and evenings (no food Saturday lunch, Sunday evening or on Mondays). To accompany your meal, you can choose from a fine selection of wines or ales including the two real ales (Marston's Pedigree and Banks Bitter).

- ⏰ Mon-Sat 11.00-23.00; Sun 12.00-22.30
- 🍴 Superb home-made dishes served most sessions
- 🅿 Large beer garden, children's play area, car park
- 🎵 Occasional quizzes, karaoke on last Friday of month, live bands outside in summer, annual bonfire
- ❓ Twycross Zoo 2 miles, Snowdome 6 miles, Middleton Hall 6 miles, Ash End House Children's Farm 8 miles, Drayton Manor Park 10 miles, The Belfry 11 miles

THE MASONS ARMS

WELFORD ROAD, LONG MARSTON, NR. STRATFORD-UPON-AVON,
WARWICKSHIRE CV37 8RG
TEL: 01789 720586

> **Directions:** Leaving the M40 at junction15, follow the A46 southwest and after a couple of miles bear left onto the A439 heading into Stratford. Following the ring road around the town, then take the B439 Bidford road. After about 3 miles Long Marston will be signposted to your left and is then a further 3 miles

Lying within the small village of Long Marston, the **Masons Arms** was originally built as a private house in 1685 and became the local hostelry in 1861. The attractive, traditionally styled inn has a spacious front garden where in warm weather you can enjoy your drinks and perhaps partake in a giant games of snakes and ladders or Jenga. Venturing inside, you will feel that you have stepped into a private sitting room, as it feels so cosy and welcoming. A popular spot in cool weather is the sofa next to the open fire, although there are plenty

of other tables and chairs scattered throughout.

Popular with the locals and visitors to the area, the superb food is one of the main attractions. A wide ranging snack menu is served each lunchtime, while most evenings there is an a la carte selection of popular favourites. Everything is tasty and clearly home-made, and offers good value for money too. To accompany your meal there is a fine wine selection while the bar is well stocked with some popular real ales, and draught beers and lagers. The skittle alley is perennially popular and the same room is available for functions and children's parties. There are regular themed evenings and every month there is live music. Owned and personally run by local girl Rachael Watts, she extends a warm welcome to all.

- 🕐 Mon-Fri 12.00-14.30, 17.00-23.00; Sat 12.00-23.00; Sun 12.00-22.30
- 🍴 Superb snack and a la carte menus
- 💷 Visa, Mastercard, Delta, Switch
- 🅿 Parking, beer garden
- 🎵 Live music and disco once a month, traditional pub games, skittle alley
- @ email: rachael@masons-arms.fsnet.co.uk
  website: www.masonsarmslongmarston.co.uk
- ❓ Anne Hathaway's Cottage 6 miles, Stratford-upon-Avon 9 miles, Ragley Hall 11 miles, Hidcote Manor Gardens 5 miles, Greenway Cycle Route, Cotswold Falconry Centre 11 miles

THE QUEENS HEAD

MAIN ROAD, NEWTON REGIS, NR. TAMWORTH,
STAFFORDSHIRE B79 0NF
TEL: 01827 830271 FAX: 01827 830609

> **Directions:** Take the B5493 southwest from Junction 11 on the M42, and after 3 miles turn left onto a minor road for Newton Regis

This substantial inn has been under the personal management of Michael and Debbie Rhodes for the last six years, and during that time they have created a hostelry that combines old world charm with modern service and value for money. Parts of the building are over 400 years old, and many period features have been retained. The basic building material is old, red brick, with a whitewashed facade and windows are small paned and picturesque. Inside **The Queens Head** the theme is continued, with low ceilings, stout oak beams, a wealth of old ornaments, and plates and prints adorning the walls. The furniture

is comfortable, with upholstered benches along the walls of the lounge, and the bar is snug and warm.

The cuisine is traditional English, with a few foreign influences thrown in. Everything is prepared on the premises from fresh produce, and you can choose from a printed menu or from a daily changing specials board. There is also a vegetarian menu, and children are more than welcome if you're eating. The specialities of the house are its steak and fish dishes, and the Sunday roast is also popular. Michael and Debbie don't accept bookings, so turn up early! You can order wine with your meal, or you can choose from four real ales (Bass, Brew X1, Banks Original and a rotating guest ale. Other drinks include Worthington Creamflow, Caffreys, Carling, Stella, Guinness, Woodpecker and Strongbow.

- Open at lunchtimes and evenings over seven days
- Good food is served Monday to Saturday between 12.00-14.00 and 18.00-21.30 and on Sunday from 12.00-14.00 and 19.00-21.00; no bookings accepted
- Car park, beer garden
- Quiz night every second Monday at 20.30, pool, crib
- rhodesqueens@aol.com
- Tamworth (historic town) 5 miles, Snowdome 6 miles, Twycross Zoo 4 miles, Battlefield Line (old railway) 6 miles, National Memorial Arboretum 12 miles

THE ROYAL OAK

GRENDON ROAD, POLESWORTH, NR. TAMWORTH,
STAFFORDSHIRE B78 1NU
TEL: 01827 331025

> **Directions:** Leaving the M42 at junction 10, from the motorway roundabout take the minor road that leads north towards Alvecote. After a mile turn right onto the B5000 which will lead you over the motorway and into Polesworth

The Royal Oak is a charming village inn that enjoys a quiet location yet is conveniently located for the Midlands motorway network. Located close to the Coventry Canal the pub proves to be popular with boaters and walkers, and a gentle stroll along the canal could be a great way to work up an appetite for some refreshments.

Entering through the brightly painted blue doors, you will find a spacious bar area that retains a great deal of traditional charm. The bar is open all day every day serving a selection of three real ales, with Marstons Pedigree being a permanent feature together with two regularly changing guest ales. Other draught offerings include M&B Mild and other stout, lager and ciders. Your friendly hosts are David and Anita, both are local, having been born in nearby Tamworth, and have firmly established themselves at The Royal Oak over the past two years, extending a warm welcome to all. Anita is a superb cook and food is served from opening time through to 6.30pm-ish Monday to Saturday with the Sunday lunch served from midday until 4pm. Everything on the printed menu and the daily specials board is home-cooked and freshly prepared to order, and such is the popularity of the place that bookings are advisable for Sunday lunch and Friday and Saturday evenings too.

- 🕐 Mon-Sat 11.00-23.00; Sun 12.00-22.30
- 🍴 Food served through the day until early evening
- Ⓟ Patio garden, car park opposite
- 🎵 Karaoke first Friday of every month
- @ email: theoak@btopenworld.com
- ❓ Snowdome 3 miles, Drayton Manor Park 5 miles, Middleton Hall 6 miles, The Belfry 8 miles, Twycross Zoo 4 miles, The Battlefield Line Historic Railway 9 miles

CHAPEL STREET, WELFORD ON AVON, WARWICKSHIRE CV37 8PX
TEL: 01789 750443

Directions: Leave the M40 at junction 15, follow the A46 southwest, then bear left onto the A439 heading into Stratford. Follow the ring road around the town, then take the B439 Bidford road. After about 3 miles Welford will be signposted to your left. Travel into the village and turn left at the Maypole.

Welford-on-Avon is a pretty Warwickshire village which gained fame for its ancient maypole. Until it was replaced by a more modern model in 1967, it had one of the tallest and oldest in the country, dating back to Shakespeare's time. Taking its name from this most famous of English playwrights, **The Shakespeare Inn** lies in the heart of the village and provides cosy, friendly surroundings in which to enjoy a drink or a bite to eat.

One of the best features is the superb beer garden which won the Whitbread Garden of the Year award and is a popular spot in sunny weather.

🕐 Mon-Sat 11.00-23.00; Sun 12.00-22.30

🍴 Traditional English and Italian dishes

🅿 Car park, beer garden

🎵 Morris dancers in summer, regular quiz nights, darts league.

@ email: info@theshakespeareinn.co.uk
website: www.theshakespeareinn.co.uk

❓ Anne Hathaway's Cottage 3 miles, Stratford-upon-Avon 6 miles, Charlecote Park 9 miles, Ragley Hall 7 miles, Mary Arden's House 6 miles, Broadway 12 miles

Inside is equally charming, with the bar and dining area furnished in a traditional style. The bar can offer a top range of ales including Hook Norton and Timothy Taylor real ales, Boddingtons Creamflow bitter and much more. There is a good wine selection, with many fine Italian wines among the selection. The food also takes on an Italian flavour, with the main menu offering a number of traditional dishes such as pasta, pizzas and lasagne. The pizzas are also available for takeaway until 10.30pm. The rest of the dishes are classic English favourites, with everything prepared daily and cooked to order using the freshest of ingredients. In summer there are regular USA style barbecues, the inspiration of owner Michelle Plotegher who hails from Florida. The Italian bias is from her husband Umberto, who was born in Northern Italy.

THE TILTED WIG

MARKET PLACE, WARWICK CV34 4SA
TEL: 01926 410466 FAX: 01926 495740

Directions: Warwick lies just 2 miles from junction 15 of the M40. Simply follow signs for Warwick Castle.

Located in the very heart of the historic market town of Warwick, **The Tilted Wig** offers all those who pass through its doors a warm welcome. The attractive Georgian coaching inn is a Grade 2 listed building retaining many of its original features. Inspiration for its name came from the nearby law courts and the legal theme is continued discreetly throughout. Inside, visitors will find an open bar area with plenty of seating (plenty more outside during good weather) combined with stone flags and stripped wood floors. The unique atmosphere is that of a wine bar, brasserie and restaurant all in one.

The menu reflects a 'Best of British' bias combined with other tasty dishes inspired by international cuisine while an extensive specials board makes use of seasonally available produce. An excellent range of beers are stocked behind the bar including four real ales, one from the local Warwickshire Beer Company, other draught beer and lagers, and bottled beers. A wide range of soft drinks and tea and coffee are also always available.

There are four en-suite letting rooms furnished to a high standard and provided with colour TV and tea and coffee making facilities. Owners Will and Caryl Freeman are intent on providing a warm welcome to all customers and are always happy to help with information on local facilities and visitor attractions.

- 🕐 Mon-Sat 11.00-23.00; Sun 12.00-22.30
- 🍴 Superb menu of snacks and hot meals
- £ Visa, Mastercard, Delta, Switch
- 🛏 2 doubles, 2 twins, all en-suite
- Ⓟ Car park
- 🎵 Live music every Thursday evening, large screen TV
- @ email: thetiltedwig@hotmail.com website: www.thetiltedwig.com
- ❓ Warwick Castle, Hatton Country World 2 miles, Packwood House 8 miles, Stratford-upon-Avon 10 miles, Mary Arden's House 10 miles, Heritage Motor Centre 9 miles

TOM O' THE WOOD

FINWOOD ROAD, ROWINGTON, WARWICK CV35 7DH
TEL: 01564 782252 FAX: 01564 782469

> **Directions:** From the M40, take the exit at junction 15 following the A46 towards Warwick. After a couple of miles turn left onto the A4177. After another 2 miles bear left onto the B4439 and Rowington is a further 3 miles.

The **Tom o' the Wood** is a pretty, red brick, country inn enjoying a relatively quiet location, just a stone's throw from the M40 and within easy reach of the busy metropolis of Birmingham. Dating back to the 18th century, it overlooks the Grand Union Canal and proves to be a popular choice with canal users, both those on foot and those travelling by boat, as well as locals and other tourists.

Inside, the lounge and bar areas are warm and cosy, with thick carpets and feature fireplaces, while the separate dining area is housed within a delightful conservatory. Due to popular demand, there are designated non-smoking areas, so you can be sure of being able to enjoy a smoke-free atmosphere if you prefer. A popular menu is served each lunchtime and evening and presents all the traditional favourites, including steaks and fish, with a specials board that makes the most of seasonal produce. To enjoy with your meal, or on its own, is a good range of beers and lagers together with guest cask beers that change periodically. In summer months visitors can enjoy the beer garden, while the younger customers try out the children's play area. If you prefer a lively evening out there is a karaoke and disco each Thursday and Sunday and a live band once a month. There are also special events arranged on most Bank Holidays.

- 🕐 Mon-Sat 12.00-23.00; Sun 10.30-22.30
- 🍴 Regular menu of traditional favourites
- 💷 Visa, Mastercard, Delta, Switch, Amex, Diners
- 🅿 Beer garden, children's play area, car park
- 🎵 Karaoke and disco Thursdays and Sundays, live band once a month, bank holiday entertainments
- ❓ Warwick Castle 5 miles, Warwick Racecourse 5 miles, Stratford-upon-Avon 12 miles, Packwood House 3 miles, Baddesley Clinton 2 miles, Grand Union Canal 1 mile

WHITE HART

RIDGE LANE, NR. ATHERSTONE, NUNEATON,
WARWICKSHIRE CV10 0RB
TEL: 01827 712038

Directions: From the M42, take the A5 towards Nuneaton from junction 10. The village of Ridge Lane will be signposted from the centre of Atherstone

Tucked away in the small village of Ridge Lane, yet within easy reach of the motorway network, you will find the **White Hart** public house. The owners, Richard and Michelle Moody, are highly experienced within the trade and in their two years of residency have firmly established themselves within the local community. Catering to local and passing trade, you can be sure of finding a warm welcome together with good food and comfortable accommodation.

Venturing inside the 18th-century inn you will find a carpeted lounge and bar which features the original lead range fireplace. The well stocked bar can offer all the usual beers and lagers with cask ales also available and occasional guest beers too. Food is served at every session and in addition to the daily specials, the regular menu offers a choice of mouth-watering steaks, fish, chicken and curry dishes. All are freshly prepared to order and everyone is sure to find something to their taste. There is sometimes live music arranged so if you prefer a lively, or a quiet night out, ring ahead for full details.

It is always nice to discover a pub that can provide bed and breakfast accommodation, and the White Hart is one of those gems. There are four guest rooms in all with three doubles and one family-sized room which can sleep up to four people.

- 🕐 Mon-Sat 11.00-23.00; Sun 12.00-22.30
- 🍴 Mouthwatering menu together with daily specials
- 🛏 3 doubles, 1 family room sleeping up to 4
- 🅿 Games room, car parking
- 🎵 Occasional live music
- ❓ Purley Chase Golf Course 1 mile, Hartshill Hayes Country Park 2 miles, Arbury Hall 6 miles, Twycross Zoo 8 miles, Drayton Manor Park 8 miles, Indoor Ski Centre 9 miles

THE WHITE LION

TREDINGTON, SHIPSTON ON STOUR, WARWICKSHIRE CV36 4NS
TEL: 01608 661522 FAX: 01608 665032

Directions: From junction 15 of the M40, follow the A429 due south through Wellsbourne. After about 14 miles bear left onto the A3400 and you will almost immediately reach Tredington.

Louise and Mark extend a warm welcome to all visitors, old and new, to the **White Lion** in Tredington, a traditional country pub set in the heart of Shakespeare Country. The imposing, part-thatched property dates back over 450 years and has become affectionately known by its locals as 'Treddy pub'. Open for food and drink all day every day the kitchen doesn't close until 10pm but the place is very popular so it may be wise to book a table at peak times to avoid disappointment.

The menu is superb, offering a delicious selection of starters, main courses and desserts, inspired by world cuisine. It is Mark who is the chef and his talents are shown off to perfection by the clever use of fresh, seasonal ingredients. There is a full selection of sandwiches if you need something quick and easy, and the classic Sunday roast, with all the trimmings, remains a firm favourite. There is also a menu of takeaway pizzas which proves popular with locals! The White Lion has a regular programme of special events with Monday being curry night. On other evenings you could pit your wits in a pub quiz (Tuesday), try your hand at a traditional game of dominoes or Aunt Sally (Thursday) or even join in with a live jamming session with Tredington's very own Ranting Cat band on Sundays. Saving the best until last, every weeknight between 5pm and 7pm is happy hour! All in all, well worth a visit.

- 🕐 Mon-Sat 10.00-23.00; Sun 10.00-22.30
- 🍴 Bar menu, specials board and takeaway pizzas
- £ Visa, Mastercard, Delta, Switch
- Ⓟ Covered beer garden, children's play area
- 🎵 Quiz each Tuesday night, live music every Sunday, monthly theme nights, darts, pool
- @ www.whiteliontredington.co.uk
- ❓ Stratford-upon-Avon 9 miles, Hidcote Manor Gardens 6 miles, Upton House 9 miles, Falconry Centre 10 miles, Broadway 15 miles, Heritage Motor Museum 10 miles

Please note all cross references refer to page numbers

STAFFORDSHIRE

The southwest of Staffordshire encompasses many changing landscapes, from the busy, industrial towns of Stafford and Burton upon Trent to the peace and quiet of Cannock Chase. Along with the Hednesford Hills, the Chase

provides a wonderful open area of woodland and moorland that is one of the county's great recreational centres. Well-supported by an interesting and informative visitors' centre, the Chase is a must for anyone visiting this part of

Ancient Cave Dwellings, Kinver Edge

Staffordshire. The southeast of Staffordshire, although lying close to the Black Country – the depressing product of the heavy industrialisation of the 18th and 19th centuries – has managed to escape in the main. One legacy of the era and a feature throughout the whole of Staffordshire, however, is the canal network. Built to link Birmingham with the Trent & Mersey Canal, the less well known Coventry Canal and the Birmingham & Fazeley Canal pass through tiny villages and hamlets and the towpaths provide the opportunity to walk in some unexpectedly scenic countryside.

Extending along the southern edge of the Peak District, the Staffordshire Moorlands certainly rival their neighbour in terms of scenic attraction. The undulating pastures of the moorlands, along with the fresh air and

Thors Cave, Manifold Valley

ancient weather-worn crags, make this the ideal place to walk, cycle or trek. It is also an area full of character, with charming scattered villages, historic market towns and a wealth of history. The Industrial Revolution also left its mark on the landscape, though the two great reservoirs of Rudyard and Tittesworth, built to provide a water supply to the growing industry and population of the Midlands, now offer peaceful havens for a wide variety of plants, animals and birds as well as recreational facilities such as fishing and boating.

The area around Stoke-on-Trent is famous the world over for its pottery industry. Originally centred on the five towns of Stoke, Tunstall, Burslem, Hanley and Longton, The Potteries were at the heart of the Industrial Revolution. Both coal and clay were found locally which gave rise to the start of the industry, though imported clay from Cornwall was later used - but it was the foresight and ingenuity of men such as Wedgwood and Minton that really turned the cottage industry into production on a much larger scale. To support the industry in and around the centre, a network of canals and, later, railways was begun. The Trent & Mersey Canal, built by James Brindley with the support of Wedgwood and his friend the Duke of Bridgewater, was finally completed in 1777 and made possible navigation from coast to coast, between the busy ports of Liverpool and Hull. Together, the Trent & Mersey Canal, the Staffordshire & Worcester Canal, begun in the same

Gladstone Pottery Museum, Longton

year, the Shropshire Union Canal to the west and the Middlewich branch of the Llangollen Canal, form a wonderful four counties ring that can be undertaken wholly or partly by boat. These canals, with their accessible towpaths, run through the very heart of the towns as well as through the often delightful countryside.

ALTON

The world-famous **Alton Towers** leisure park is the main attraction here, but even this spot has its quieter, lesser known corners. Originally the home of the Earls of Shrewsbury, who also owned much of the surrounding area, the 19th century mansion by Pugin is now just a gutted shell. The surrounding gardens and parkland (which contain most of the attractions) are older and were laid out by Capability Brown. Hundreds of workmen were employed to convert a whole valley into what is still a magnificent mix of formal gardens and parkland. As well as many fountains and pools there are also numerous paths which lead to charming follies such as a Swiss Chalet and a Gothic temple.

The village of Alton has plenty to offer the visitor. The view up from the valley bottom to the **Castle**, perched on a sandstone rock above the River Churnet, has given this area of Staffordshire the nickname of 'Rhineland', and the steep climb up to **Toot Hill Rock** is rewarded by magnificent views. The Castle, in its present form, was built mainly by Pugin, who also built the now restored Italianate railway station. Note, too, the old lock-up and water mill.

BIDDULPH

John Wesley was a frequent visitor to this isolated moorland town but the history of Biddulph goes back to long before the days of Methodism. After the Norman Conquest the manor of Biddulph was granted by William the Conqueror to Robert the Forester, an overlord of what was then the extensively forested area of Lyme. The Biddulphs, a staunchly Catholic family, took control of the area. John Biddulph fought under the Royal flag during the Civil War and was killed at the Battle of Hopton Heath. His son entrusted the defence of Biddulph Hall to Lord Brereton who withstood a determined siege until 1644 when he was finally subjected to heavy artillery. The Hall was then demolished to prevent its being re-garrisoned.

Biddulph Grange (National Trust) belonged to the Cistercian monks of the Abbey at Hulton until the Dissolution and its garden is one of the most unusual and remarkable in the whole country. It was created by James Bateman in the mid-1800s as a series of connected parts to show specimens from his extensive collection which he had harvested from all parts of the globe. Highlights include the Egyptian Court and the Great Wall of China.

BURTON UPON TRENT

The 'capital' of East Staffordshire, Burton upon Trent is famous for its brewing industry. It began many centuries ago, and even the monks of the Benedictine Abbey, founded here in 1100, were not the first to realise that the Burton well water was specially suited to brewing. William Bass began brewing in Burton in 1777, and by 1863 the brewery had grown to produce half a million barrels of beer each year on a 750-acre site. In 1998 Bass acquired the Burton premises of Carlsberg-Tetley, creating the biggest brewery site in the UK – 830 acres, brewing 5.5 million barrels yearly. The brewery is open for tours, and the entry fee includes a tour of the **Bass Museum of Brewing** in Horninglow Street, and up to three pints of beer or lager. As well as being offered the opportunity of seeing, sniffing and sampling the traditionally brewed beer, visitors can tour the machinery, inspect the fleet of old vehicles (including the famous Daimler Worthington White Shield Bottle Car) and admire the splendid Bass shire horses.

Cannock Chase

A Benedictine Abbey, founded by a Saxon earl called Wulfric Spot, was established on the banks of the River Trent, where the **Market Place** now stands. In the 12th century, the monks constructed a large stone bridge of some 36 arches across the River Trent – today's bridge replaced the medieval structure in 1864. The area along the banks of the Trent, between Burton Bridge and the later structure of Ferry Bridge, which opened in 1889, is known as the **Washlands**. Rich in native wildlife, the Washlands is a haven for all manner of birds, small mammals, trees and plants.

CANNOCK CHASE

Though close to areas of dense population, Cannock Chase is a surprisingly wild place of heath and woodland that is designated an Area of Outstanding Natural Beauty. Covering some 20,000 acres, the Chase was once the hunting ground of Norman kings and, later, the Bishops of Lichfield. Deer are still plentiful. Conifers now dominate but it is still possible to find the remains of the ancient oak forest and, in the less well-walked marshy grounds, many rare species survive. A popular place for leisurely strolls and fine views, the Chase is also ideal for more strenuous walking and other outdoor recreational activities.

Amid all this natural beauty, there are

also reminders of the 20th century and, in particular, the unique military cemeteries near **Broadhurst Green**, where some 5,000 German soldiers from the First World War lie buried.

The **Museum of Cannock Chase** at the Valley Heritage Centre is only one of the many wonderful parts of Cannock Chase. Opened in May 1989, the Centre is set in the corn store of a former colliery where the pit ponies' feed was kept. Its galleries provide a variety of exhibitions, with rooms dedicated to the natural history of the Hednesford Hills and Castle Ring hill fort.

CHEDDLETON

The restored **Cheddleton Flint Mill**, in the rural surroundings of the Churnet valley, makes an interesting visit. The water-powered machinery was used to crush flint that had been brought in by canal and then transported, again by water, to Stoke, where it was used in the hardening of pottery. The small museum includes a rare 18th century 'haystack' boiler and a Robey steam engine. There are also collections of exhibits relating to the preparation of raw materials for the pottery industry. Trips by narrow boats along the Caldon Canal can be taken from the mill.

The village station is home to the **Churnet Valley Railway and Museum**, which will give great delight to all railway enthusiasts. The Museum has a nostalgic collection of beautifully preserved locomotives and other railway memorabilia, and there are steam train rides to Leekbrook Junction and the lovely hamlet of Consall Forge.

To the west of Cheddleton is **Deep Hayes Country Park**, which lies in a secluded valley by the Caldon Canal and Staffordshire Way. From the ridge there are breathtaking views but, for the less energetic, there is a very pleasant walk around two pools which has many offshoots into lovely countryside.

CONSALL

This is a beautiful spot hidden in a

Caldon Canal

particularly deep section of the Churnet Valley downstream from Cheddleton. The little cottages keep close company with the small bridges over the **Caldon Canal**. Originally known as Consall Forge, the hamlet took its name from an old iron forge that existed here in the first Elizabethan Age. As iron making became uneconomic here, the forge altered its operation and became one of the major lime making centres after the completion of the Caldon Canal.

Reached through Consall village is **Consall Nature Park**, an RSPB reserve that is a quiet and peaceful haven with much to delight the avid birdwatcher.

ECCLESHALL

For over 1,000 years **Eccleshall Castle** was the palace of the bishops of Lichfield but, at the beginning of the 19th century, it became a family home when the Carter family moved here from Yorkshire. The present simple sandstone house is typical of the best architecture of the William & Mary period and incorporates part of the earlier 14th century Castle. The interior of the house has been augmented by successive members of the family, one of whom added a magnificent Victorian staircase and dome. Perhaps to remind them of the county from which they came, the Carters have collected a very interesting number of 19th century paintings by Yorkshire artists. The gardens were created around the ruins of the old castle and have a great deal of romantic appeal.

A little way north of Eccleshall, on the A519 at Cotes Heath, is **Mill Meece Pumping Station**, where two magnificent steam engines that once pumped more than three million gallons of water each day are kept in pristine condition.

FEATHERSTONE

Just to the south of the village is **Moseley Old Hall**, which visitors can be forgiven for thinking belongs to the 19th century. In fact, it dates from the first Elizabethan Age and, inside, much of the original panelling and timber framing is still visible. The Hall once sheltered King Charles II for a short time following his defeat at the Battle of Worcester in 1651 and it is for this that the house is best remembered. In 1940, the house was acquired by the Wiggin family and in 1962 it became the property of the National Trust. At that time it had no garden to speak of, but fairly soon two experts recreated the garden in the style of the century. The outstanding feature is the knot garden with its box hedges and gravel beds. There is interest everywhere in this wonderful garden, which is full of rare 17th century plants and herbs. In the barn is an exhibition showing the escape of King Charles.

GNOSALL

Some beautiful ash and sycamore trees form a delightful shaded arch over the road through this village (the name is pronounced 'Nawzell') and it also has its very own ghost! On the night of January 21st 1879 a man was attacked at Gnosall canal bridge by an alarming black monster with enormous white eyes. The police were quite sure it was the ghost of a man–monkey who had haunted the bridge for years after a man was drowned in the canal. It is worth staying a while in the village, ghost permitting, to have a look around the fine collegiate **Church of St Lawrence**.

Despite its name, a large portion of the **Shropshire Union Canal**, some 23 miles, lies within the county of Staffordshire. Indeed, much of this southern section passes through wonderful countryside. Extending from Ellesmere Port, Cheshire, on the Manchester Ship Canal to Autherley Junction near Wolverhampton, the Shroppie, as it is affectionately known, has a long history.

Built by three separate companies, at three different times, the Canal was begun as early as 1772 but not finished until 1835, a few months after the death of Thomas Telford, who had worked on its construction. In order to compete with the new railways, the canal had to be built as simply and economically as possible and so, unlike many canals before it, the Shropshire Union's route was short and straight, cutting deep through hills and crossing lower ground on embankments rather than talking the longer route on level ground.

GREAT HAYWOOD

This ancient village is famous for having the longest packhorse bridge in England. Built in the 16th century, the **Essex Bridge** (named after the famous Elizabethan Earl who used nearby Shugborough Hall when hunting in the area) still has 14 of its original 40 arches spanning the River Trent.

Most visitors to the village also take time to see one of the most impressive attractions in the county, **Shugborough Hall**, the 17th century seat of the Earls of Lichfield. This magnificent 900-acre estate includes Shugborough Park Farm, a Georgian farmstead built in 1805 for Thomas, Viscount Anson, and now home to rare breed animals and to demonstrations of traditional farming methods such as hand milking, butter and cheese making and shire horses at work. The former servants' quarters have been restored to the days of the 19th century and offer an insight into life below stairs. The mansion itself is a splendid piece of architecture, altered several times over its 300 years, but always retaining its distinct grandeur. Outside, in the beautiful parkland, can be found an outstanding collection of neoclassical monuments.

HANCHURCH

Trentham Gardens were landscaped by Capability Brown and given a more formal style by Sir Charles Barry, whose work can be observed in the lovely Italian gardens. Although the Hall was demolished in 1911, this style can still be recognised in such buildings as the orangery and sculpture gallery which remain today and form a framework for the outstanding conference, exhibition and banqueting centre that is Trentham. There is usually unrestricted access to 800 acres of woodland, lake and gardens, with opportunities for woodland walks, boating and jet skiing.

HEDNESFORD

This former mining town lies on the edge of Cannock Chase and its oldest building, The Cross Keys Inn, was built around 1746. The Anglesey Hotel, built in 1831 by Edmund Peel of Fazeley, was originally designed as a form of summerhouse in a Tudor style with stepped gables and this too lies on the heart of Hednesford.

Nearby, the **Hazel Slade Reserve** shows the adaptability of nature with an old-fashioned countryside of small fields, hedges, streams, marshes and woodland. In the 1960s the old broadleaf wood was felled for timber; hedges were planted and cattle grazed the cleared fields. However, a small area of the wood managed to recover and grew from the stumps and seeds that remained in the ground. Then, five years later, a pool and marsh started to form as the land began to subside as a result of the local mining activity. The Reserve is a popular place for fishermen as well as those interested in natural history.

Rising over 700 feet above sea level, the **Hednesford Hills** are a prominent local landmark that brings the countryside of Cannock Chase into the heart of Hednesford. Originally covered in oak and birch, these 300 acres of heathland have been the scene of varied activities over the years. They have been quarried for sand and gravel, mined for coal and used for military training. The land is now a registered common and the hills are a tract of wild landscape with a plethora of heathland plants, abundant wildlife and the opportunity for recreation for the people who live nearby.

The hills have other sporting connections, too. Cockfighting once took place at **Cockpit Hill** though the exact location of the old cockpit is unknown. In the 1900s, prize fighters prepared themselves at the nearby Cross Keys Inn for boxing bouts on the hills and racehorses were trained on the land. Race meetings were held here regularly until 1840 when the racetrack at Etchinghill, near Rugeley, became more popular. In particular, three Grand National winners were stabled and trained on the Hednesford Hills: Jealousy won the race in 1861, Eremon in 1907 and Jenkinstown in 1910.

INGESTRE

The beautiful **Church of St Mary the Virgin**, in this small estate village, is something of a surprise. Standing close to the Jacobean Ingestre Hall, the sophisticated church was built in 1676 and has been attributed to Sir Christopher Wren. One of the few churches that Wren designed outside London, it has an elegant interior with a rich stucco nave ceiling and some of the earliest electrical installations in any church. The chancel, which is barrel vaulted, is home to a delightful garlanded reredos and there are many monuments to the Chetwynds and Talbots, who were Earls of Shrewsbury from 1856 and had their seat in the village.

LEEK

Known as the 'Capital of the Moorlands', Leek is an attractive textile centre on the banks of the River Churnet, noted for its range and variety of antiques shops. It was here that French Huguenots settled, after fleeing from religious oppression, and established the silk industry that thrived due to the abundance of soft water coming off the nearby moorland. Until the 19th century, this was a domestic industry with the workshops on the top storeys of the houses; many examples of these 'top shops' have survived to this day. Leek also became an important dyeing town, particularly after the death of Prince Albert, when 'Raven Black' was popularised by Queen Victoria, who remained in mourning for her beloved husband for many years.

William Morris, founder of the Arts and Crafts movement, lived and worked in Leek for many months between 1875 and 1878. Much of his time here was spent investigating new techniques of dyeing but he also revived the use of traditional dyes. His influence can be seen in the art here and also in the architecture. **Leek Art Gallery** is the place to go to find out more about the wonderful and intricate work of the famous Leek School of Embroidery that was founded by Lady Wardle in the 1870s.

Every road coming into the town seems to converge on the old cobbled **Market Place** with its butter cross, and the road to the west leads down to the Parish Church. Dedicated to Edward the Confessor (the full name is St **Edward's and All Saints' Church**), the original Church was burnt down in 1297 and

Hen Cloud, The Roaches

rebuilt some 20 years later, though the building is now largely 17th century. The timber roof of the nave is well worth a second look and is the Church's pride and joy – it is said that each of the cross beams was hewn from a separate oak tree. In the west part of the nave, an enormous 18th century gallery rises up, tier on tier, giving the impression of a theatre's dress circle!

To the north side of the Church is an area still known locally as 'Petty France'; it holds the graves of many Napoleonic prisoners of war who lived nearby.

Another building worthy of a second glance is the imposing **Nicholson Institute**, with its copper dome. Completed in 1884 and funded by the local industrialist Joshua Nicholson, the Institute offered the people of Leek an opportunity to learn and also expand their cultural horizons. The town's **War Memorial**, built in Portland stone and with a clock tower, has a dedication to the youngest Nicholson son, who was killed in the First World War. Leek was the home of James Brindley, the 18th century engineer who built much of the early canal network. A water-powered corn mill built by him in 1752 in Mill Street has been restored and now houses the **Brindley Water Museum**, which is devoted to his life and work.

The **River Churnet**, though little known outside Staffordshire, has a wealth of scenery and industrial archaeology and, being easily accessible to the walker, its valley deserves better recognition. The river rises to the west of Leek in rugged gritstone country but for most of its length it flows through softer red sandstone countryside in a valley that was carved out during the Ice Age. Though there are few footpaths directly adjacent to the riverbank, most of the valley can be walked close to the river using a combination of canal towpaths and former railway tracks.

Four miles to the north of Leek on the A53 rise the dark, jagged gritstone outcrops of **The Roaches**, **Ramshaw Rocks** and **Hen Cloud**, and just below The Roaches there is another delightful stretch of water, **Tittesworth Reservoir**, which is extremely popular with trout fishermen. It has some super trails, a visitor centre with an interactive exhibition, a restaurant and a gift shop.

LICHFIELD

Despite its 18th century prominence Lichfield lagged behind other towns in extensive rebuilding programmes and consequently it still retains its medieval grid pattern streets with elegant Georgian houses and, mixed in among them, black and white Tudor cottages. First settled by the Celts and also close to the crossroads of the two great Roman roadways, Ryknild Street (now the A38) and Watling Street (now the A5), Lichfield was one of the most important towns of ancient days; the King of Mercia offered St Chad the seat of Lichfield and, on his death, the town became a place of pilgrimage and an important ecclesiastical centre.

The first cathedral was built here in

669 but no traces of this building, or the later Norman structure, remain. The **Lichfield Cathedral** seen today dates from the 12th century and is particularly famous for the three magnificent spires which dominate the City skyline. Inside there are many treasures, including the beautiful 8th century illuminated manuscript *The Lichfield Gospels* and Sir Francis Chantrey's famous sculpture *The Sleeping Children*.

The surrounding Cathedral Close is regarded by many as the most original and unspoilt in the country. Since it is separated from the rest of the city by **Stowe and Minster Pools**, it is also a peaceful haven of calm.

At the very heart of Lichfield is the **Lichfield Heritage Centre**, part of St Mary's Centre in the Market Place. A church has stood on this site since the 12th century and the present building, the third, dates from 1868. As with many ecclesiastical buildings, the decline in

the church-going population made St Mary's redundant and, to save it from being demolished altogether, the Centre was formed. A stroll round here is a fascinating experience and for the energetic, there are spectacular views across the city from the viewing platform on the spire. There are exhibitions on the history and everyday life of the city as seen through the eyes of its inhabitants over the centuries and it also includes the story of the siege of Lichfield Cathedral during the Civil War and displays of the city's silver, ancient charter and archives.

The City has been a place of pilgrims and travellers for centuries and, in 1135, **St John's Hospital** was founded to offer shelter to those passing through Lichfield. One of the finest Tudor brick buildings in the country, the Hospital is now a home for the elderly. The **Hospital Chapel**, with its magnificent stained glass window by the designer of the celebrated east window at Coventry Cathedral, John Piper, is open daily.

Lichfield's most famous son is Dr Samuel Johnson, the poet, novelist and author of the first comprehensive English dictionary. The son of a bookseller, Johnson was born in 1709 in Breadmarket Street,

Lichfield Cathedral

Erasmus Darwin Centre

Apart from the historic pleasure that Lichfield gives there is also plenty of parkland to enjoy and, in particular, the **Beacon Park and Museum Gardens**. The 75-acre Park encloses playing fields and a small boating lake and, in the Museum Gardens, can be found a statue of Commander John Smith, captain of the ill-fated *Titanic*, sculpted by Lady Katherine Scott, widow of Scott of the Antarctic.

Anna Seward, the landscaper of Minster Pool, is another of Lichfield's famous sons and daughters. She lived in the Bishop's Palace and was a poet and letter writer as well as being at the centre of a Lichfield-based literary circle in the late 1700s. Erasmus Darwin, the doctor, philosopher, inventor, botanist and poet, and the closest friend of Josiah Wedgwood, lived in a house in Beacon Street on the corner of The Close. The **Erasmus Darwin Centre**, just three minutes from the Cathedral, is a fascinating place to visit, with touch-screen computers to access Darwin's writings and inventions, and a garden where herbs and shrubs that would have been familiar to the doctor are grown. Erasmus was the grandfather of Charles Darwin, and had his own theories about evolution. David Garrick, probably the greatest actor-manager of the 18th century theatre, had a home which stands opposite the west gate of the Cathedral.

Lichfield is a festival city, the premier event being the **Lichfield International Arts Festival** held in July.

and the house is now home to the **Samuel Johnson Birthplace Museum**. Open every day except Sundays, the Museum, as well as exhibiting artefacts relating to his life and works, also has a series of tableaux showing how the house looked in the early 1700s.

Memorials to Dr Johnson's stepdaughter Lucy Porter can be seen in the medieval St Chad's Church, which has a Norman tower. In the churchyard is a well in the place where St Chad used to baptise people in the 7th century. The ancient practice of well-dressing was revived at St Chad's in 1995 to celebrate the 50th anniversary of Christian Aid and is now an annual event.

MADELEY

Situated on an ancient packhorse route from Newcastle-under-Lyme, this village's name comes from the Anglo-Saxon 'maden lieg', which means 'clearing in the woods'. The focal point of this enchanting place, which has been designated a conservation area, is **The Pool**, formed by damming the River Lea to provide water power for the corn mill that still stands at its northern end. The pool is a haven for a variety of bird life. Madeley's grandest building is the **Old Hall**, an excellent example of a 15th century squire's timber-framed residence. The village's large sandstone church can be seen through the trees from the mill pond. Standing in a raised churchyard, with ancient yew trees, **All Saints Parish Church** was originally Norman but was extensively enlarged in the 1400s; the chapel was rebuilt in 1872.

OAKAMOOR

This village was once the home of the Thomas Bolton & Sons copper works that produced some 20,000 miles of copper wire for the first transatlantic cable in 1856. Little now remains of the works, which were demolished in the 1960s, but the site of the mill has been turned into an attractive picnic site complete with the very large mill pond. Nearby **Hawksmoor Nature Reserve** and bird sanctuary covers some 300 acres of the Churnet Valley and is managed by a local committee.

RUDYARD

In fond memory of the place where they first met in 1863, Mr and Mrs Kipling named their famous son, born in 1865, after this village. The nearby two mile long **Rudyard Lake** was built in 1831 by John Rennie to feed the Caldon Canal. With steeply wooded banks the lake is now a leisure centre where there are facilities for picnicking, walking, fishing and sailing. On summer weekends and Bank Holidays, visitors can enjoy a magical 3-mile return trip alongside the lake behind the vintage locomotives of the Rudyard Lake Steam Railway. The west shore of the Reservoir is also a section of the Staffordshire Way, the long distance footpath which runs from Mow Cop to **Kinver Edge**, near Stourbridge. This is a sandstone ridge covered in woodland and heath, and with several famous rock houses which were inhabited until the 1950s.

Back in Victorian days, Rudyard was a popular lakeside resort – in 1877 more than 20,000 people came here to see **Captain Webb**, the first man to swim the English Channel, swim in the Reservoir.

SANDON

Near the village stands the ancestral home of the Earl of Harrowby, **Sandon Hall**. Rebuilt in 1850 after the earlier house had been damaged by fire, the Hall is surrounded by 400 acres of parkland, which include a notable arboretum. The Hall is steeped in history and, along with the impressive interior, makes an interesting and informative visit. The family, too, has led a fascinating life, with seven generations in parliament and three successive members of the family holding office in the Cabinet. The museum tells of their lives and also includes costumes, toys and the duelling pistols of William Pitt the Younger.

SHALLOWFORD

Set in beautiful grounds in this tiny hamlet near Norton Bridge, **Izaak**

Izaak Walton's Cottage

Walton's Cottage is a pretty 17th century half-timbered cottage which was once owned by Izaak Walton, famous biographer and author of *The Compleat Angler*. Fishing collections are on show, and there's a small souvenir shop. Within the grounds are an authentic 17th century herb garden, a lovely picnic area and orchard.

STAFFORD

The Saxon origins of the county town of Staffordshire are still visible in the extensive earthworks close to the Castle and the foundations of a tiny chapel in the grounds of St Mary's Church. **Stafford Castle** is the impressive site of a Norman fortress where visitors can follow the castle trail, wander around the medieval herb garden and explore the visitor centre built in the style of a Norman Guardhouse. The Castle grounds are often used for historical re-enactments by such groups as the Napoleonic Society and are the site for Sealed Knot battles as well as other outdoor entertainment. Stafford originally had a medieval town wall and evidence of it can still be seen today in the names of the town's main streets. However, only the **East Gate** remains of the structure. Stafford lies on the banks of the River Sow, and **Green Bridge** marks the site of the ancient ford across the river. There has been a bridge on this spot since the late 1200s but the gate in the town's medieval walls that was also at this point was demolished in 1777. Just to the east of the Bridge is

Victoria Park, opened in 1908 and later extended to incorporate land reclaimed from the River Sow. There are many pleasant walks through the Park, which includes a mill pond and a weir, in particular to the **Windmill at Broad Eye**.

A place well worth visiting during any stay in Stafford is **The Ancient High House**, a beautiful Elizabethan house built in 1595 and now the largest surviving timber-framed town house in England. Through painstaking efforts over several years, Stafford Borough Council have restored this breathtaking piece of architecture to its former glory. Today the building houses the Museum of the Staffordshire Yeomanry and the Tourist Information Centre. The **Shire Hall Gallery** (1798) on the market square was the town courthouse and still retains the original panelled courtrooms. It is now a venue for contemporary exhibitions and children's workshops, and has a teashop and a workshop.

Close to the High House is the **Collegiate Church of St Mary**, an unusual building which dates in part from the late 1100s, but has received additions in the early English, Gothic and Victorian styles. The huge tower arches in the nave seem to divide the building into two, which is, in fact, exactly what they were intended to do, as St Mary's is two churches under one roof. The nave was the parish church of Stafford with its own altar while the chancel beyond was used by the Deans of the College of St Mary whose duty it was to pray for deceased members of the

Royal family. Although the College was abolished in 1548, the screens which divided the Church remained until 1841 and today the Church is still referred to as the Collegiate. Sir Izaak Walton was baptised here on 21st September 1593 and his bust can be seen on the north wall of the nave.

St Mary's Mews dates back to the mid-19th century and is a Grade II listed building. The architect was the renowned Gilbert Scott, the famous church restorer of the 1850s. Other notable buildings include The Infirmary, designed by Benjamin Wyatt and completed in 1772; the Noell Almshouses dating back to 1680, and Chetwynd House, the 17th century town house of the Chetwynd family and now used as the town's main Post Office.

STOKE-ON-TRENT

The city was established as late as 1910 when Fenton joined the five towns (Tunstall, Burslem, Hanley, Longton and Stoke) immortalised by the novels of Arnold Bennett. Once fiercely independent, the towns became progressively involved with each other as improvements in roads, water supplies and other amenities forced them towards amalgamation. The new city's crest, of an ancient Egyptian potter at his wheel in one quarter, sums up the fortune on which the wealth of the area was created. Each of the old towns is also represented in the crest and the joint motto translates to "Strength is stronger for unity".

century. For those interested in pottery and industrial architecture, Stoke-on-Trent is a wonderful place to visit, with many museums and factories open to the public to tell the story of the city. The **Spode Museum & Visitor Centre** in Church Street is one of several famous establishments open to visitors.

Hanley, one of the five towns of The Potteries, and part of the Stoke-on-Trent conurbation, was the birthplace of Arnold Bennett, Sir Stanley Matthews and John Smith (the captain of the ill-fated *Titanic*). **The Potteries Museum & Art Gallery** houses the world's finest collection of Staffordshire ceramics and offers many more attractions, including a natural history gallery and a lively programme of exhibitions, talks, tours and workshops. **Burslem**, in the northern suburbs, is the home of **Burleigh Earthenware Pottery**, founded in 1851 and famous for its elegant blue and white patterns. Also in Burslem is the **Royal Doulton Visitor Centre**, which contains the world's largest display of Royal Doulton figures and many other treasures from the company's rich heritage. **Etruria**, to the west of the city centre, was created by Josiah Wedgwood in 1769 as a village for the workers at the pottery factory he built in this once rural valley. Though the factory has gone (it moved to Barlaston in the 1940s), Etruria Hall, Wedgwood's home, is still standing in

Stoke-on-Trent Pottery

It was the presence of the essential raw materials for the manufacture and decoration of ceramics, in particular marl clay, coal and water, that led to the concentration of pottery manufacture in this area. Though production started in the 1600s it was the entrepreneurial skills of Josiah Wedgwood and Thomas Minton, who brought the individual potters together in factory-style workplaces, that caused the massive leap forward in production that took place in the 18th century. Their factories were large but there were also hundreds of small establishments producing a whole range of more utilitarian chinaware; production in the Potteries reached its height towards the end of the 19th what is now the National Garden Festival site. The pottery industry dominated the village and the **Etruria Industrial Museum** displays a steam-powered potters' mill as well as other exhibits connected with the industry.

TAMWORTH

A modern, busy town, Tamworth is actually much older than it first appears. Straddling the famous Roman Watling Street (now the A5), it has a fascinating and turbulent past. The first reference to the town dates back to the 8th century when it was the capital of the Kingdom of Mercia. King Offa built a palace here. Raiding Danes managed to destroy the town twice and it was later invaded by other Scandinavians, who left evidence of their visit in some of the street names such as Gungate. Alfred's daughter, Ethelfleda, was busy here, too, and excavations in the town centre have revealed Saxon fortifications. Dominating Tamworth today is the fine Norman motte and bailey **Castle** set in the Pleasure Grounds, which have truly magnificent floral terraces. The sandstone castle, with its superb herringbone wall, dates originally from the 1180s, having replaced a wooden tower on the present artificial mound constructed shortly after the Norman Conquest. The vast **Parish Church of St Editha**, founded in 963, is notable for its marvellous stained glass, including the work of William Morris and Burne-Jones.

The **Town Hall**, built in 1701, is charming, with open arches and Tuscan columns below. The building was paid for by Thomas Guy, the local Member of Parliament, who is probably more famous as the founder of the London hospital that bears his name. Thomas Guy also gave the town its 14 almshouses in **Lower Gungate**, which were rebuilt in 1913.

UTTOXETER

Today, the town is perhaps best known for its racecourse, a popular National Hunt track which lies to the southeast of town. Highlight of the course's 20 days of racing is the stamina-sapping **Midlands Grand National** held in the spring. Uttoxeter is a traditional, rural market town, with a busy livestock and street market on Wednesdays. There are several pleasant, old, timbered buildings in Uttoxeter but fires in 1596 and 1672 destroyed most of the town's architectural heritage. As well as a visit to the Heritage Centre, housed in some old timber-framed cottages in Carter Street, **St Mary's Church** should also appear on a sightseer's itinerary; it has a typical 'preaching box' dating from 1828.

WILLOUGHBRIDGE

This remote hamlet, on the slopes of the Maer Hills, was once a fashionable spa after warm springs were discovered by Lady Gerard. Those days have long since gone but a trip to the **Dorothy Clive Garden** on the Shropshire border is well worth making.

THE ANCIENT BRITON

GREENBANK ROAD, TUNSTALL, STAFFORDSHIRE ST6 7EZ
TEL: 01782 252496/837697

> **Directions:** Tunstall lies at the northern extremity of the conurbation that forms
> The Potteries. From junction 15 of the M6 follow the A500 north turning right
> onto the B5999 for Tunstall. In the centre of Tunstall take the A527 towards
> Biddulph but almost immediately, when it bears sharp left, continue straight on
> into Greenbank Road

The Ancient Briton, which can be found close to the centre of Tunstall, on the north edge of The Potteries, was only built in 1930. The pub actually has a rather impressive claim to fame though. The house opposite was once the home of Robbie Williams and The Ancient Briton was the first pub he sang karaoke in before going on to his incredibly successful pop career. Despite being placed firmly on the celebrity hunter's map, the pub was actually in a poor state when the McCaffery family took over in late 2002. However, Michael and Maggie, with daughters Jane and Jacqueline, and son-in-law

Neil, have turned the place around and it is alive and kicking again. It is gradually being refurbished throughout with new lighting and upholstery already completed.

Boasting a spacious interior, the pub can accommodate the many customers that come here to enjoy the tasty home-cooked food which is served all day. The regular menu offers lots of traditional dishes, with a specials board giving Maggie and Jane the opportunity to create something a little more special with seasonally available produce. There is a non-smoking dining area for which bookings are recommended, and children are welcome. The bar stocks a regularly changing guest ale together with popular lagers and beers on draught.

- Mon-Sat 11.00-23.00; Sun 12.00-22.30
- Wide ranging selection served all day except Sunday
- Patio area, children's play area planned
- Ceramica Visitor Centre 1 mile, Little Moreton Hall 6 miles, The Wedgwood Story Visitor Centre 9 miles, Bridgemere Garden World 12 miles

Staffordshire

THE BLACK LION

12 HOLLOW LANE, CHEDDLETON, LEEK, STAFFORDSHIRE ST13 7HP
TEL: 01538 361647

Directions: To reach Cheddleton, take the A500 from junction 15 of the M6 and after a couple of miles turn right onto the A50. Four miles further on turn left onto the A520 Leek road. Cheddleton is then about 8 miles

The Black Lion is a truly delightful hidden gem, tucked away in the back roads it is well worth taking the trouble to seek out. The premises date back to the 12th century when they were built to house the men who were building the adjoining Church of St Edward. In fact there is another religious link, with the upstairs function room having been used as the local Catholic church up until 50 years ago. As you approach, you cannot fail to appreciate the cosy country feel, with a neatly painted front, rustic tables and chairs outside, and walls

covered with sprawling ivy. Venturing inside, the characterful feel continues, with real fires, stripped wood doors, and lots of knick-knacks on display.

The place has recently been taken over by Kerry and Paul, a local couple who are new to the trade, but with a little gem like The Black Lion, are sure to have a great success on their hands. Opening all day, a tasty menu is served from midday until 8pm Monday to Saturday (lite bites only Tuesday and Wednesday) with a classic roast lunch served on Sunday. The chef specialises in serving traditional local dishes such as lobby (a stew), liver and onions and rabbit pie. Meanwhile, the bar can offer a choice of up to four real ales.

- ○ Mon-Sat 11.00-23.00; Sun 12.00-22.30
- ❚ Food served until 8pm Mon-Sat and Sunday lunch
- ℗ Beer garden, function room, car park
- ♪ Folk club meets here each Tuesday
- ? North Staffordshire Steam Railway, Tittesworth Reservoir 6 miles, Biddulph Grange Gardens 9 miles, Little Moreton Hall 12 miles, Peak District National Park 5 miles

BOWLING GREEN

LEEK ROAD, CELLARHEAD, STAFFORDSHIRE ST9 0JQ
TEL: 01782 550204 FAX: 01782 551544

> **Directions:** Cellarhead is just east of Newcastle-under-Lyme. From junction 16 of the M6 take the A500 towards Stoke and pick up signs for Hanley and Ashbourne A52. Cellarhead then lies about 6 miles east of Hanley on the A52

Built in the 18th century, the **Bowling Green** is a former coaching inn which lay on two busy coaching routes, between Buxton and Stafford, and Stoke and Ashbourne. It once had stables and the teams of horses would be changed here while the drivers and passengers were refreshed with food and drink.

Today, it still lies on the same busy crossroads and continues to cater to travellers in need of refreshment. Open at every session (closed Monday lunchtime in winter), and all day Friday to Sunday the bar serves a wide range of beer, lager and cider with three real ales also on tap – Worthington, Bass and a rotating guest ale. Food is served each lunchtime and evening, except Sunday evenings, with a printed menu and daily specials board. There is a dedicated non-smoking restaurant which can seat up to 36 diners, and children are welcome here. The spacious dining area looks out over the beer garden and patio, and in fine weather many customers like to eat al fresco.

The Bowling Green is run by two couples, Keith, Ruth, Michael and Margaret, and although they have only been in residence 12 months they bring with them many years experience in the trade. They are not able to offer accommodation within the pub, but there is a small caravan site to the rear. Ring for details.

- 🕐 Mon-Thur 11.30-15.00, 18.00-23.00; Fri-Sat 11.30-23.00; Sun 12.00-22.30
- 🍴 Printed menu and daily specials
- £ Visa, Mastercard, Delta, Switch
- 🚐 5 pitch caravan site
- Ⓟ Large beer garden, children's play area planned, car park
- 🎵 Charity pub quiz Sundays, free pool and cheap ale Wednesdays
- @ keith@bowling-green.fsnet.co.uk
- ❓ North Staffordshire Railway 5 miles, Ilam Park 13 miles, Ashbourne 17 miles, The Wedgwood Story Visitor Centre 9 miles, Alton Towers 11 miles

THE CROWN AT MOBBERLEY

TEAN ROAD, CHEADLE, STAFFORDSHIRE ST10 1TW
TEL/FAX: 01538 722422

> **Directions:** From junction 15 of the M6 take the A500 towards Stoke. After a couple of miles turn right onto the A50 Uttoxter road and after the junction with the A520 turn left onto the A521 and follow it to Cheadle. At Cheadle turn right onto the A522 and Mobberley is then just over a mile

The Crown at Mobberley is prominently situated on a corner site, directly on the A522, just south of Cheadle. A sizeable car park makes this ideal for those travelling by car and children are welcome both to eat in the restaurant and to enjoy the play area in the beer garden. The location, on the old Leek to Uttoxter coach road, means that the pub was a coaching inn and post house during the 18th century. Retaining a great deal of period charm,

both inside and out, it is family run and has a relaxed, friendly atmosphere. The tenants are Christine and Neville Parkes and they have been running the place together with their son David for the past eight years.

The bar offers a choice of two real ales together with a good range of draught lagers, cider and stout. However, it is the great food that is probably the main attraction here. The menu is wide ranging, from salads and sandwiches, to steaks and roasts, with a bar menu, senior citizens menu, and an a la carte selection too. Prices are reasonable and everyone is sure to find something that tickles their taste buds. Meals can be enjoyed in the main dining area or the non-smoking Blue Room.

🕐 Mon 18.00-23.00; Tue-Thur 11.00-15.00, 18.00-23.00; Fri-Sat 11.00-23.00; Sun 12.00-22.30; open all day bank holidays

🍴 Wide ranging menu offering superb choice

£ Visa, Mastercard, Delta, Switch

P Beer garden, children's play area, car park

♫ Darts, dominoes, crib

? Alton Towers 5 miles, Foxfield Light Railway 5 miles, Wedgwood Visitor Centre 11 miles, Shugborough Hall 17 miles, Bridgemere Garden World 18 miles

DOG AND PARTRIDGE

UTTOXETER ROAD (A522), LOWER TEAN, STAFFORDSHIRE ST10 4LN
TEL/FAX: 01538 722468

Directions: From the M6 take junction 13 or 14 and travel into the centre of Stafford. From here take the A518 and follow it all the way to Uttoxeter. Then turn onto the A522, which will be signposted for Cheadle, and you will reach Lower Tean after just 6 miles

With origins in the 18th century, it is not too surprising to learn that the **Dog and Partridge** was once a coaching inn with its own smithy. In those days the ale house was known by locals as Taskers, after the men who worked in the smithy. Continuing to cater to travellers, as well as the local community, the pub is a large, traditional country inn with a great deal of character. The interior is cosy and welcoming and although there is no longer a smithy, there is a superb conservatory which looks out over the beer garden. Seating

up to 75 diners, the non-smoking conservatory dining area is elegantly styled and ideal for a special meal out. The menu is excellent, with a wide range of dishes on the a la carte menu catering to all tastes, while the bar menu offers tasty snacks and lighter offerings. Food is served at every session, although it is bar meals only on Sunday and Monday evenings.

The bar stocks a choice of two real ales, with Marstons Pedigree and Worthington kept on tap. There is also a good wine list. The owners, Malcolm and Hazel, have chosen the Dog and Partridge to be their first venture into the trade and in their eight months here have gone from strength to strength.

- Mon-Wed 19.00-23.00; Thur-Sat 12.00-14.00, 19.00-23.00; Sun 12.00-14.00, 19.00-22.30
- Superb conservatory restaurant
- Visa, Mastercard, Delta, Switch
- Beer garden, children's play area, car park
- Quiz monthly in winter, live entertainment most Fridays
- Uttoexeter Racecourse 7 miles, Sudbury Hall 12 miles, Ashbourne 12 miles, Alton Towers 6 miles, Foxfield Light Railway 6 miles, Wedgwood Visitor Centre 11 miles

THE HOLLYBUSH INN

DENFORD ROAD, DENFORD, NR. LEEK, STAFFORDSHIRE ST13 7JT
TEL: 01538 371819

Directions: Take the A53 south from the centre of Leek for 2 miles, then at Longsdon turn left. Denford is then signposted

What a lovely inn **The Hollybush Inn** is! It sits with the Caldon Canal to the front and the Leek branch of the canal to the rear, and is a favourite stopping point for people cruising the waters. Dating back to the 17th century, it was actually a cornmill before it became a pub. Today visitors will find a picturesque, whitewashed building with small-paned windows and an inn sign that incorporates a clock. The inside is equally delightful and everything an English inn should be; the floors are part quarry tiles, there are old oak beams, open fires, copper and brass ornaments and comfortable seating. The restaurant area is roomy and well appointed, seating up to 20 people, though you can also eat in the conservatory or elsewhere in the hostelry

if you wish.

There is a printed menu and a specials board, and all the dishes are prepared in the inn's own kitchens from fresh ingredients that are sourced locally where possible. Try the speciality of the house, home-made beef and ale pie, or a dish that is infamous throughout the area, the Hollybush grill. To accompany your meal, you can choose from a selection of wines, or you can order from the bar. The range of drinks on offer includes Courage Best, Directors, Burton, Bass 4X Mild, Worthington Creamflow, Carling, Grolsch, Black Sheep, London Pride, Youngs Specials, Tiger, Strongbow and Guinness. The Hollybush Inn has been in the hands of the Prime family since 1979, and run by Steve and Linda since January 2000. A warm welcome awaits you.

- Mon-Sat 11.00-23.00; Sun 12.00-22.30
- Available all day seven days a week
- Large car park, beer garden
- Live entertainment every Thursday evening
- North Staffordshire Railway 2 miles, Leek 3 miles, Deep Hayes Country Park 1 mile, Flint Mill, Cheddleton 2 miles, Biddulph Grange 6 miles

THE LAMPLIGHTER

60 TAPE STREET, CHEADLE, STOKE-ON-TRENT,
STAFFORDSHIRE ST10 1ES
TEL/FAX: 01538 752259

> **Directions:** Cheadle is 7 miles east of Stoke-on-Trent. It can be reached by taking the A500 from junction 15 of the M6 then turning right onto the A50 Uttoxeter road. After about four miles Cheadle will then be signposted along the A521 to the left

It's hard to believe that just 12 months ago, when Sue Hodgkinson arrived at **The Lamplighter**, that it really was on its last legs. However the place has now taken on a new lease of life with a complete refurbishment throughout and now firmly on the local map as a popular place to enjoy good ale, fine food and excellent hospitality. Built in the Victorian era it was known for many years as The Station Hotel - a strange choice of name as there isn't a railway line through the town. The striking frontage leads to a comfortable interior

which has been attractively decorated and furnished whilst retaining a distinct period feel.

Each weekday The Lamplighter opens at 8.30am (open from 8.00am on Saturday) serving tasty breakfasts which have become something of a speciality. Children are most welcome and the pub attracts many walkers and other early risers. The more usual menu of bar meals and snacks is available at lunchtimes during the week with a delicious selection of home-cooked dishes on offer. During normal licensing hours, at lunchtime and in the evening (all day Friday to Sunday), the bar serves a good selection of draught keg bitters, lagers, cider and stout, together with two real ales from Thwaites brewery.

- 🕐 Mon-Thur 11.00-15.00, 18.00-23.00; Fri-Sat 11.00-23.00; Sun 12.00-22.30
- 🍴 Open for breakfast Monday to Saturday
- 💷 Visa, Mastercard, Delta, Switch
- 🅿 Car park
- 🎵 Quiz on Tuesdays, rock night once a month, live entertainment Saturdays
- ❓ Foxfield Light Railway 3 miles, Wedgwood Visitor Centre 10 miles, Alton Towers 5 miles, Ashbourne 12 miles, Sudbury Hall 14 miles, Ilam Park 11 miles

THE LORD SHREWSBURY

NEW ROAD, ALTON, STAFFORDSHIRE ST10 4AF

TEL: 01538 702218

Directions: From the M6 follow the A500 towards Stoke from junction 15 and after a couple of miles head southast along the A50. At Meir, bear left onto the A523 and follow signs for Cheadle. Then continue east along the B5032 and Alton will be signposted to the left after about 5 miles

The Lord Shrewsbury is an impressive looking building which started life as a coach house and stables owned by the Earl of Shrewsbury, who himself gained fame for founding Alton Towers. It has now been a pub for over 150 years but was only given its present name by the current owners, Andrew and Paula Price, on their arrival in Spring 2003. Ably assisted by various family members in the running of the pub, one of the first things they did was completely refurbish the interior to

create a plush, modern, city-style environment with high quality décor and furnishings. Open all day through the main tourist season, food is served all day too with a regular printed menu supplemented by a specials board. Meals can be enjoyed in the main restaurant or throughout the other bar areas, and children are welcome. A well stocked cellar offers a minimum of three real ales, together with other beers, lagers and much more.

Conveniently located for Alton Towers, and for exploring the delightful Staffordshire countryside and the Peak District, there are six, comfortable en-suite guest rooms with plans for creating a further four. Rates are the same throughout the year and include a hearty breakfast.

- Mon-Sat 11.00-23.00; Sun 12.00-22.30 (Mon-Thur 18.00-23.00 Nov-June)
- Quality restaurant open all day
- Visa, Mastercard, Delta, Switch, Amex
- 6 en-suite guest room (4 more planned)
- Children's games room, large car park
- Disco once a month
- Alton Towers 1 mile, Ashbourne 8 miles, Uttoxeter Racecourse 8 miles, Sudbury Hall 12 miles, The Wedgwood Story Visitor Centre 14 miles, Peak District National Park 8 miles

MOSS ROSE INN

BUXTON ROAD, LEEK, STAFFORDSHIRE ST13 7LN
TEL: 01538 371501

> **Directions:** Leek can be located from the M6 by taking the A500 from junction 16 southeast towards Stoke. On the outskirts of the town, Leek will be signposted along the A53. The Moss Rose is a mile beyond the town, heading towards Buxton

The Moss Rose Inn is a traditional country pub enjoying a rural location just a short drive from the centre of Leek. These attractive, whitewashed premises date back to the 18th century when it started life as a coaching inn complete with blacksmiths, and it was formerly known as The Forresters Inn. The interior is cosy and relaxed and the new tenants Ian and Traci extend a friendly welcome to customers old and new.

The pub enjoys a super reputation for serving delicious home-cooked food, and Traci prepares a wide ranging menu of home-made dishes each lunchtime and evening (no food Sunday evenings). There is a regular printed menu, supplemented by a blackboard of daily specials, and on Sundays there is a superb traditional Sunday lunch with a choice of two or three roast meats. There is a small no smoking dining area although meals can be taken throughout the bar areas and outside on the patio. The bar stocks a good selection with three real ales on tap including Marstons Bitter and Marstons Pedigree plus a rotating guest ale. There is also Banks Traditional Mild and other popular beers and lagers. A popular pub quiz is held each Sunday night.

- 🕐 Mon-Fri 11.00-15.00, 18.00-23.00; Sat 12.00-23.00, Sun 12.00-15.00, 18.00-22.30
- 🍴 Tasty home cooked menu of popular dishes
- 🅿 Patio, car park
- 🎵 Quiz Sunday nights, jamming session Saturday nights
- ❓ Brindley Mill 1 mile, Biddulph Grange Gardens 8 miles, Buxton 11 miles, Peak District National Park 1 mile, North Staffordshire Railway 4 miles

Staffordshire

THE NAVIGATION INN

NEWPORT ROAD, GNOSALL, STAFFORD ST10 0BN
TEL: 01785 822327 FAX: 01785 824822

Directions: From the M6, leave at junction 13 and head towards the centre of Stafford. As you reach the centre of the town, pick up the A518 Newport road. Gnosall will be reached after about 6 miles.

Located directly on the A518, at the western end of the large village of Gnosall, **The Navigation** is a delightful pub with a lovely conservatory overlooking the Shropshire Union Canal. It was built in the 18th century at the same time as the nearby mill which is notable for being the place where self-raising flour was first produced. The freshly painted brick frontage is adorned with colourful hanging baskets and four large union jacks, so you are unlikely to miss it as you pass by.

Venturing inside, you will find a spacious bar area, a locals' bar with pool table, and a superb dining area located within a conservatory overlooking the canal. You can enjoy light meals and snacks from the bar menu all day long, while in the restaurant they serve a more extensive a la carte menu. There is plenty to choose from, with vegetarian options, a children's selecion and OAP deals. Meals can also be taken outside in the pretty beer garden in warmer weather while younger visitors can make the most of the children's play area. The location makes this a popular haunt for locals, tourists and walkers, and the pub proves popular with all. In fact, if you happen to be travelling by canal, the location is Bridge 35 on the Shropshire Union, and there are moorings alongside the pub. If you prefer a lively evening out then there is a monthly pub quiz and in summer there are occasional BBQs, weather permitting.

🕐 Mon-Sat 12.00-15.00, 18.00-23.00; Sun 12.00-22.30

🍴 Snack menu available all day

💷 Visa, Mastercard, Delta, Switch, Amex, Diners

🅿 Children's play area, beer garden

🎵 Monthly pub quiz, summer BBQs, pool, darts

❓ Shropshire Union Canal, Stafford Castle 8 miles, Shugborough 12 miles, Cannock Chase 10 miles, Weston Park 8 miles, Ironbridge 16 miles, Royal Air Force Museum 12 miles

THE OXFORD ARMS

MORETON PARADE, MAYBANK, NEWCASTLE-UNDER-LYME,
STAFFORDSHIRE ST5 0JD
TEL: 01782 616129 FAX: 01782 628531

Staffordshire

Directions: Maybank lies just to the east of Newcastle-under-Lyme. To get there, take the A500 east from junction 15 of the M6 and follow signs for Stoke. Just after the junction with A53 Maybank will be signposted to the left

Situated amidst the leafy suburbs of Maybank Marsh, **The Oxford Arms** offers a unique combination of both quality dining and high-class live entertainment. The proprietor, Mark Anthony Fallon, is a well-respected music agent and highly skilled chef. With over 20 years' experience in the licensed trade and entertainment business he has sought to create a venue that offers everything a community could want all under one roof.

Dating back to the 1930s, there was once a colliery and steel works located behind the pub, but sadly these are long gone. Inside visitors will find a spacious, recently refurbished public bar complete with large screen TV for all the major sporting events. There is a relaxed, comfortable snug which also serves as a non-smoking restaurant area, a games rooms with pool table and jukebox, and finally a lounge room which can hold up to 220 people and is the venue for the live entertainment which is held most nights of the week. Mark uses his culinary skills to offer a varied menu of carefully selected dishes catering to all tastes. Food is available most lunchtimes and early evenings (no food Saturday evening or all day Sunday) and children are welcome in the snug. The Oxford stocks a fine array of cask beers, with Speckled Hen a regular feature, together with two rotating guest ales and a good selection of keg bitters, lagers and stout.

- ⏰ Mon-Sat 11.00-23.00; Sun 12.00-22.30
- 🍽 Select menu of tasty dishes
- 💷 Visa, Mastercard, Delta, Switch
- 🅿 Car park, games room
- ♫ Prize quiz Sundays, karaoke Monday and Friday nights, live music Wednesday, Thursday and Saturday
- @ email: mark@fallonents.freeserve.co.uk website: www.oxfordarms.co.uk
- ? Ceramica Visitor Centre 2 miles, The Wedgwood Story Visitor Centre 6 miles, Foxfield Light Railway 8 miles, Alton Towers 15 miles, Stapeley Water Gardens 14 miles

THE QUEENS AT FREEHAY

COUNSLOW ROAD, CHEADLE, STAFFORDSHIRE ST10 1RF
TEL/FAX: 01538 722383

Directions: Leaving the M6 at junction 15, take the A500 towards Stoke turning onto the A50 Uttoxeter road after a couple of miles. After crossing the A520 bear left onto the A521 which will lead you to Cheadle

Tucked away in the quiet Staffordshire town of Cheadle is the delightful **Queens at Freehay** public house. The charming building dates back to the 18th century and enjoys a pretty setting surrounded by mature trees and a well looked after garden.

Stepping over the threshold, visitors will be pleasantly surprised to find a refreshingly modern interior with bright décor and elegant tables and chairs. This is very much a family-run establishment with Anne and Graham Yates arriving in

1999, subsequently handing things over to their son Adrian a couple of years later, while still helping out where they can.

The family have created a well-liked eating and drinking place with high quality food that is renowned throughout the surrounding area. The a la carte menu offers something to suit every taste and appetite and there are also two daily specials board, one dedicated to fresh fish dishes. The fine cuisine can be enjoyed every lunchtime and evening and bookings are recommended at all times. The dining room is non-smoking and children are welcome. The bar offer a good choice of draught lagers, ciders and beers with two real ales, Bass and Worthington, also kept on tap.

- Mon-Sat 12.00-15.00, 18.00-23.00; Sun 12.00-15.00, 18.30-22.30; closed Christmas Day, Boxing day, New Years Eve night and New Years Day night
- Delicious food with a variety of menus
- Visa, Mastercard, Delta, Switch
- Small beer garden, car park
- Foxfield Light Railway 3 miles, Alton Towers 4 miles, Wedgwood Visitor Centre 9 miles, Uttoxeter Racecourse 11 miles, Sudbury Hall 14 miles, Ashbourne 13 milesmiles

RED LION INN

LICHFIELD ROAD, HOPWAS, TAMWORTH, STAFFORDSHIRE B78 3AF
TEL/FAX: 01827 62514

Directions: Tamworth can be found just to the west of the M42, and reached by following the A5. From the centre of town take the A51 signposted to Lichfield and you will find Hopwas after a further 2 miles

Set slightly back from the main Lichfield Road, the **Red Lion Inn** is an impressive, sizeable Victorian property surrounded by a large car park. From the road you would probably not realise that it actually backs onto the canal, and the most is made of this location with a superb beer garden with lots of tables. Inside you will find a bright modern bar and plenty of room for dining too. The public bar has recently been redecorated, again with a fresh, contemporary style.

Your host is John Runcorn and he has been running the Red Lion since 2001 and has over 26 years experience in the licensed trade. In his time here he has established a far reaching reputation for his superb cuisine, with John doing most of the cooking himself. The wide ranging menu and daily specials board are served from midday through until the evenings with the pub also opening for breakfasts from 10am. Although the pub is quite spacious, such is its popularity that it is advisable to book at weekends. The dining area is non-smoking but meals can also be taken in the bar and outside in the beer garden in fine weather. Families are made especially welcome and children can join their parents inside the pub and choose from their own menu. The well stocked bar offers plenty of liquid refreshment with three real ales kept on tap.

- 🕐 Mon-Sat 10.00-23.00; Sun 12.00-22.30
- 🍽 Superb menu available all day
- £ Visa, Mastercard, Delta, Switch
- Ⓟ Canal-side beer garden, car park
- ❓ Coventry Canal, Snowdome 2 miles, Staffordshire Regiment Museum 3 miles, Drayton Manor Park 4 miles, The Belfry 9 miles, Ash End House Children's Farm 8 miles

RED LION INN

Staffordshire

TOWNEND LANE, WATERFALL, STAFFORDSHIRE ST10 3HZ
TEL: 01538 308279

Directions: To reach Ashbourne from the M1 take the A52 from junction 25 through Derby and on to Ashbourne. Carry straight on through Ashbourne and after 5 miles bear right onto to A523 Leek road. Turn right at Waterhouses and follow signs for Waterfall

The Red Lion Inn enjoys an enviable location within the picturesque village of Waterfall on the edge of the Peak District National Park. Dating back to the late-19th century it is constructed of local stone and is built into a small hill which has led to the creation of an unusual tiered beer garden. It is only a small place but venturing inside you find there is bags of traditional character and a cosy, welcoming atmosphere.

🕐 Mon-Tue 19.00-23.00; Wed-Fri 12.00-15.00, 19.00-23.00 (closed Wed-Fri lunch mid-Sept-May); Sat 12.00-15.00, 19.00-23.00; Sun 12.00-15.00, 19.00-22.30

🍴 Wide-ranging home-cooked menu

🅿 Beer garden, patio area, car park

🎵 Folk night once a month

@ email: redlionwaterfall@onetel.net.uk website: web.onetel.net.uk/~redlionwaterfall

❓ Ilam Park 4 miles, Ashbourne 8 miles, North Staffordshire Railway 6 miles, Tittesworth Reservoir 9 miles, Alton Towers 6 miles, The Wedgwood Story Visitor Centre 15 miles

The owners, Brian and Kathleen Hunt, have been here for just a year and although it is their first venture into the trade have established themselves as friendly hosts. Kathleen is in charge of the kitchens and serves a varied menu of bar snacks and traditional hot dishes. Bookings are advisable for Sunday lunch which is always busy. This is a free house and the bar stocks many of the most popular selections for liquid refreshment. There are usually two real ales, Bass Bitter and M&B Mild, and also available on draught are Carling Premier, Strongbow, Guinness and Worthington Creamflow. Once a month, usually on the last Wednesday, there is live folk music from 9pm.

THE SWAN INN

FRADLEY JUNCTION, ALREWAS, NR. BURTON UPON TRENT,
STAFFORDSHIRE DE13 7DN
TEL: 01283 790330

> **Directions:** Head into the very centre of Tamworth from junction 10 of the M42
> and then pick up the A513 which heads north past the villages of Comberford and
> Elford. After 8 miles, at the junction with the A38, continue straight across and
> Fradley Junction will be signposted to the left.

The Swan has looked out over the junction of the Trent & Mersey and Coventry canals for over two centuries. It has played an important part in the everyday life of the canals, being originally constructed to serve the workmen that dug the canals then later used as a stabling point for boat horses. The charming Grade 2 listed building of whitewashed brick is located within a conservation area and is fondly known by the locals as "The Mucky Duck" and reputed to be one of the most photographed pubs in the country. The interior is cosy and full of character, having vaulted, brick ceilings held up by pillars, comfortable furniture, subdued

wall lighting and two open fires.

The owners are Jackie Burton and Jason Parker, together they work hard to create a welcoming establishment serving good food and fine ales to locals, visitors and canal users. There is a fine bar menu available throughout the day, offering a wide-ranging selection of meals and snacks, supplemented by a daily specials board. The Sunday lunch carvery has a following all of its own, and you are advised to arrive in good time to ensure you don't miss out. The bar stocks a good choice of ales, with Ansells, Burton and Marston Pedigree kept on tap all year round.

The canal provides the opportunity for a pleasant walk before your meal, with boat hire available next door for those who want to get more hands on.

- Mon-Sat 11.00-23.00; Sun 12.00-22.30
- Varied menu available
- Visa, Mastercard, Delta, Switch
- Ample car parking, boat moorings
- Trent & Mersey Canal, National Memorial Arboretum 1 mile, Burton-upon-Trent 8 miles, Staffordshire Regimental Museum 5 miles, Drayton Manor Park 11 miles, Lichfield City 6 miles.

99 The Anchor Inn, Bolsover, Derbyshire	**112** The Nelson Arms, Middleton by Wirksworth, Derbyshire
100 The Anchor Inn, Tideswell, Derbyshire	**113** New Inn, Woodville, Derbyshire
101 Bulls Head, Ilkeston, Derbyshire	**114** The Old Glove Works, Glossop, Derbyshire
102 The Bull's Head, Ashford-in-the-Water, Bakewell, Derbyshire	**115** The Peacock Inn, Cutthorpe, Chesterfield, Derbyshire
103 The Cross Keys, Castle Donington, Derby, Derbyshire	**116** The Princess Victoria, Matlock Bath, Derbyshire
104 The Duke William, Matlock, Derbyshire	**117** The Punchbowl, West Hallam, Derbyshire
105 The Elm Tree Inn, Elmton, Derbyshire	**118** Red Lion Hotel, Wirksworth, Derbyshire
106 Hardwick Inn, Hardwick Park, Chesterfield, Derbyshire	**119** The Royal Oak, Tibshelf, Derbyshire
107 The Jolly Sailor, Hemington, Derbyshire	**120** The Seven Oaks Inn & Restaurant, Stanton-by-Dale, Ilkeston, Derbyshire
108 The Kelstedge Inn, Kelstedge, Derbyshire	**121** The Swan Inn, Milton, Derbyshire
109 The Ketch, Kniveton, Derbyshire	**122** The White Cow, Ilkeston, Derbyshire
110 The Live and Let Live, Cotmanhay, Ilkeston, Derbyshire	**123** The White Hart Hotel, Ashbourne, Derbyshire
111 The Moon Hotel, Spondon, Derbyshire	

Please note all cross references refer to page numbers

DERBYSHIRE

Traditionally, Derbyshire marks the start of the north of England and the county was also at the forefront of modern thinking at the beginning of the Industrial Revolution. The chief inheritor of this legacy is Derby, the home of Rolls-Royce and Royal Crown Derby porcelain, and it remains a busy industrial centre today. An early landmark of this new age is Richard Arkwright's mill and associated village at Cromford.

However, the county is dominated by the Peak District National Park that covers much of its area. The first of the ten National Parks, it is often divided into White and Dark peak as the landscape changes from deep limestone valleys to bleak, isolate moorland.

Along with numerous attractive villages and small towns, ancient monuments and caves and cavers, the park is home to two of the finest stately homes not just in Derbyshire but also in the country – Haddon Hall and Chatsworth.

The southern section of the Peak District is probably best known for beautiful Dovedale. The large car park near Thorpe which gives general access to the Dale is often crowded, but there is plenty of room for everyone and the wonderful valley, just a few hundred yards from the car park, is well worth experiencing. It is also the place to have a go at crossing a river on stepping stones, something that has delighted children for many, many years. The River Dove is also a Mecca for keen fishermen.

PLACES OF INTEREST

Alfreton 72	Glossop 88
Ambergate 72	Heanor 89
Ashbourne 72	Ilam 89
Ault Hucknall 73	Ilkeston 90
Bakewell 74	Kedleston 90
Bamford 76	Matlock 90
Belper 77	Matlock Bath 91
Birchover 78	
Bolsover 78	Monyash 93
Buxton 79	Repton 93
Calke 81	Rowsley 94
Castleton 82	South Wingfield 95
Chesterfield 83	
Creswell 84	Sudbury 95
Dale Abbey 84	Swarkestone 95
Derby 85	Thorpe 96
Edale 86	Tideswell 96
Edensor 86	Tissington 96
Elvaston 87	Wirksworth 97
Eyam 88	

Black Tor & Loose Hill, High Peak

The ancient custom of well-dressing is almost exclusively confined to the limestone areas of the county. The porous rock, through which rainfall seeped leaving the surface completely dry just a few hours after heavy rainfall, meant that, for the people of these close-knit communities, the well or spring was of utmost importance. If this dried up, the lives of the whole community were at risk.

The area of northeast Derbyshire and the District of Bolsover centres around Chesterfield. This was the heart of the county's coal-mining area and many of the towns and villages reflect the prosperity the mines brought in Victorian times. Sadly, the vast majority of the collieries are now closed; there was for a while a period of decline, but visitors today will be surprised at the wealth of history and fine architecture to be seen throughout the region.

The Peak District National Park was the

Monsal Dale Viaduct

first of Britain's National Parks to be established, in 1951, and ever since then

its 555 square miles of glorious scenery has been protected from 'inappropriate development'. Of all the world's national parks, it is the second most popular – only Mount Fuji in Japan attracts more visitors each year.

Referred to as the Dark Peak as well as the High Peak, the northern area of the Peak District National Park is not as foreboding as its name might suggest. These high moors are ripe for exploring on foot, and a walk from the Kinder Reservoir will lead to the western edge of Kinder Scout. This whole area is really a series of plateaux, rather than mountains and valleys, with the highest point on Kinder Scout some 2,088 feet above sea level. In this remote and wild area the walker can feel a real sense of freedom - however, it is worth remembering that the moors, with

Well Dressing, Youlgreave

their treacherous peat bogs and unpredictable mists which can rise quickly even in summer, should not be dismissed as places for a casual ramble.

To the eastern side of this region are the three reservoirs created by flooding of the upper valley of the River Derwent. Howden, Derwent, and Ladybower provide water for the East Midlands but their remote location, along with the many recreational activities found there, make them popular places to visit. The Derwent dam is particularly famous as the site of practice exercises for the Dambusters of the Second World War.

ALFRETON

This attractive former coal-mining town stands on a hill close to the Nottinghamshire border. On the charming High Street can be found the George Hotel, a fine Georgian building that looks down the length of the street. There are also a number of other 18th century stone built houses, the most impressive of which is **Alfreton Hall** (private), the centrepiece of an attractive public park. In soft mellow stone, the Hall was built around 1730, with 19th century additions. The park is quite extensive, boasting its own cricket ground and a horse-riding track around its perimeter. In **King Street** there is a house of confinement, or Lock-up, which was built to house lawbreakers and catered mainly for the local drunkards. The close confines of the prison with its two cells, minute windows and thick outer walls must have been a very effective deterrent.

AMBERGATE

Where the River Amber joins the mighty Derwent, Ambergate is one of the main gateways to the Peak District for travellers going north on the A6. The village is surrounded by deciduous woodland, including the fine **Shining Cliff Woods**, an important refuge for wildlife. The railway, road and canal here are all squeezed into the tight river valley, and the railway station, standing 100 feet above the road, was one of the few triangular stations in Britain. Built

in the late 19th century, the church of St Anne was a gift to the village from the Johnson family of the Ambergate Wire Works, now known as the business concern Richard Johnson and Nephew.

ASHBOURNE

Ashbourne is one of Derbyshire's finest old towns, with a wealth of wonderful Georgian architecture as well as some older buildings, notably the **Gingerbread Shop** which is timber framed and probably dates from the 1400s. The triangular cobbled **Market Square** was part of the new development begun in the 1200s that shifted the town to the east, away from the church. Weekly markets have been held in the square since 1296, and still take place every Saturday. It was in this market place, once lined with ale houses, that Bonnie Prince Charlie proclaimed his father as King James III, and so started the Jacobite Rebellion. Traditional Ashbourne gingerbread is said to be made from a recipe that was acquired from French prisoners of war who were kept in the town during the Napoleonic Wars.

Also worthy of a second glance is the **Green Man and Black's Head Royal Hotel**. The inn sign stretches over the St John's Street and was put up when the Blackamoor Inn joined with the Green Man in 1825. Though the Blackamoor is no more, the sign remains and it claims to be the longest hotel name in the country. Of Georgian origin, the amalgamated hotel has played host to

James Boswell, Dr Johnson and the young Princess Victoria. Ashbourne was, in fact, one of Dr Johnson's favourite places; he came to the town on several occasions between 1737 and 1784. He also visited the hotel so often that he had his own chair with his name on it! The chair can still be seen at the Green Man.

A stroll down **Church Street**, described by Pevsner as one of the finest streets in Derbyshire, takes the walker past many interesting Georgian houses – including the Grey House which stands next to the **Grammar School**. Founded by Sir Thomas Cockayne on behalf of Elizabeth I in 1585, the school was visited on its 400th anniversary by the present Queen. Almost opposite the Grey House is **The Mansion**, the late-17th century home of the Reverend Dr John Taylor, oldest friend of Dr Johnson. Next to The Mansion are two of the many almshouses established in Ashbourne during the 17th and 18th centuries.

In **St Oswald's Parish Church** Ashbourne has one of the most impressive and elegant churches in the country, described by George Eliot as "the finest mere parish church in England". James Boswell said that the church was "one of the largest and most luminous that I have seen in any town of the same size". St Oswald's stands on the site of a minster church mentioned in the Domesday Book, though most of what stands today dates from rebuilding work in the 13th century.

The alabaster tombs and monuments to the Bradbourne and Cockane families in the north transept chapel are justly famous. Perhaps the best-known monument is that to Penelope Boothby, who died in 1791 at the tender age of five. Thomas Banks' white Carrara marble figure of the sleeping child is so lifelike that she still appears to be only sleeping. The moving epitaph reads: "She was in form and intellect most exquisite; The unfortunate parents ventured their all on this frail bark, and the wreck was total". It is said that Penelope's parents separated at the child's grave and never spoke to each other again.

Ashbourne is home to the famous Shrovetide football game played on Shrove Tuesday and Ash Wednesday. The two teams, the 'Up'ards' (those born north of the Henmore Brook) and the 'Down'ards' (those born south of it) begin their match at 2pm behind the Green Man Hotel. The game continues until well into the evening. The two goals are situated three miles apart, along the Brook, on the site of the old mills at Clifton and Sturston. It is rare for more than one goal to be scored in this slow-moving game.

AULT HUCKNALL

The strange name of this village probably means 'Hucca's high nook of land', and this pleasant place, standing on a ridge close to the Nottinghamshire border, is home to the magnificent Tudor house, **Hardwick Hall** (National Trust).

It is one of Derbyshire's Big Three stately homes alongside Chatsworth and Haddon, all three glorious monuments to the great landowning families who played so great a role in shaping the history of the county. The letters E S can be seen carved in stone on the outside of the house: E S, or Elizabeth of Shrewsbury, was perhaps better known as Bess of Hardwick. This larger-than-life figure had attachments with many places in Derbyshire, and the story of her life makes for fascinating reading. The house stands as a monument to her wealth and good taste, and is justly famous for its magnificent needlework and tapestries, carved fireplaces and friezes, which are considered as among the finest in Britain.

Though Bess is the first person that springs to mind with regard to Hardwick Hall, it was the 6th Duke of Devonshire who was responsible for the Hall's antiquarian atmosphere. He inherited the property in 1811 and, as well as promoting the legend that Mary, Queen of Scots stayed here, he filled the house with furniture, paintings and tapestries from his other houses and from Chatsworth in particular.

BAKEWELL

The only true town in the Peak District National Park, Bakewell attracts many day-trippers, walkers and campers as well as locals who come to take advantage of its many amenities. The beautiful medieval five-arched bridge spanning the River Wye is still in use today as the main crossing point for traffic. A stone-built town set along the banks of the River Wye, Bakewell enjoys a picturesque setting among well-wooded hills. With only 4,000 inhabitants it is nevertheless generally acknowledged as the capital of the **Peak District National Park**.

For many, it is a dessert that has made the name of Bakewell so famous, but please remember it is referred to locally as a *pudding* and most definitely not as a tart! Its invention is said to have been an accident when what was supposed to have been a strawberry tart turned into something altogether different. The cooking mishap took place in the kitchens of the Rutland

Harwick Hall

Arms Hotel which was built in 1804 on the site of a coaching inn. One of the hotel's more famous guests was the novelist Jane Austen, who stayed there in 1811. The Rutland Arms featured in her book *Pride and Prejudice*, while Bakewell itself appears as the town of Lambton.

Bakewell is the market town for this whole central area of the Peak District – markets were held here well before the granting of a charter in

River Wye, Bakewell

1330. In fact, its importance during the 11th century was such that, as recorded in the Domesday Book of 1086, Bakewell had two priests. Monday is now Bakewell's market day and the cattle market, one of the largest in Derbyshire, is an important part of the area's farming life. The annual **Bakewell Show** started in 1819 and has gone on to become one of the foremost agricultural shows in the country. Across the River Wye stands the enormous, new Agricultural and Business Centre, where the livestock market takes place.

The large parish **Church of All Saints** was founded in Saxon times, as revealed by the ancient preaching crosses and stonework. Its graceful spire, with an octagonal tower, can be seen for miles around. One of the few places in Derbyshire in the Domesday book to

record two priests and a church, the churchyard and church itself contain a wonderful variety of headstones and coffin slabs and, near the porch, a most unusual cross. Over 1,200 years old, it stands an impressive 8 feet high. On one side it depicts the Crucifixion, on the other are the Norse gods Odin and Loki.

Behind the church is the lovely **Old House Museum**, housed in a building on Cunningham Place which dates back to 1534. It is thought to be the oldest house in Bakewell. This beautiful building narrowly escaped demolition but has been lovingly restored by the **Bakewell Historical Society** and now displays its original wattle and daub interior walls. Now established as a folk museum, it houses a fascinating collection of rural bygones.

The town is full of delightful, mellow

stone buildings, many of which date from the early 1600s and are still in use today. The **Old Town Hall** is now the Tourist Information Centre of the Peak District. Few buildings remain from the days when Bakewell was a minor spa town, but the **Bath House**, on Bath Street, is one such building. Built in 1697 for the Duke of Rutland, it contained a large bath which was filled with the spa water and kept at a constant temperature of 59 degrees Fahrenheit.

Only a mile to the south of Bakewell down the Matlock Road, on a bluff overlooking the Wye, the romantic **Haddon Hall** stands hidden from the road by a beech hedge. The home of the Dukes of Rutland for over 800 years, the

Haddon Hall

Hall has enjoyed a fairly peaceful existence, in part no doubt because it stood empty and neglected for nearly 300 years after 1640, when the family chose Belvoir Castle in Leicestershire as their main home. Examples of work from

every century from the 12th to the 17th are evident in this architectural treasure trove, while the 16th century terraced gardens are one of the chief delights of the Hall, thought by many to be the most romantic in England. The Hall's chapel is adorned with medieval wall paintings; the kitchens are the oldest extant part of the house, and feature time-worn oak tables and dole cupboards. The oak-panelled Long Gallery features boars' heads (to represent Vernon) and peacocks (Manners) in the panelling.

BAMFORD

This charming village stands at the heart of the Dark Peak below **Bamford Edge** and close to the **Upper Derwent Valley Dams**. When the Derwent and Howden Dams were built in the early years of the 20th century, the valley of the Upper Derwent was flooded, submerging many farms under the rising waters. The 1,000 or so workers and their families were housed at Birchinlee, a temporary village which came to be known locally as 'Tin Town' because of its plethora of corrugated iron shacks. During the Second World War the third and largest reservoir, the **Ladybower**, was built. This involved the inundating of two more villages – Derwent and Ashopton. The dead from Derwent's church were re-interred in the churchyard of St John the Baptist in Bamford. The living were rehoused in Yorkshire Bridge, a purpose-built hamlet located below the embankment of the Ladybower Dam. There is a Visitor Centre at **Fairholmes** (in the Upper Derwent Valley) which tells the story of

Ladybower Resevoir

these 'drowned villages'.

The **Derwent Dam**, built in 1935, was the practice site for the Dambusters, who tested dropping their bouncing bombs here.

Bamford's **Church of St John the Baptist** is unlike any other in Derbyshire. Designed in 1861 by the famous church architect William Butterfield, it has a slender tower and an extra-sharp spire. Also worthy of note, particularly to lovers of industrial architecture, is **Bamford Mill**, just across the road by the river. This cotton mill was built in 1820; it retains its huge waterwheel and also has a 1907 tandem-compound steam engine.

The village lies in the heart of hill-farming country, and each Spring Bank Holiday Bamford plays host to one of the most famous of the Peak District Sheepdog Trials.

BELPER

Famous for its cotton mills, the town is situated alongside the **River Derwent** on the floor of the valley. In 1776, Jedediah Strutt, the wheelwright son of a South Normanton farmer, set up one of the earliest water-powered cotton mills here to harness the natural powers of the river to run his mills. With the river providing the power, and fuel coming from the nearby South Derbyshire coalfield, the valley has a good claim to be one of the cradles of the Industrial Revolution. Earlier, in 1771, Strutt had gone into profitable partnership with Richard Arkwright to establish the world's first water-powered cotton mill at Cromford. Great benefactors to Belper for 150 years, the Strutt family provided housing, work, education and even food from the model farms they established in the surrounding countryside.

The mills are still standing and, along with them, some unique mill-workers' cottages. To discover more about the cotton industry, a visit to the **Derwent Valley Visitor Centre** is a must. It records the influence of the Strutt family on the town and of Samuel Slater,

Strutt's apprentice who emigrated to America in 1789, built a mill there and went on to become 'the Father of American manufacturers'.

The oldest mill still surviving is the two-storey **North Mill** at Bridgefoot, near the magnificent crescent-shaped weir in the Derwent and the town's bridge. Built in 1876, the mill has cast-iron columns and beams, and hollow tile floors which provided a warm-air central heating system. It is now the visitor centre.

The massive, neighbouring redbrick **East Mill** was constructed in 1912, but is now largely empty. A Jubilee Tower in terracotta was erected on the mill site in 1897 to mark Queen Victoria's sixty years on the throne. Train travellers through Belper are among those treated to a glimpse of George Stephenson's mile-long cutting, walled in gritstone throughout and spanned by no fewer than ten bridges. When completed in 1840 it was considered the engineering wonder of its day. In addition to all its industrial history the town goes back to well before the Industrial Revolution. It was mentioned in the Domesday Book (as *Beau Repaire* - the beautiful retreat), and in 1964 the remains of a Roman kiln were found here.

The River Gardens are a pleasant place for a stroll among the beautifully tended gardens. Rowing boats can be hired for a trip along the Derwent. The Gardens are a favourite with the film industry, having been used in Ken Russell's *Women in Love*, as well as

television's *Sounding Brass* and *In the Shadow of the Noose*.

BIRCHOVER

The strange **Rocks of Rowtor**, behind The Druid Inn, are said to have been used for Druidical rites. The Rev Thomas Eyre, who died in 1717, was fascinated by these rocks and built the strange collection of steps, rooms and seats which have been carved out of the gritstone rocks on the summit of the outcrop. It is said that the Reverend Eyre would take his friends there to admire the view across the valley below – a view which nowadays is obscured by trees.

The equally strange outcrops of **Robin Hood's Stride** and **Cratcliff Tor** are nearby. A medieval hermit's cave, complete with crucifix, can be seen at the foot of Cratcliff Tor hidden behind an ancient yew tree.

BOLSOVER

The approach to Bolsover from the north and east is dominated by the splendid, sandstone structure of **Bolsover Castle** (English Heritage), which sits high on a limestone ridge. A castle has stood here since the 12th century, though the present building is a fairytale 'folly' built for Sir Charles Cavendish during the early 1600s on the site of a ruined castle. By the mid-1700s much of the building had been reduced to the ruins seen today, though thankfully the splendid keep has withstood the test of time.

Pevsner remarked that not many large

houses in England occupy such an impressive position as Bolsover Castle, which stands on the brow of a hill overlooking the valley of the River Rother and Doe Lea. The first castle at Bolsover was built by William Peverel, illegitimate son of William the Conqueror, as part of his vast Derbyshire estates. Nothing remains of that Norman building. Visitors can explore the Little Castle, or Keep, which is decorated in an elaborate Jacobean style with wonderful fireplaces, panelling and wall paintings.

BUXTON

With a population of barely 20,000, the elegant Georgian town of Buxton is nevertheless the largest settlement within the boundaries of the Peak District National Park. (The second largest town, Bakewell, has fewer than 5,000 inhabitants.) Buxton's gracious architecture can be attributed mainly to the efforts of the 5th Duke of Devonshire, who hoped to establish a northern spa town that would rival, possibly surpass, the attractions of Bath in the southwest. In both locations it was the Romans who first exploited the healing waters of apparently inexhaustible hot springs as a commercial enterprise. The Romans' name for Buxton was *Aquae Arnemetiae* – the Spa of the Goddess of the Grove.

The waters still bubble up at Buxton, always maintaining an incredibly constant temperature of 82 degrees Fahrenheit (28 degrees Centigrade). Buxton water is reputed to be particularly pure and especially effective in mitigating the symptoms of rheumatism. Countless sufferers from rheumatism are on record attesting that the balmy Buxton water helped to soothe their painful symptoms: Mary, Queen of Scots, a political prisoner detained at nearby Chatsworth but allowed out on day release to Buxton, was one of them.

In the 18th century, the 5th Duke of Devonshire commissioned the building of **The Crescent** to ensure that visitors would flock here. Designed by John Carr of York, the building is similar to the architecture found in Bath and, after suffering from neglect, underwent a huge

Buxton Opera House

restoration programme. As with many places, the coming of the railway to Buxton in 1863 marked the height of the town's popularity. Nothing, however, could be done to alter the harsh climate, and the incessant rainfall meant that the Duke's dream of making Buxton the 'Bath of the North' was never truly realised.

Among the other notable architectural features of the town are **The Colonnade** and the **Devonshire Royal Hospital**. They were originally built as stables for hotel patrons of The Crescent and, after their conversion by the 6th Duke in 1858, the largest unsupported dome in the world was built to enclose the courtyard in 1880.

Originally built in 1905, the attractive **Opera House** was restored in 1979 to its grand Edwardian style. After being used as a cinema for many years, it is once again the host of live performances and, as well as offering a comprehensive and popular programme throughout the year, also has one of the largest stages in England.

The attractive **Pavilion Gardens** have a conservatory and octagon within the grounds – antique markets and arts shows are often held here, and it is a very pleasant place to walk around any time of year. Laid out in 1871 by Edward Milner, with money donated by the Dukes of Devonshire, the 23 acres include formal gardens, serpentine walks and decorative iron bridges across the River Wye. The conservatory was reopened in 1982 following extensive renovation; there is also a swimming pool filled with warm spa water.

St John the Baptist church was built in Italian style in 1811 by Sir Jeffrey Wyatville. That same year Wyatville laid out The Slopes, the area below the Market Place in Upper Buxton. The grand **Town Hall** was built between 1887 and 1889 and dominates the Market Place. Further down Terrace Road is the **Buxton Museum**, which reveals the long and varied history of the town and its surrounding area. **St Anne's Church**, built in 1625, reflects the building work performed here before Buxton's 18th century heyday when limestone was the most common construction material rather than the mellow sandstone that dominates today.

Buxton is surrounded by some of the most glorious of the Peak District countryside. These moorlands also provide one of the town's specialities – heather honey. Several varieties of heather grow on the moors: there is ling, or common heather, which turns the land purple in late summer; there is bell-heather which grows on dry rocky slopes; and there is cross-leaved heather which can be found on wet, boggy ground.

To the west of the town lies **Axe Edge**, the highest point of which rises to 1,807 feet above sea level. From this spot on a clear day (and the weather here is notoriously changeable) the panoramic views of Derbyshire are overwhelming. Just beyond, at 1,690 feet above sea level, the **Cat and Fiddle Inn** is the second highest pub in England. **Axe Edge Moor**, which receives an average annual rainfall of over four feet, is strictly for hardened walkers. It should come as no surprise that this Moor is the source of several rivers which play important roles in the life of the Peak District. The **River Dove** and the **River Manifold**, which join at Ilam, rise not far from one another; the **River Wye** rises above Buxton to join the Derwent further south; the **River Goyt**, a major source of the Mersey, rises to the west of Axe Edge. The entire length of the River Goyt can be walked, from its source to its confluence with the River Etherow to the north and just outside the boundaries of the National Park.

Those who venture to **Errwood Reservoir** will be surprised to see rhododendrons growing near the banks of a man-made lake. They once stood in the grounds of Errwood Hall, which was built in the 1830s for the Grimshawe family. The house was demolished before the Reservoir was flooded, but the gardens were left to grow wild. Not far away can be seen the strange-looking Spanish Shrine. Built by the Grimshawes in memory of their Spanish governess, it is a small stone building with an unusual beehive roof.

Also to the west of town, **Poole's Cavern** on Green Lane is a natural limestone cave which was used by tribes from the Neolithic period onwards. It was visited by Mary, Queen of Scots and the 'chair' she used is pointed out during the regular tours of the cave. Above the cavern and about 20 minutes' walk away is **Grin Low Country Park** and the prominent folly and scenic viewpoint, built in 1896, known as **Solomon's Temple**.

CALKE

In 1985 the National Trust bought **Calke Abbey**, a large Baroque-style mansion built in 1701 on the site of an Augustinian priory founded in 1133. However, it was not until 1989 that the Trust were able to open the house to the public, for this was no ordinary house at all. It was dubbed "the house that time forgot", as since the death of the owner, Sir Vauncy Harpur-Crewe, in 1924 nothing had been altered in the mansion! In fact, the seclusion of the house and also the rather bizarre lifestyle of its inhabitants had left many rooms and objects untouched for over 100 years. There was even a spectacular 18th century Chinese silk state bed that had never been unpacked.

Today, the Trust has repaired the house and returned all 13,000 items to their original positions so that the Abbey now looks just as it did when it was bought in 1981. The attention to detail has been so great that none of the rooms has been redecorated. Visitors can enjoy the silver display and trace the route of 18th century servants along the brewhouse tunnel to the house cellars. Calke Abbey stands in its own large park with gardens, a chapel and stables that are also open to the public. There are three walled gardens with their glasshouses, a restored orangery, vegetable garden, pheasant aviaries and the summer flower display within the unusual 'auricular' theatre.

Derbyshire

CASTLETON

Situated at the head of the Hope Valley, Castleton is sheltered by the Norman ruin of **Peveril Castle** with its spectacular views over Castleton and the surrounding countryside. The Castle, originally called Castle of the Peak, was built as a wooden stockade in 1080 by William Peveril, illegitimate son of William the Conqueror. It was later rebuilt in stone and the keep added by Henry II. It remains the only surviving example of a Norman castle in Derbyshire, and is among the best preserved and most complete ruins in Britain. Approaching Castleton from the west along the A625, the road runs through the **Winnats Pass**, a narrow limestone gorge. Thought to have been formed under the sea, from currents eroding the seabed, the gorge has been used as a road for centuries and is still the only direct route to the village from the west.

The hills to the west of Castleton are famous for their caves. The **Blue John Mine and Caverns**, which have been in the hands of the Ollerenshaw family for many years, are probably one of Derbyshire's most popular attractions, offering amazing trips down into the depths. Above ground, in the gift shops various items can be bought made from the distinctive Blue John fluorspar with its attractive purplish veining. The village's **Ollerenshaw Collection** of huge vases and urns made from the same unique stone is open to the public. Once prized by the Romans, it is said that Petronius paid the equivalent of around £40,000 for a wonderfully ornate vase carved from the stone.

At the bottom of Winnats Pass lies **Speedwell Cavern**, a former lead mine which used boats on an underground canal to ferry the miners and iron ore to and from the rockface. Visitors can follow the same boat journey underground in the company of a guide. **Peak Cavern**, reached by a delightful riverside walk, has the widest opening of any cave in Europe., and up until the 17th century, little cottages used to stand within the entrance. The ropemakers who lived in these tiny dwellings used the cave

Castleton Village

entrance, dry in all weathers, for making rope: the ropewalk, which dates back some 400 years, can still be seen. Guides re-enact the process of making rope, and one rope-maker's cottage is still extant. Recently the cave was used by the BBC who filmed an episode of *The Chronicles of Narnia* series here. Over the years successive Kings and Queens would entertain deep within the belly of the cave, which would be festooned with candles and other open flames – visitors can see the ledge on which the Royal musicians would perch. Peak Cavern was originally known as The Devil's Arse, but the fastidious Victorians felt this was 'inappropriate' and changed it to the name it carries today.

No description of Castleton would be complete without a mention of **Mam Tor**. The name means 'Mother Hill', and locally the tor is referred to as Shivering Mountain, because the immense cliff face near the summit is constantly on the move owing to water seepage. A climb to the top of the ridge is well worth while, as the views are splendid – in particular of the two diverse rock formations which separate the White (limestone) Peak from the northern Dark (gritstone) Peak.

CHESTERFIELD

This friendly, bustling town on the edge of the **Peak District National Park** grew up around its open-air market which was established over 800 years ago and claims to be England's largest. The market is as popular as ever and is held every Monday, Friday and Saturday, with a flea market each Thursday.

The town centre has been conserved for future generations by a far-sighted council, and many buildings have been saved, including the Victorian **Market Hall** built in 1857. The traditional cobbled paving was restored in the Market Place, and New Square was given a complete facelift. There are several Tudor buildings in the heart of

St Mary & All Saints' Church

Chesterfield, most notably the former Peacock Inn which is now home to the **Peacock Heritage Centre** and the tourist information office.

Visitors to the town are drawn to a peculiarly graceful spire reaching high into the skyline; twisting and leaning, it is totally confusing to the eye. The **Crooked Spire** of St Mary & All Saints' Church has dominated the skyline for so long that local folk have ceased to notice its unusual shape. Superstition surrounds it, and sadly the real story behind its unusual appearance has been lost over the years. The truth probably lies in the wake of the Black Death during the 14th century, when the people of Chesterfield were building their beautiful new church and awe-inspiring steeple. Many must have fallen to the plague, among them skilled craftsmen who knew how to season wood. The survivors built the spire out of green timber which over the years has distorted under the heavy lead covering. However, some stories say it was the Devil, who, pausing for a rest during one of his flights, clung to the spire for a moment or two. Incense from the Church drifted upwards and the Devil sneezed, causing the spire to twist out of shape.

This magnificent spire rises to 228 feet and leans 9 feet 4 inches from its true centre-point. It is eight-sided, but the herringbone pattern of the lead slates trick the eye into seeing 16 sides from the ground.

CRESWELL

Lying close to the Derbyshire-Nottinghamshire border, the limestone gorge known as **Creswell Crags** is well worth visiting. Formed thousands of years ago by the erosion of a river which cut through the limestone, this rock, which is porous and subject to erosion

underground as well as on the surface, contributes by its very nature to the forming of natural chambers. The subterranean movement of water created a vast network of caves, which were subsequently exposed and used by Neanderthal man as shelters. Tours can be taken from the Visitor Centre, where there is also a display of artefacts found in the area. Testimony to the artistry of the later inhabitants of these caves was the discovery of a bone carved with the head of a horse. The carving is about 13,000 years old and can now be seen in the British Museum. The largest cavern, **Church Hole Cave**, extends some 170 feet into the side of the gorge; it was here that hand tools were found.

DALE ABBEY

The village takes its name from the now ruined abbey that was founded here by Augustinian monks in the 13th century. Beginning life in a very humble manner, local legend has it that a Derbyshire baker came to the area in 1130, carved himself a niche in the sandstone and devoted himself to the way of the hermit. The owner of the land, Ralph FitzGeremunde, discovered the baker and was so impressed by the man's devotion that he bestowed on him the land and tithe rights to his mill in Borrowash. The sandstone cave and the romantic ruined 40 feet high window archway are popular attractions locally and a walk around the village is both an interesting and a pleasurable experience. Nearby **Hermit's Wood** is an ancient area of woodland with beech, ash, oak and lime trees. It is wonderful at any time of year, but particularly in the spring when the woodland floor is covered with a carpet of bluebells.

To the north of the village stands the **Cat and Fiddle Windmill**, built in the 1700s and a fine example of the oldest type of mill. The stone roundhouse is capped with a box-like wooden structure which houses the machinery and which is fitted onto an upright post round which it can rotate to catch the wind.

DERBY

Essentially a commercial and industrial city, Derby's position, historically and geographically, has ensured that is has remained one of the most important and interesting cities in the area. Consequently there is much for the visitor to see, whether from an architectural or historical point of view. There are, however, two things almost everyone, whether they have been to the city before or not, associate with Derby: Rolls-Royce engines and Royal Crown Derby porcelain. When in 1906 Sir Henry Royce and the Hon CS Rolls joined forces and built the first **Rolls-Royce** (a Silver Ghost) at Derby, they built much more than just a motor car. Tours of the **Royal Crown Derby** factory offer an intriguing insight into the high level of skill required to create the delicate flower petals, hand gild the plates and hand paint the Derby Dwarves.

The city's **Cathedral of All Saints**

possesses a fine 16th century tower, the second highest perpendicular tower in England, and among the treasures inside are a beautiful wrought-iron screen by Robert Bakewell and the tomb of Bess of Hardwick Hall. Originally Derby's Parish Church, it was given cathedral status in 1927.

One of Derby's most interesting museums is **Pickford House**, situated on the city's finest Georgian street at number 41. It is a Grade I listed building, erected in 1770 by the architect Joseph Pickford as a combined family home and place of work. Pickford House differs from the majority of grand stately homes; unlike most it does not have a wealth of priceless furniture and works or art. Instead, visitors are able to gain an insight into everyday middle-class life during the 1830s.

Just a short walk from Pickford House is the **Industrial Museum**, and what better place could there be to house a museum devoted to the preservation of Derby's industrial heritage than the beautiful old **Silk Mill,** a building which stands on one of the most interesting sites in the country and which preceded Richard Arkwright's first cotton mill by over 50 years.

The **City Museum and Art Gallery** is also well worth visiting. Opened in 1879, it is the oldest of Derby's museums and the displays include natural history, archaeology and social history exhibits. One section of the museum is devoted to a Military Gallery and relates to Derby's local historical regiments. The walk-in

Derby Town Centre

First World War trench scene attempts to capture the experience of a night at the front. A ground-floor gallery houses the city's superb collection of fine porcelain, manufactured in Derby from the mid-18th century. The **Derby Heritage Centre** has local history displays, a tea room and a souvenir shop housed in one of the city's oldest buildings. Another of the city's treats is the **Derbyshire Constabulary Memorabilia Museum**, which has a display of uniforms and weapons dating from the mid-1600s to the present day.

EDALE

In the valley of the River Noe, Edale marks the start of the **Pennine Way**. Opened in 1965, this long-distance footpath follows the line of the backbone of Britain for some 270 miles from here to Kirk Yetholm, just over the Scottish border. Though the footpath begins in the lush meadows of this secluded valley, it is not long before walkers find themselves crossing wild and bleak moorland before heading further north to Bleaklow. Many travellers have spoken of Derbyshire as a county of contrasts, and nowhere is this more apparent than at Edale. Not only does the landscape change dramatically within a short distance from the heart of the village, but the weather can alter from brilliant sunshine to snowstorms in the space of a couple of hours.

Tourism first came to Edale with the completion of the Manchester to Sheffield railway in 1894, though at that time there was little in the way of hospitality for visitors. Today there are several hotels, camping sites, a large Youth Hostel and adventure and walking centres.

EDENSOR

This model village (the name is pronounced Ensor) was built by the 6th Duke of Devonshire between 1838 and 1842 after the original village had been demolished because it spoilt the view from Chatsworth House. The village church was built by Sir George Gilbert Scott; in the churchyard is buried the late President Kennedy's sister Kathleen, who had married into the Cavendish family. Both she and her husband, the eldest son of the 10th Duke, were killed during the Second World War.

The home of the Dukes of Devonshire, **Chatsworth House**, known as the 'Palace of the Peak', is without doubt one of the finest of the great houses in Britain. The origins of the House as a great showpiece must be attributable to the redoubtable Bess of Hardwick, whose marriage into the Cavendish family helped to secure the future of the palace. Her husband, Sir William Cavendish, bought the estate for £600 in 1549, and it was Bess who completed the new House after his death. Over the years, the Cavendish fortune continued to pour into Chatsworth, making it an almost unparalleled showcase for art treasures. Every aspect of the fine arts is here, ranging from old master paintings to furniture, tapestries, porcelain and some magnificent alabaster carvings.

The gardens of this stately home also have some marvellous features, including the Emperor Fountain, which dominates the Canal Pond and reaches a height of 290 feet. There is a maze and a Laburnum Tunnel and, behind the house, the famous

Cascades. The overall appearance of the park as it is seen today is chiefly due to the talents of Capability Brown, who was first consulted in 1761.

ELVASTON

Elvaston is gathered around the edge of the **Elvaston Castle** estate, home of the Earls of Harrington. The magnificent Gothic castle seen today replaced a 17th century brick and gabled manor house; part of the original structure can be seen on the end of the south front. Designed by James Wyatt, the castle was finished in the early 1800s but, unfortunately, the 3rd Earl died in 1829 and had little time to enjoy his new home. The grounds were originally laid out and designed for the 4th Earl by William Barron. Barron, who was born in Berwickshire in 1805, started work in 1830 on what at first appeared to be an impossible task. The

Chatsworth House

4th Earl wanted a garden 'second to none', but the land available, which had never been landscaped, was flat, waterlogged and uninspiring with just two avenues of trees and a walled kitchen garden (but no greenhouses or hot houses). First draining the land, Barron then planted trees to offer shelter to more tender plants. From there the project grew. In order to stock the gardens, Barron began a programme of propagation of rarer tree species and, along with the tree-planting methods he developed specially to deal with Elvaston's problems, his fame spread. The gardens became a showcase of rare and interesting trees, many to be found nowhere else in Britain. Now owned by Derby County Council, the gardens, after years of neglect, have been completely restored and the delights of the formal gardens, with their fine topiary, the avenues and the kitchen garden can be enjoyed by all visitors to the grounds, which are now a Country Park.

No visit to Elvaston would be complete without a walk down to the Golden Gates. Erected in 1819 at the southern end of the formal gardens, the gates were brought from the Palace of Versailles by the 3rd Earl of Harrington. Little is known of the Gates' history, but they remain a fine monument and are the symbol of Elvaston.

EYAM

Pronounced 'Eem', this village will forever be known as the **Plague Village**. In 1666, a local tailor received a bundle of plague-infected clothing from London. Within a short time the infection had spread and the terrified inhabitants prepared to flee the village. However, the local rector, William Mompesson, persuaded the villagers to stay put and, thanks to his intervention, most neighbouring villages escaped the disease. Eyam was quarantined for over a year, relying on outside help for supplies of food which were left on the village boundary. Out of a total of 350 inhabitants, only 83 survived.

The home of the Wright family for over 300 years, **Eyam Hall** is a wonderful, unspoilt 17th century manor house that is now open to the public.

GLOSSOP

At the foot of the Snake Pass, Glossop is an interesting mix of styles: the industrial town of the 19th century with its towering Victorian mills and the 17th century village with

Eyam Village

its charming old cottages and cobbled streets.

From Glossop, the A57 East is an exhilarating stretch of road with hairpin bends, known as the **Snake Pass**. The road is frequently made impassable by landslides, heavy mist and massive snowfalls in winter but, weather permitting, it is an experience not to be missed. For much of the length of the turnpike road that Thomas Telford built across Snake Pass in 1821, the route follows the line of an ancient Roman road, known as **Doctor's Gate**, which ran between Glossop and a fort at Brough. The route was so named after it was rediscovered, in the 16th century, by Dr Talbot, a vicar from Glossop.

HEANOR

The hub of this busy town centres on the market place, where the annual fair is held, as well as the twice-weekly market (Fridays and Saturdays). Away from the bustle of the market are the **Memorial Gardens**. This peaceful setting always promises a magnificent spread of floral arrangements, herbaceous borders and shrubberies.

To the south of Heanor is the **Shipley Country Park**, on the estate of the now demolished Shipley Hall. In addition to its magnificent lake, the Country Park boasts over 600 acres of beautiful countryside which should keep even the most enthusiastic walker busy. Well known as both an educational and holiday centre, there are facilities for horse riding, cycling and fishing.

Restoration over the years has transformed former railways into wooded paths, reservoirs into peaceful lakes, and has re-established the once-flowering meadows and rolling hills which had been destroyed by colliery pits.

ILAM

Now a model village of great charm, Ilam was originally an important settlement belonging to Burton Abbey. Following the Reformation in the 16th century, the estate was broken up and Ilam came into the hands of the Port family. In the early 1800s the family sold the property to Jesse Watts Russell, a wealthy industrialist. As well as building a fine mansion, **Ilam Hall**, for himself, Russell also spent a great deal of money refurbishing the attractive cottages. Obviously devoted to his wife, he had the Hall built in a romantic Gothic style and, in the centre of the village, he had the Eleanor Cross erected in her memory. Ilam Hall is now a Youth Hostel.

Many places in the Peak District have provided the inspiration for writers over the years and Ilam is no exception. The peace and quiet found here helped William Congreve create his bawdy play *The Old Bachelor*, whilst Dr Johnson wrote *Rasselas* whilst staying at the Hall. Ilam lies in the valley of the River Manifold and is a popular starting point for walks along this beautiful stretch of river. In summer the Manifold disappears underground north of the village to reappear below Ilam Hall.

ILKESTON

The third largest town in Derbyshire, Ilkeston received its royal charter for a market and fair in 1252; both have continued to the present day. The history of the town, however, goes back to the days when it was an Anglo-Saxon hilltop settlement known as Tilchestune. Once a mining and lace-making centre, its history is told in the **Erewash Museum**, housed in a fine Georgian house on the High Street. Other fine examples of elegant 18th century houses can be found in East Street while in Wharncliffe Road there are period houses with art nouveau features.

Ilkeston commands fine wide views from the hillside above the valley of the **Erewash**, which here bounds the county. The town's church-crowned hilltop is a landmark that can be seen from far afield.

KEDLESTON

Kedleston Hall has been the family seat of the Curzon family since the 12th century and, until it was taken over the by National Trust, it had the longest continuous male line in Derbyshire and one of the longest in the country. The present elegant mansion was built between 1759 and 1765 by Robert Adam and remains one of the finest examples of his work. Since taking over the property, the National Trust have embarked on a major restoration programme. The three-mile Long Walk was created in 1776. Along with the house itself, there is the park with its lakes, boat house and fishing pavilion to explore.

MATLOCK

As the northern, gritstone landscape of the Peak District is often referred to as the Dark Peak, the southern, limestone plateaux have gained the equally obvious name of White Peak. Though the hilltops are often windswept and bleak, the numerous dales, cut deep into the limestone, provide a lush and green haven for all manner of wild and plant life. Several of the rivers are famous for their trout, particularly the Lathkill, which was greatly favoured by the keen angler and writer Izaak Walton.

Matlock is a bustling town nestling in the lower valley of the River Derwent, and is the administrative centre of Derbyshire as well as being a busy tourist centre bordering the Peak District National Park. There are actually eight Matlocks making up the town, along with several other hamlets. Most have simply been engulfed and have lost their identity as the town grew, but Matlock Bath, the site of the spa, still maintains its individuality.

Matlock itself, at one time, had the steepest-gradient (1-in-5½) tramway in the world; it was also the only tram system in the Peak District. Opened in 1893, the tramcars ran until 1927 and the Depot can still be seen at the top of Bank Street. The old Ticket Office and Waiting Room at Matlock station have been taken over by the Peak Rail Society and house the Society's shop and exhibitions explaining the history and aims of the society. **Peak Rail** has its southernmost terminus just a few minutes' walk from the mainline station; from here the railway runs through the charming rural station of Darley Dale to the terminus at Rowsley South. Run entirely by volunteers, this lovely old

Park & Gardens, Matlock

steam train operates on different days throughout the year. A restaurant car is fitted for every journey. The full journey (one way) takes just 20 minutes, and passengers can alight to enjoy the picnic area at the entrance to Rowsley South Station, or the exhibition coach at Darley Dale platform to learn about the history of the re-opening of the line. Special events are held throughout the year, and engine-driving courses can be taken – the perfect gift for the steam enthusiast!

Inside Matlock's **Church of St Giles** can be seen the faded and preserved funeral garlands or 'virgin crants' that were once common all over Derbyshire. Bell-shaped, decorated with rosettes and ribbons and usually containing a personal item, the garlands were made in memory of a deceased young girl of the parish. At her funeral the garlands were carried by the dead girl's friends and, after the service, would be suspended from the church rafters above the pew she had normally occupied.

High up on the hill behind the town is

the brooding ruin of **Riber Castle**. The castle was built between 1862 and 1868 by John Smedley, a local hosiery manufacturer who became interested in the hydropathic qualities of Matlock. He drew up the designs for the building himself and spent lavishly on its interior décor. Smedley constructed his own gas-producing plant to provide lighting for the Castle and it even had its own well.

Following the death of first Smedley and then his wife, the castle was sold and for a number of years it was a boys' school. During the Second World War the castle was used as a food store before it was left to become a ruined shell. Today the building and surrounding grounds are home to a sanctuary for rare breeds and endangered species; the **Wildlife Park** has been particular successful at breeding lynx, and boasts the world's largest collection of these magnificent animals.

MATLOCK BATH

As with many other spa towns up and down the country, it was not until the

Regency period that Matlock Bath reached its peak. As well as offering cures for many of the ills of the day, Matlock Bath and the surrounding area had much to offer the visitor. The spa town was compared to Switzerland by Byron and it was also much admired by Ruskin, who stayed at the New Bath Hotel in 1829.

One of the great attractions of the town is **The Aquarium**, which occupies what was once the old **Matlock Bath Hydro** established in 1833. The original splendour of the Bath Hydro can still be seen in the fine stone staircase and also in the thermal large pool which is now without its roof. The pool, maintained at a constant temperature of 68 degrees Fahrenheit, was where the rheumatic patients came to immerse themselves in the waters and relieve their symptoms. Today, the pool is home to a large collection of Large Mirror, Common and Koi Carp, while the upstairs consulting rooms now house tanks full of native, tropical and marine fish. Down by the riverbank and housed in the old Pavilion can be found the **Peak District Mining Museum and Temple Mine**, the only one of its kind in the world. Opened in 1978 and run by the Peak District Mines Historical Society, the Museum tells the story of lead mining in the surrounding area from as far back as Roman times to the current time. The Museum also houses a huge engine, dating from 1819, which was recovered from a mine near Winster.

For many, model railways are an interesting and absorbing hobby that friends and family find hard to understand but **The Model Railway** on show in Temple Road is more a work of art than just another model railway. It is a reconstruction of the Midland Railway Company's track through some of the most scenic areas of the Peak District. Combining magnificent dioramas with locomotives and carriages based on the designs of 1906, the trains, slowed down to a speed in scale with the models, travel the realistic route.

Found in the Victorian Railway Station buildings is the **Whistlestop Countryside Centre**, which aims to inform and educate the public on the wildlife of the county as well as manage wildlife conservation. Set up by the Derbyshire Wildlife Trust and run by volunteers, the Centre has an interesting and informative exhibition and a gift shop and the staff are qualified to lead a range of environmental activities.

For spectacular views of Matlock Bath, nothing beats a walk on **High Tor Grounds**. There are 60 acres of nature trails to wander around, while some 400 feet below, the River Derwent appears like a silver thread through the gorge. A popular viewing point for Victorian visitors to the town, today rock climbers practise their skills climbing the precipitous crags of the Tor.

On the opposite side of the valley are the beautiful wooded slopes of Masson Hill, the southern face of which has become known as the **Heights of Abraham**. This particular name was chosen after General Wolfe's victory in Quebec – this part of the Derwent valley being seen to resemble the gorge of the St Lawrence River and the original Heights of Abraham lying a mile north of Quebec. Today it is a well-known viewing point, reached on foot or, more easily, by cable car.

In 1812, the **Great Rutland Show Cavern**, on the slope, was opened to the public, a new experience for tourists of the time, and it was visited by many notables, including the Grand Duke Michael of Russia and Princess Victoria. Following this success, in 1844, the **Great Masson Cavern** was opened and construction of the **Victoria Prospect Tower** was begun. Built by redundant lead miners, the Tower became a new landmark for the area and today still provides a bird's eye view over Derbyshire.

To the south of the town centre is a model village with a difference; **Gulliver's Kingdom** theme park makes a great day out for all the family.

MONYASH

Monyash was once at the centre of the Peak District's lead mining industry and had its own weekly market (the charter being granted in 1340); the old market cross still stands on the village green.

Today, Monyash, which is situated at the head of **Lathkill Dale**, is busy during the season with walkers keen to explore the valley of the River Lathkill, a road-free beauty spot with ash and elm woods that was designated a National Nature

Reserve in 1972. The River Lathkill, like others in the limestone area of the Peak District, disappears underground for parts of its course. In this case the river rises in winter from a large cave above Monyash, known as **Lathkill Head Cave**. In summer, the river emerges further downstream at Over Haddon

REPTON

This village, by the tranquil waters of the River Trent, is steeped in history. The first recorded mention of Repton was in the 7th century when it was established as the capital of the Saxon kingdom of Mercia. A monastery, housing both monks and nuns, was founded here sometime after 653, but the building was sacked by the Danes in 874. A battleaxe, now on display in the school museum, was excavated a little distance from the church. It had apparently lain undisturbed for well over 1,000 years.

The parish **Church of St Wystan** is famous for its Anglo-Saxon chancel and crypt, but it also contains many of the major styles of medieval architecture. When the chancel and part of the nave were enlarged in 1854, the original Anglo-Saxon columns were moved to the 14th century porch. The crypt is believed to be one of the oldest intact Anglo-Saxon buildings in England. The burial place of the Kings of Mercia, including St Wystan in 850, the crypt was rediscovered by chance in 1779 by a workman who was digging a hole for a grave in the chancel floor.

The ancient **Cross**, still at the central

crossroads in the village, has been the focal point of life here for centuries.

Parts of an Augustinian priory, founded in 1170, are incorporated in the buildings of **Repton College**, itself founded in 1557. Sir John Port had specifically intended the college to be a grammar school for the local poor children of Etwall, Repton and Burnaston. Today, Repton stands as one of the foremost public schools in the country. Interestingly, two of its headmasters, Dr Temple and Dr Fisher, went on to become Archbishops of Canterbury. A third archbishop, Dr Ramsey, was a pupil at the school under Dr Fisher's guiding light. Film buffs will recognise the 14th century gatehouse and causeway, as they featured in both film versions of the popular story *Goodbye, Mr Chips*.

ROWSLEY

This small village at the confluence of the Rivers Wye and Derwent is home to the impressive **Peacock Hotel**. Built originally as a private house, it is aptly named since the carved peacock over the porch is actually part of the family crest of the Manners family, whose descendants still live at nearby Haddon Hall.

On the banks of the River Wye lies **Caudwell's Mill**, a unique Grade II listed historic flour mill. A mill has stood on this site for at least 400 years;

the present mill was built in 1874, powered by water from the River Wye, and was run as a family business for over a century up until 1978. Since then the Mill has undergone extensive restoration by a group of dedicated volunteers and, using machinery that was installed at the beginning of this century, the Mill is once again producing wholemeal flour. Other mill buildings on the site have been converted to house a variety of craft workshops, shops and a restaurant.

On Chatsworth Road near the terminus of the Peak Rail line, **Peak Village** is an extensive factory outlet shopping centre offering a range of ladies' and men's fashion, sports and outdoor wear, home furnishings, jewellery, toys and books, and eateries. Also on site is the charming **Wind in the Willows** attraction, created by an award-winning team of craftsmen and designers

Monyash Village

to bring the adventures of Ratty, Mole, Badger and Mr Toad to life.

SOUTH WINGFIELD

Above the village, on the rise of a hill, stand the graceful ruins of the 15th century **Wingfield Manor**. Built by Ralph Lord Cromwell, the manor house was used as Mary Queen of Scots' prison on two separate occasions in 1569 and 1584 when she was held under the care of the Earl of Shrewsbury. The local squire, Anthony Babington, attempted to rescue the Queen and lead her to safety but the plot failed and, instead, led to them both being beheaded. One of the less well-known of Derbyshire's many manor houses and mansions, the history and architectural interest provided by the ruins make it one of the more fascinating homes in the area. A wander around the remains reveals the large banqueting hall with its unusual oriel window and a crypt which was probably used to store food and wine. Whatever its use, it is a particularly fine example and rivals a similar structure at Fountains Abbey.

SUDBURY

Sudbury is the estate village to **Sudbury Hall**, the late-17th century mansion and home of a branch of the Vernon family who lived at Haddon Hall. The house is intriguing, the garden restful. Gifted to the National Trust in 1967, the Hall is an unexpected mixture of architectural styles. A splendid example of a house of Charles II's time, the interior of Sudbury

Hall contains elaborate plasterwork and murals throughout, wood carvings by Grinling Gibbons, and some fine examples of mythological paintings by Laguerre. Of particular interest is the **Museum of Childhood**, which is situated in the servants' wing and provides a fascinating insight into the lives of children down the ages. Other displays range from a wealthy family's nursery and an Edwardian schoolroom to a 'chimney climb' and coal tunnel for the adventurous. The formal gardens and meadows lead to the tree-fringed lake. Wildlife abounds, including kestrels, grey herons, grass snakes, dragonflies, newts, frogs, toads, little and tawny Owls and woodpeckers. Special events are held throughout the year.

SWARKESTONE

It was at **Swarkestone Bridge** in 1745 that Bonnie Prince Charlie's hopes of seizing the English crown were finally dashed. To everyone's surprise, his advance guard had successfully penetrated so far south and victory seemed within his grasp. But when the Jacobite soldiers reached the bridge with its seven arches and three-quarter-mile long causeway crossing the River Trent they were confronted by a strong force of King George's troops. If Prince Charles's soldiers had managed to force their way across the river at this point, they would have faced no other natural barriers along the 120-mile march to London. As it transpired, the Scottish army retreated and fled north. Bonnie Prince Charlie himself managed to escape but the Jacobite Rebellion was all over bar the shouting.

THORPE

Thorpe lies at the confluence of the Rivers Manifold and Dove, and is dominated by the conical hill of **Thorpe Cloud** which guards the entrance to **Dovedale**. Although the Dale becomes over-crowded at times, there is always plenty of open space to explore on the hill as well as excellent walking. For much of its 45-mile course from Axe Edge to its confluence with the River Trent, the **River Dove** is a walker's river and is indeed mostly inaccessible by car. The steep sides to its valley, the fast-flowing water and the magnificent white rock formations all give Dovedale a special charm. Dovedale, however, is only a short section of the valley. Above Viator Bridge it becomes **Mill Dale** and further upstream again are **Wolfscote Dale** and **Beresford Dale**.

TIDESWELL

One of the largest villages in the area, Tideswell takes its name from a nearby ebbing and flowing well. Over 900 feet above sea level, the surrounding countryside offers many opportunities to wander, stroll, or take a leisurely (or energetic) hike through some varied and impressive scenery.

Known as the 'Cathedral of the Peak', the magnificent 14th century **Church of St John the Baptist** has a wealth of splendid features. The tower is impressive, the windows are beautiful, there is a fine collection of brasses inside and the 'Minstrel of the Peak', William Newton, is buried in the churchyard.

Today the village is home to a number of craftspeople working in buildings converted from other uses. The excellence of their work is apparent not only in the items they display but also in the splendid well-dressing they help to enact annually on the Saturday nearest St John the Baptist's Day (24th June).

TISSINGTON

Sitting at the foothills of the Pennines, Tissington is perhaps most famous for its ancient festival of well-dressing, a ceremony which dates back to at least 1350. Today this takes place in the middle of May and draws many crowds who come to see the spectacular folk art created by the local people.

There are plenty of theories as to why well dressing began or was revived at Tissington. One centres on the purity of the Tissington wells during the Black Death which swept through the country in the mid-1300s. During this time some 77 of the 100 clergy in Derbyshire died and the surviving villagers simply returned to the pagan custom of well-dressing. Another plausible theory dates back only as far as the great drought of 1615, when the Tissington wells kept flowing though water everywhere was in very short supply. Whichever theory is true, one thing is certain, that in the last 50 years or so many villages who had not

Stepping Stones, Dovedale

the area or country lanes to make an enjoyable circular country walk. The Tissington Trail passes through some lovely countryside and, with a reasonable surface, is also popular with cyclists. Along the route can also be found many of the old railway line buildings and junction boxes and, in particular, the old Hartington station, which is now a picnic site with an information centre in the old signal box.

dressed a well for centuries, if ever, are now joining in the colourful tradition.

A total of six wells are dressed at Tissington: the Hall, the Town, the Yew Tree, the Hands, the Coffin and the Children's Wells. Each depicts a separate scene, usually from the Bible.

Home of the FitzHerbert family for 500 years, **Tissington Hall** is a distinguished and impressive stately home which was built by Francis FitzHerbert in 1609. The estate consists of 2,400 acres comprising 13 farms, 40 cottages and assorted lettings. The Hall boasts a wealth of original pieces, artwork, furnishings and architectural features tracing the times and tastes of the FitzHerbert family (now headed by Sir Richard FitzHerbert) over the centuries. Tissington Hall and Gardens are open to the public on 28 afternoons throughout the summer.

Following the old Ashbourne to Parsley Hay railway line, the **Tissington Trail** is a popular walk which can be combined with other old railway trails in

WIRKSWORTH

Nestling in the lush green foothills of the Peak District where north meets south, Wirksworth is home to a distinctive **Heritage Centre** which takes visitors through time from the Romans in Wirksworth to the present day. Quarrying, lead-mining and local customs such as clypping the church (a ceremony in which the parish church is encircled by the congregation holding hands around it) and well-dressing are explored with interactive and fascinating exhibits. One of the town's most interesting sights is the jumble of cottages on the hillside between The Dale and Greenhill, in particular the area known locally as 'The Puzzle Gardens'. **Babington House** dates back to Jacobean Wirksworth. Another former lead-merchant's house, **Hopkinsons House**, was restored in 1980 as part of a number of restoration schemes initiated by the Civic Trust's Wirksworth Project. The ancient **Parish Church of St Mary's** is a fine building standing in a tranquil close and bounded by Elizabethan 'Gell Almshouses' and the former (Georgian) grammar school. The church holds one of the oldest stone carvings in the country: known as the **Wirksworth Stone**, it is a coffin lid dating from the 8th century.

The **National Stone Centre** tells 'the story of stone', with a wealth of exhibits, activities such as gem-panning and fossil-casting, and outdoor trails tailored to introduce topics such as the geology, ecology and history of the dramatic Peak District landscape. Nearby, the **Steeple Grange Light Railway Society** runs along a short line over the High Peak Trail between Steeplehouse Station and Dark Lane Quarry. Power is provided by a battery-electric locomotive; passengers are carried in a 'manrider' salvaged from Bevercotes Colliery in Nottinghamshire. Visitors to **North End Mills** are able to witness hosiery being made as it has been for over half a century; a special viewing area offers an insight into some of the items on sale in the Factory Shop.

THE ANCHOR INN

15 MARKET PLACE, BOLSOVER, DERBYSHIRE S44 6PN
TEL: 01246 241324

Directions: Bolsover lies to the east of the M1 between junctions 29 and 30. Exit at junction 30 and follow the A616 southeast, turning at Clowne onto the B6417. At the junction with the A632 turn right into Bolsover

Close to Bolsover Castle, just off the market place, you will find the popular **Anchor Inn**. Dating to the 17th century the hostelry has recently come under the new ownership of Mark and Diane Smith who are a pleasant, out-going couple making their first venture into the licensed trade. They have inherited a friendly pub that is well-liked in the surrounding area and already firmly established as a popular haunt for the locals.

Here you will find a large bar, on two levels, together with a small tap room and separate TV room. The well stocked bar offers Tetleys Cask together with popular beers and lagers such as Carlsberg Export, John Smiths and

Tetley Smooth. Mark is a real ale fan and gradually building up a reputation for the quality of his fine ales. There is a superb menu of delicious snacks and main meals available all day Monday to Saturday and at Sunday lunch. You will find everything from freshly made sandwiches to steaks, omelettes and chilli, and all priced very reasonably indeed. In the afternoons there are even extra special meal deals too. There is also a daily specials board, and you can be assured that everything is prepared using the freshest ingredients. In warmer weather, drinks and meals can be enjoyed al fresco in the beer garden.

For a lively evening out, you can put your wits against the local competition in a friendly pub quiz, or try out your singing talents in the karaoke.

- ⏰ Mon-Sat 11.00-23.00; Sun 12.00-22.30
- 🍴 Wide ranging selection of meals and snacks
- 💷 Visa, Mastercard, Delta, Switch
- 🅿 Beer garden, nearby public car park
- 🎵 Quiz on Thursdays, Karaoke Friday and Saturday
- ❓ Bolsover Castle, Sutton Scarsdale Hall 3 miles, Hardwick Hall 5 miles, Sherwood Forest 12 miles, Peak District National Park 12 miles, Sheffield 14 miles

THE ANCHOR INN

FOUR LANE ENDS, TIDESWELL, NR. BUXTON, DERBYSHIRE SK17 8RB
TEL: 01298 871371

Directions: From junction 29 of the M1 follow the A617 into Chesterfield then picking up the A619 Buxton road. After 9 miles, just after Baslow, turn right onto the A623. After about 7 miles, Tideswell will be signposted to the left.

One of the oldest villages in the Peak District is Tideswell, and with its magnificent parish church, sometimes called "the cathedral of the Peak", it is certainly well worth a visit. While you're there, why not have a drink or meal at **The Anchor**? This pretty roadside inn has origins in the 15th century, then became an alehouse run by tenants of the Duke of Devonshire, and eventually a busy coaching inn in the mid-18th century. It has changed little over the years and still evokes earlier times when life was lived at a slower pace. But be warned – there are reputedly two ghostly residents in the

form of a 15-year old boy and his grandmother.

Stepping over the threshold you will discover that many delightful period features have been retained, such as the open fires and thick beams. The pub is run by Peter and Michelle, both experienced chefs, so you can be assured of a delicious meal any lunchtime or evening. The menu offers a choice of carefully selected dishes, catering to all tastes and appetites, and is very reasonably priced. For something a little more exotic there are regular themed nights where the menu takes on a more international flavour. The bar stocks a good range of liquid refreshment; Robinsons is the resident real ale with a couple of guest beers which change each month. In winter months you will also find mulled wine is available.

- Mon-Sat 12.00-15.00, 18.30-23.00; Sun 12.00-22.30; closed Mondays November to March
- Good selection of meals and snacks
- Visa, Mastercard, Delta, Switch
- Car parking, beer garden
- Eyam 4 miles, Blue John Mine and Caverns 8 miles, Buxton 6 miles, Chatsworth 8 miles, Longshaw Estate 8 miles, Bakewell 6 miles, Haddon Hall 8 miles

BULLS HEAD

LITTLE HALLAM HILL, ILKESTON, DERBYSHIRE DE7 4LY
TEL: 0115 932 9931

Directions: The town of Ilkeston lies between Derby and Nottingham. It can be reach from junction 25 of the M1 by following the minor road through Stanton-by-Dale directly into the town.

Standing on Little Hallam Hill in Ilkeston the **Bulls Head** public house is a very impressive place both inside and out. Dating back in parts to the 17th century, this large and welcoming establishment is an attractive landmark on the street. Rod Haycock has been running the place since 1990 and has been in the trade for most of his working life. As a former motorbike racer, Rod has adorned the pub with a great deal of racing memorabilia, and motor cyclists are always made most welcome.

- 🕐 Mon-Sat 11.00-15.00, 18.00-23.00; Sun 12.00-15.00, 18.00-22.30
- 🍴 Lunchtime menu only
- Ⓟ Beer garden, patio, parking
- ♫ Live performers each Sunday evening
- @ rodhaycock@btconnect.com
- ❓ Shipley Country Park 2 miles, American Adventure Theme Park 1 mile, Denby Potteries 7 miles, Nottingham 8 miles, East Midlands Airport 12 miles

The pub is open at every session and food is available every lunchtime from 11.30am until 2pm. The Sunday carvery is particularly popular and there are two sittings, at 12.30 and 1.30pm, for which bookings are recommended. The regular menu offers up a wide selection of traditional English favourites – scampi, plaice, haddock, chicken, gammon, eggs and sausage, all served with heaps of chips and fresh vegetables – as well as lasagne, curry and chilli con carne, a variety of filled rolls, jacket potatoes and salads. To wash them down with there's a good choice of ales, lagers, cider, stout, wines and spirits. With live music every Sunday night, this is a friendly and lively pub.

THE BULL'S HEAD

CHURCH STREET, ASHFORD-IN-THE-WATER, NR. BAKEWELL,
DERBYSHIRE DE45 1QB
TEL: 01629 812931

Directions: Leaving the M1 at junction 29, follow the A617 into Chesterfield. Here, pick up the A619 Buxton road. After 9 miles, just after Baslow, the A619 is a left turn at a roundabout. Continue to Bakewell and then turn right onto the A6 where you will find Ashford-in-the-Water after another mile.

The Bull's Head is an historic coaching inn which dates back to the 17th century, and retains much of its historic character both inside and out. At one time Ashford-in-the-Water was a busy village with as many as eighteen coaches passing through each day bound for London, Nottingham and Manchester. Now the village is perhaps best known for its well dressings, while the pub enjoys a more leisurely pace catering to locals and tourists.

Run by Debbie and Carl Shaw for nearly four years, the pub is almost a family tradition, having previously been run by Debbie's uncle and before that, by her grandparents. Carl has many years experience as a chef, and together they have created a friendly, welcoming establishment serving fine ales and tasty food. The blackboard menu is superb with everything from the bread to the cheese biscuits being home-made. Only the freshest ingredients are used and all meals are cooked to order so don't be surprised if there is a small wait before your meal is served. No bookings are taken and tables are simply allocated on a first come first served basis. Quality wines are served by the bottle and there are usually at least two real ales on tap. This is a small, friendly pub which is much loved by locals and anyone who has had the good fortune to stumble upon it. It is well worth going a little out of your way to try.in all, well worth a visit.

🕐 Mon-Sat 11.00-15.00, 18.00-23.00; Sun 12.00-15.00, 19.00-22.30

🍽 Good quality, well-priced menu

💷 Visa, Mastercard, Delta, Switch

🅿 Beer garden

❓ Bakewell 2 miles, Haddon Hall 4 miles, Chatsworth 5 miles, Longshaw Estate 9 miles, Eyam 5 miles, Buxton 10 miles, Heights of Abraham 11 miles, Peak Steam Railway 8 miles

THE CROSS KEYS

90 BONDGATE, CASTLE DONINGTON, NR. DERBY,
DERBYSHIRE DE74 2NR
TEL: 01332 812214

Directions: Leave the M1 at junction 24 and take the A50 west for 2 miles. Castle Donington is the signposted along a unmarked road to the south.

The Cross Keys is housed in a building which is over 300 years old, right in the heart of the large village of Castle Donington. It's a substantial, whitewashed inn with well proportioned windows, tall chimneys, hanging baskets and a car park to the side. John and Bev Macauley have only been here a few months, but they have already established themselves at was previously their local. A friendly, outgoing couple they ensure that a warm, genuine welcome is extended to everyone.

The interior is exactly how an old village pub should be - cosy and inviting, with dark, low beams, subdued lighting, and polished, comfortable furniture. There's carpeting on the lounge floor and old tiles in the bar, making for that olde worlde, traditional look. There's a selection of real ales available behind the bar - Marston's Pedigree, Bass, Theakston's Best, and a guest ale which changes every week. You can also choose from a good selection of other beers and lagers. There is a fine menu of tasty snacks served each weekday lunchtime, with the most popular items being the tasty burgers and the superb home-made pizzas. There is also a specials board of mainly traditional English dishes, freshly prepared by Bev, and updated weekly. Food can be enjoyed throughout the bar areas and outside in summer months. Pizzas are also served Mon-Fri from 7-10.30pm, and Sat & Sun from 12 untill 30 mins before closing time .

The Cross keys is a sporty pub, and serves as the local headquarters for both the rugby and cricket teams. It's the ideal place to stop off for a quiet drink or bar lunch and you can always be sure of a friendly welcome with lively banter.

- Mon 17.00-23.00; Tue-Fri 12.00-14.30, 17.00-23.00; Sat 12.00-23.00; Sun 12.00-22.30

- Bar snacks and pizzas available lunchtimes

- Beer garden, car park

- Donington Park Motor Racing 1 mile, American Adventure Theme Park 10 miles, Shipley Country Park 10 miles, Elvaston Castle Country Park 4 miles, Calke Abbey 5 miles, East Midlands Airport 1 mile

Derbyshire

THE DUKE WILLIAM

91 CHURCH STREET, MATLOCK, DERBYSHIRE DE4 3BZ
TEL/FAX: 01629 582585

Directions: From junction 28 of the M1, turn west onto the A38 for 4 miles. Just after Alfreton turn right at the large roundabout and then immediately left onto the A615. This will take you directly into Matlock.

The Duke William can be found just over a mile from the centre of Matlock, heading towards Cromford, and is a fine old, stone building enjoying an elevated position. Dating back to 1737, this former coaching inn lies in the oldest part of the town, opposite the original village green, and there is also a lovely footpath that leads to Matlock Bath.

This is a friendly establishment run by Peter and Louise Groves and the couple have been here for two years, having previously run a restaurant in the area. Open at every session and all day Saturday and Sunday, the bar serves a wide range of real ales, including

Mansfield Cask Mild and Bitter, Marstons Pedigree, Banks Bitter and a monthly guest ale. The menu is superb, with a regular printed selection supplemented by numerous blackboards which are updated daily. Everything is prepared using the freshest of ingredients and offers excellent value for money. It is worth leaving room for the dessert selection alone, with the toffee apple crumble being one option that is hard to resist. The cosy, traditional interior provides a separate non-smoking restaurant area, and meals can be taken in any part of the pub. Children are welcome and in warmer weather they can make use of the outdoor play area.

A small caravan and camping site to the rear of the pub provides room for up to five of each. There are showers and toilet facilities on site and meals can, of course, can be enjoyed within the pub.

- Mon-Fri 12.00-15.00, 17.30-23.00; Sat 12.00-23.00; Sun 12.00-22.30
- Wide ranging menu with ever changing specials board
- Visa, Mastercard, Delta, Switch
- Small caravan and camping site behind the pub
- Children's playground, car park
- Live music every Saturday
- Heights of Abraham 1 miles, Gulliver's Kingdom 2 miles, Peak Steam Railway 1 miles, Chatsworth 8 miles, Cromford Mill 2 miles, Lea Gardens 3 miles.

THE ELM TREE INN

ELMTON, NR. CRESWELL, WORKSOP, NOTTINGHAMSHIRE S80 4LS
TEL: 01909 721261

Directions: From junction 30 of the M1, follow the A616 southeast towards Warsop. Passing through Clowne, Elmton is signposted right along a minor road.

The Elm Tree Inn is one of the most picturesque inns in Derbyshire. It dates back over 500 years, and with its warm stone and colourful hanging baskets, it is everything a country inn should be. The interior brims with character and period details which have been lovingly preserved by the owners and are well maintained by the manager, Richard Banks. There are low beamed ceilings, subdued wall lighting, comfortable furniture, and a wealth of framed prints, memorabilia and brassware.

The Old Barn Owl Restaurant is housed in a converted barn behind the main building, and is open on Friday and Saturday evenings as well as Sunday lunchtimes. The menu for this restaurant includes dishes such as salmon in filo pastry, lamb steak with minted gravy, grilled sirloin steak, tenderloin of pork and griddle chicken breast, plus a selection of vegetarian dishes. Everything is prepared by the inn's own chef, who prides himself on using only the freshest of produce. The Sunday lunches include a range of roasts, with chicken or fish if you prefer.

You can still eat within the inn itself for the rest of the week, with food served from 11.30am until 9.30pm, from a snack menu and an ever changing specials board that is sure to contain something for everyone. Choose from such delights as beef and ale pie, mixed grills, and the amazing "Almighty Cod"! To accompany your meal, wine is available by the bottle or glass. Six real ales – including Black Sheep, Black Sheep Special, Old Speckled Hen, Tetley and a weekly changing guest ale - are on offer at the bar, plus Tetley Smooth, Grolsch, Guinness, Carlsberg, Stella, Scrumpy Jack and Strongbow.

- 🕐 Mon-Sat 11.00-23.00; Sun 12.00-22.30
- 🍴 Food available all day until 9.30pm
- £ Visa, Mastercard, Delta, Switch
- Ⓟ Large beer garden, car park
- @ robinsons@elmtreeinnelmton.freeserve.co.uk
- ❓ Sutton Scarsdale Hall 5 miles, Creswell Craggs 2 miles, Bolsover Castle 3 miles, Hardwick Hall 8 miles, Sherwood Forest 9 miles, Clumber Park 11 miles

HARDWICK INN

HARDWICK PARK, NR. CHESTERFIELD, DERBYSHIRE S44 5QJ
TEL: 01246 850245 FAX: 01246 856365

Derbyshire

Directions: Two and a quarter miles from M1 junction 29. At roundabout take A6175 towards Clay Cross; after 400 metres turn left signed Stainsby and Hardwick Hall (ignore any further signs to Hardwick Hall). At sign to Stainsby follow road to left. After a little over a mile turn left at the staggered road junction

The Hardwick Inn is one of the most historic inns in Derbyshire - so much so that it belongs to the National Trust, and a book has been written about its history! It dates from the late 16th century, and is thought to have been established by Elizabeth Talbot, Countess of Shrewsbury, better known as Bess of Hardwick. It's a large building of mellow, local stone, with leaded windows, gables and a large beer garden to the front. Behind the inn there is a large landscaped garden with views over open countryside which is a delightful place to laze away a sunny afternoon. When you step into The Hardwick Inn, you seem to be stepping back in time,

with the numerous bar areas retaining a relaxed, comfortable feel. Tradition is important here too, though modern service and efficiency have not been sacrificed to preserve it. The present occupiers, Peter and Pauline Batty, are the third generation of the same family to run the place.

There are five ales available, including such favourites as Old Peculier, Speckled Hen and Theakstons XB and there is an amazing range of over 170 malt whiskies, with wines galore also on offer. People come from miles around to sample the food. Bar meals are served and there's a splendid carvery restaurant serving classic English dishes including steak and kidney pies. Booking in advance is advisable.

Children are welcome, and there's nowhere better for a family meal or quiet, relaxing drink!

- 🕐 Mon-Sat 11.00-23.00; Sun 12.00-22.30
- 🍽 Bar meals and a la carte
- £ Visa, Mastercard, Delta, Switch, Amex, Diners
- P Beer garden, car parking
- @ email: batty@hardwickinn.co.uk website: www.hardwickinn.co.uk
- ❓ Stainsby Mill 1 mile, Hardwick Hall 1 mile, Sherwood Forest 10 miles, Sutton Scarsdale Hall 3 miles, Newstead Abbey 8 miles, Denby Potteries 14 miles

THE JOLLY SAILOR

MAIN STREET, HEMINGTON, DERBYSHIRE DE74 2RB
TEL/FAX: 01332 810448

Derbyshire

> **Directions:** Located just a stone's throw from the M1 and East Midlands airport. From junction 24 take the minor road east towards Castle Donington and you will come to Hemington after just a mile.

Peter and Margaret have been in the licensed trade for almost 25 years, and have owned **The Jolly Sailor** for the last thirteen. Hemington is a true hidden village, tucked away in the countryside close to the Nottinghamshire border, but it is well worth seeking out to sample the delights of this lovely inn. Though the building looks modern it actually dates back in parts to the 17th century and may have once been weavers' cottages.

The interior is in keeping with its early origins and has old beams hung with pint pots and an open fire in the comfortable lounge. The décor is bright and fresh and a pleasant change to the dark dreary pubs that you sometimes find. The separate non-smoking restaurant is also light and airy and a delightful place in which to enjoy your evening meal. There is seating for up to 26 diners and advance booking is recommended to avoid disappointment. The room is also available for hire for meetings or small parties. The menu offers a wide choice of home-made dishes and is served Monday to Saturday lunchtime 12.00 - 2pm, Friday and Saturday early evening 6.00pm - 8.30pm..

The Jolly Sailor is a freehouse and so if it's a drink you're after then there is plenty of choice. There are no less than six real ales, including Marston Pedigree, Bass and Abbot, plus a good range of draught lagers, cider and stout. This is a first class establishment that is spotlessly clean, and offers good value for money in comfortable surroundings. You can be sure of a warm welcome if you pay a visit.

- 🕐 Mon-Fri 11.30-14.30, 16.30-23.00; Sat 11.30-23.00; Sun 12.00-22.30
- 🍴 Varied menu of bar meals and snacks
- £ Visa, Mastercard, Delta, Switch
- Ⓟ Car park
- ❓ Donington Park Motor Racing 4 miles, Grand Prix Collection 3 miles, East Midlands Airport 4 miles, Calke Abbey 9 miles, Derby 10 miles, Nottingham 12 miles

THE KELSTEDGE INN

MATLOCK ROAD, KELSTEDGE, CHESTERFIELD S45 0DX
TEL: 01246 590448

Derbyshire

Directions: From junction 28 of the M1, turn west onto the A38 for 4 miles. Just after Alfreton turn right at the large roundabout and then immediately left onto the A615. This will take you directly into Matlock. Here, turn right onto the A632 and you will reach the village of Kelstedge after about 4 miles.

Not far from the eastern edge of the Peak District, within the pleasant village of the same name, you will find the **Kelstedge Inn**. Dating from the mid-18th century it has all the appeal of a traditional country pub and enjoys a large corner site at the brow of a steep hill. It is an attractive building of local stone, with thick walls and pretty small paned windows. It is everything an English pub should be – warm and cosy in winter, and cool and welcoming in summer – while an adjoining barn has been converted to provide comfortable accommodation.

Sylvia and Simon Oxspring have been in charge for the past three years and under their care the inn maintains an enviable reputation in the local area as a popular place for a drink or a meal. The interior is every bit as attractive as the exterior, with open fires, highly polished wood and comfortable furniture, and there is a spacious 25-seater non-smoking restaurant area. Sylvia is the chef and she presents a varied blackboard menu of classic dishes ranging from light snacks to more hearty meals. The well-stocked bar offers three resident cask ales together with other popular beer, lager and ciders.

The adjoining barn houses comfortable bed and breakfast accommodation, with a total of six rooms all with en-suite facilities. One has a four-poster bed, ideal for a romantic stay, one is suitable for disabled guests, while two rooms can be joined to make a family suite.

- Mon-Fri 11.00-15.00, 18.00-23.00; Sat 11.00-23.00; Sun 12.00-22.30
- Weekly updated blackboard menus
- Visa, Mastercard, Delta, Switch, Amex, Diners.
- 5 doubles, 1 twin, all en-suite
- Beer garden, car parking, children's play area
- Haddon Hall 9 miles, Peak Steam Railway 4 miles; Chatsworth 7 miles, Heights of Abraham 4 miles, Gulliver's Kingdom 5 miles, Hardwick Hall 9 miles

THE KETCH

KNIVETON, ASHBOURNE, DERBYSHIRE DE6 1JF
TEL: 01335 342341

> **Directions:** The inn sits on the outskirts of Kniveton, which is 3 miles north east of Ashbourne on the B5035

Seen on a warm summer's day, there is no finer sight than this inn with its many window boxes and tubs positively frothing with flowers and greenery. The building was formerly a farmhouse before becoming a pub and in the past it has been called the Ketchum Inn and the Greyhound, but now it is firmly **The Ketch**, a popular place for locals and tourists alike.

It's a free house, owned and managed by husband and wife team Alan and Carol Fowler, who have been in the trade for 16 years and in charge at The Ketch for the last six. The outside is neat and smart, with stone and whitewash lending the place a traditional look while inside it is spotless and beautifully maintained. The fittings and furniture are in pine, and the place is carpeted throughout. Framed prints hang on the walls and an open fire keeps the bar area cosy and warm on the coldest of days. From the well stocked bar you can order Worthington Creamflow, Guinness, Carling, Grolsch, Bass Mild and Blackthorn cider and in addition, there are always two real ales on offer. Alan does the cooking and there's a good menu and specials board with the speciality of the house being cuts from a "Lamb Henry" (a half shoulder of lamb) and the curries are always popular too. The dining area can seat up to 60 in comfort with some non-smoking areas. In front of the inn there's a small caravan park with five electric hook ups, which takes camper vans and caravans only, and there's a good sized car park. The Ketch is a peach of an inn, homely and warm, with a great ambience.

- 🕐 Open lunchtimes and evenings, and all day Sunday during the summer months
- 🍴 Wide-ranging menu catering to all tastes
- £ Visa, Mastercard, Delta, Switch
- 🚐 Small caravan park for towing caravans and camper vans
- Ⓟ Beer garden, car park, children's play area
- ❓ Peak District National Park 1 mile, Ilam Park 5 miles, Alton Towers 9 miles, Darley Moor 5 miles, Carsington Water and Visitor's Centre 2 miles

THE LIVE AND LET LIVE

18 CHARLOTTE STREET, COTMANHAY, ILKESTON,
DERBYSHIRE DE7 8JL
TEL: 01159 305450

Directions: Cotmanhay forms the northern suburbs of Ilkeston. From the M1 take the A610 east from junction 28 for nearly 2 miles before turning towards Ilkeston along the A6096. After 2 miles turn right onto the A6007 and Cotmanhay will be found on your right.

The Live and Let Live is a cosy pub where tourists and passers-by can be assured of a friendly welcome. Popular with the local community it actually came recommended to us for its good food and hospitality by a visitor from Hull! It has recently been taken over by Melvyn and Marlene Hawkins; the couple come from the local area and this is their first venture into the trade.

Marlene has established herself in the kitchens and prepares a lunchtime menu of popular bar meals, with a traditional roast lunch on Sundays. Everything is sensibly priced and served in good sized portions too. You can wash down your meal with a pint of real ale or a selection from the other draught lagers, keg bitters, cider and stout, that is available. Families are welcome and there is a children's room where the little darlings can find plenty to keep them occupied. Outside there is a patio, where meals and drinks can be taken in fine weather, and this in turn backs onto a local park. In summer there are occasional barbecues held here – ring for details. Each Wednesday there is a popular pub quiz which is free to enter, and the evening is rounded off with a disco.

- Mon-Sat 11.00-23.00; Sun 12.00-22.30
- Lunchtime menu only
- Small car park, patio garden, children's room
- Free quiz and disco each Wednesday
- American Adventure Theme Park 1 mile, Shipley Country Park 2 miles, Denby Potteries 5 miles, Derby 10 miles, Kedleston Hall 13 miles, Nottingham 9 miles

THE MOON HOTEL

STATION ROAD, SPONDON, DERBYSHIRE DE21 7NE
TEL: 01332 545921

Directions: Spondon lies on the eastern outskirts of Derby. It is most easily reached from junction 25 of the M1 by following the A52 for 5 miles west.

Just a couple of miles from the centre of Derby, close to the railway station in Spondon, lies the **Moon Hotel**. The charming timbered building presents an attractive front to the road and stands within a good sized plot offering plenty of car parking. Taken over just six months ago by Chantal Mordue, and run by Kirk Stevens, the pair have given the inside a complete overhaul with extensive refurbishments having been carried out throughout. The spacious bar areas are naturally light and airy and the new furnishings and décor are modern and tasteful. However, the cosy atmosphere of an English pub has been retained with the place having a friendly, comfortable feel.

A good sized bar means that every customer will have no problem getting served and it is stocked with a fine range of ales, beers and lagers catering to all tastes. A superb carvery is served every lunchtime and early evening offering a selection of roasts and tasty fresh vegetables together with a vegetarian option. Children are more than welcome and they have their own menu to choose from. Through the afternoon there is also a good selection of bar snacks on offer. The size of the place means that bookings are not required and there are a number of designated non-smoking areas. For those that like a lively Friday night out then you can enjoy a live band here each week. The function room can accommodate up to 170 and there is a small entrance charge.

- ⏰ Mon-Sat 11.30-23.00; Sun 12.00-22.30
- 🍴 Bar snacks and carvery served daily
- £ Visa, Mastercard, Delta, Switch
- 🅿 Car park
- 🎵 Live band each Friday
- ❓ Derby 2 miles, Kedleston Hall 7 miles, Donington Park Racetrack 8 miles, Shipley Country Park 7 miles, Denby Potteries 10 miles, Calke Abbey 10 miles

THE NELSON ARMS

MAIN STREET, MIDDLETON BY WIRKSWORTH, MATLOCK,
DERBYSHIRE DE4 4LU
TEL/FAX: 01629 825154

Directions: Follow the A38 southwest for 6 miles west from junction 28 of the M1. At Ripley turn right onto the A610 then right again onto the A6 so you are approaching Matlock from the south. After about 5 miles turn left onto the A5012 and Middleton will be signposted to the left.

The Nelson Arms enjoys a quiet location tucked away from the busy tourist routes, on the edge of the Peak District. Historically, this was a mining area and the pub was originally called The Messenger, taking its name from the person who would carry news between the various local shafts. Today it is a friendly village pub where a warm welcome is always extended to new faces. The interior is traditionally styled with wooden furniture and an open fire in winter months. Here you can enjoy a

tasty bite to eat with the lunchtime menu offering mainly snacks and a more extensive menu available in the evenings until 8.30pm (no food Sunday evening). If you fancy a pint of real ale with your meal, Marston Pedigree is a permanent feature, accompanied by a guest ale that changes with every barrel. The Nelson Arms is owned and run by Judith Mitchell, who takes great pride in cooking all the food herself, while her husband Neil is gradually updating the facilities. Be careful if you have a yearning for a ordering a Budweiser as it is the name of the pub's dog!

Comfortable accommodation sleeping up to four, is available in an adjoining studio which has recently been converted from a barn. Available for single night stays or longer rentals subject to availability.

- Mon-Sat 11.30-23.00; Sun 12.00-22.30
- Good selection of snacks and main meals
- Visa, Mastercard, Delta, Switch
- Studio apartment sleeping four
- Front and rear beer gardens, car park
- Live entertainment twice monthly, Sunday quiz night, pool, Sky TV, Boules
- Riber Castle Wildlife Park 3 miles, Heights of Abraham 2 miles, Gulliver's Kingdom 2 miles, Peak Steam Railway 3 miles, Cromford Mill 1 miles, Carsington Water 3 miles, Haddon Hall 9 miles

NEW INN

2 HIGH STREET, WOODVILLE, SWADLINCOTE, DERBYSHIRE DE11 7EH
TEL: 01283 21753

Derbyshire

Directions: From junction 22 of the M1 take the A511 towards Ashby-de-la-Zouch. Continuing on towards Burton upon Trent, past the town of Swadlincote, and the village of Woodville is then just a further 2 miles.

The New Inn is a substantial building located right on Woodville's main street. It dates back to the late-18th century and was the first pub bought by the brewers Bass in 1843. The old, warm coloured bricks combine with the original windows and pretty porch to create a pleasing aspect. Inside it is well laid out with a spacious bar and dining area, all carpeted throughout to add to the cosy atmosphere.

The place has been in the hands of the Rogers family for 30 years, with the present licensees, Glen and Michelle Rogers, having been at the helm for the past three years and placing their own

- 🕐 Mon-Thur 12.00-15.30, 18.00-23.00; Fri 12.00-16.00, 18.00-23.00; Sat 12.00-23.00; Sun 12.00-16.00, 19.00-22.30
- 🍴 Tasty menu of snacks and hot meals served at most sessions
- 💷 Visa, Mastercard, Delta, Switch
- 🅿 Bowling Green, beer garden, patio
- 🎵 Regular themed nights in restaurant, pub games
- ❓ Calke Abbey 9 miles, Staffordshire Regiment Museum 10 miles, Staunton Harold Church 6 miles, Donington Park Motor Racing 10 miles, Twycross Zoo 9 miles

stamp on the place. The bar is well stocked with a wide range of beers, spirits and wines together with two real ales, a range of lagers and two ciders on offer. If you're looking for a bite to eat then there's a comprehensive menu that offers reasonably priced dishes in hearty portions. A superb carvery is served not only for Sunday lunch but also on Wednesday evenings. An a la carte menu can be enjoyed on most other nights, with Thursdays usually being a themed food evening. Please note that on Saturday lunchtime only cold snacks are served.

The New Inn has one unusual feature - it's own bowling green, and there is nothing nicer on a summer evening than, glass in hand, watching a bowl rolling towards the jack. If you play a bit yourself, you could even get a game!

THE OLD GLOVE WORKS

RIVERSIDE MILL, GEORGE STREET, GLOSSOP, DERBYSHIRE SK13 8AY
TEL: 01457 858432 FAX: 01457 858437

Directions: The town of Glossop lies at the north-eastern edge of Derbyshire. It can be easily reached by following the M67 to its eastern extreme and onto the A628. as you enter Hollingworth turn right onto the A57 which will lead you directly to Glossop.

The Old Glove Works in Glossop is housed within a former mill and is just a few hundred metres from the main street, next to the river. It is a popular venue, well known throughout the area as a cask ale bar and for its lively entertainment. The free house was taken over by Sharon and Russell Dalton in 1998 and their first task was to completely refurbish it to create the fine establishment here today. The couple do not run the place single-handed though. Possibly the most popular member of

staff is Boddington, the English Mastiff!

There is a terraced area at the front and a secluded patio area at the back in addition to the spacious bar area inside. The bar is long to ensure that everyone can be served, and offers up to six regularly changed cask ales. The quality of the ale has been recognised with an award from a national publican's magazine and an entry in the Good Beer Guide. A varied selection of hot meals and snacks is served each weekday lunchtime with hot roast beef muffins available on Friday evenings.

The main attraction here is the variety of entertainment; there is usually live music on Thursday nights and Sunday afternoons with a resident DJ on Friday and Saturday. Major sporting events are shown on a big screen TV. Over 25's only.

- ○ Mon-Wed 12.00-20.00; Thur-Sat 12.00-midnight; Sun 12.00-22.30
- ◐ Bar menu served weekday lunchtimes
- £ Visa, Mastercard, Delta, Switch, Amex
- P Patio garden, front terrace, function room available, parking
- ♫ Live entertainment Thursday and Sunday, resident DJ Friday and Saturday nights until late
- @ email: m18rus@hotmail.com website: www.thegloveworksglossop.com
- ? Peak District National Park, Lyme Park 11 miles, Blue John Caverns 16 miles, Holmfirth 16 miles, Manchester 15 miles, Buxton 14 miles

THE PEACOCK INN

SCHOOL HILL, CUTTHORPE, CHESTERFIELD, DERBYSHIRE S42 7AS
TEL/FAX: 01246 232834

Directions: From the M1, exit at junction 29 and take the A617 dual carriageway into the heart of Chesterfield. From the centre of the town pick up the B6051 which leads northwest towards the Peak District, and after a couple of miles Cutthorpe will be signed to the left.

Located in the picturesque village of Cutthorpe, just four miles from Chesterfield, is the delightful **Peacock Inn**. This former coaching inn is a large sprawling building surrounded by four acres of its own grounds. For visitors travelling by car there is plenty of parking space and you are welcome to bring children.

The17th-century stone-built pub gives no indication of what you are going to find inside, but we feel sure you will be pleasantly surprised. There are a number of inter-connecting rooms, many

🕐	Mon 18.00-23.00, Tue-Sat 12.00-15.00, 18.00-23.00; Sun 12.00-22.30
🍴	Delicious menu of home-cooked dishes available most sessions
£	Visa, Mastercard, Delta, Switch
🚐	Caravan park
P	Large car park
🎵	Live singers each Tuesday night
?	Linacres Reservoirs 1 mile, Longshaw Estate 7 miles, Peak District National Park 6 miles, Sutton Scarsdale Hall 8 miles, Sheffield 13 miles, Matlock Bath 13 miles

of them set with tables and chairs and suitable for dining. At one end a barn conversion houses the main restaurant which is a vision of cream – cream painted walls, exposed ceiling beams, and luxurious cream tablecloths. Clearly the food is a popular attraction, and with one look at the menu its not hard to see why. There is a excellent variety from the sandwiches and jacket potatoes to the inspired a la carte selection, with everything freshly prepared to order. Food is served Tuesday to Sunday lunchtimes and Wednesday to Saturday evenings. Bookings are pretty much essential at weekends. At the bar there is a good selection to keep both the wine and real ale connoisseurs happy, together with all the other usual lagers and spirits.

THE PRINCESS VICTORIA

174/176 SOUTH PARADE, MATLOCK BATH, DERBYSHIRE DE4 3NR
TEL: 01629 57462

Directions: From the M1 follow the A38 for 3 miles due west. Then, at the roundabout turn onto the A61 and immediately left onto the A615 following signs for Matlock Bath. It is then just 8 miles along this road.

The Princess Victoria was originally built in the late-18th century as the home of a Yorkshire mill owner and didn't become a public house until the mid-19th century. It has been run by Katrina and Phil Jones for the past two and half years, with Katrina's parents running the place for 15 years before that. The couple are well established favourites within the local community with the Princess enjoying a far reaching reputation for serving fine food. The blackboard menu offers a variety of tempting dishes from midday until 9pm every day. Meals can be taken throughout the bar areas though there is also a restaurant upstairs which opens in the evenings and for Sunday lunches.

- 🕐 Mon-Sat 11.00-23.00; Sun 12.00-22.30
- 🍺 Superb blackboard menu available all day Mon-Sat
- 💷 Visa, Mastercard, Delta, Switch, Amex
- 🎵 Quiz Tuesday nights, live music each Saturday, additional activities in summer months
- ❓ Peak Railway, Riber Castle Wildlife Park 1 mile, Gullivers Kingdom Adventure Park 2 miles, Market House 4 miles, Haddon Hall 6 miles, Chatsworth 12 miles

Customers can enjoy an a la carte menu within the restaurant although bookings are required at weekends. Children are welcome during the early evening.

The bar itself stocks a selection of five real ales, with Batemans XB, XXXB and Dark Mild together with Abbot Ale being the permanent fixtures. A fifth guest ale is regularly rotated and there are plenty of other draught lagers, cider and stout to choose from. On Tuesday nights you can take part in the pub quiz, while on Saturday nights there is usually live music.

THE PUNCHBOWL

43 THE VILLAGE, WEST HALLAM, ILKESTON, DERBYSHIRE DE7 6GR
TEL: 0115 932 0050

> **Directions:** Leaving the M1 at junction 26, follow the A610 to the west. After a couple of miles turn left onto the A6096 into the centre of Ilkeston. Take the A609 west for two miles, then West Hallam will be signposted to the left

Stephen and Michele Gascoigne have been mine hosts at **The Punchbowl** since 1998, and have turned the hostelry into a charming and welcoming establishment that is popular with both locals and visitors alike. Originally a farmhouse, dating back to 1754, it later became a coaching inn and the former cow sheds were converted into a comfortable dining area in 1989.

The interior is clean and welcoming, with walls painted in restful colours and a ceiling that has picturesque exposed beams. This is the kind of inn where it is a positive pleasure to stretch out your legs and enjoy a relaxing drink, or sit down to a well cooked and presented meal. It's also very child friendly.

The food is marvellous - tasty, beautifully cooked on the premises and well presented, with ample and filling portions. There are bar meals available at lunchtime with a popular roast dinner served on Sundays and the speciality of the house is home-made steak and kidney pie. The Punchbowl is renowned for the range of real ales behind its well stocked bar. You can enjoy Marston's Pedigree, Burton, Tetley or a weekly updated guest ale, together with a full range of beers, cider and stout such as Tetley Smooth, Carlsberg, Stella, Dry Blackthorn, Guinness, Murphys or Ansell's Mild. There is also a good range of wines and spirits.

The Punchbowl is an inn that combines the best of traditional values with friendly service and value for money.

- 🕐 Mon-Sat 12.00-15.00, 18.00-23.00; Sun 12.00-15.00, 18.00-22.30
- 🍴 Bar meals every lunchtime and evening, restaurant open in the evenings
- £ Visa, Mastercard, Delta, Switch
- Ⓟ Beer garden, children's play area
- ❓ American Adventure Theme Park 1 mile, Shipley Country Park 1 mile, Kedleston Hall 7 miles, Ilkeston 3 miles, Denby Potteries 6 miles, Donington Park Racetrack 12 miles

RED LION HOTEL

THE MARKET PLACE, WIRKSWORTH, DERBYSHIRE DE4 4ET

TEL: 01629 822214

Directions: To locate Wirksworth leave the M1 at junction 28 and follow the A38 into Ripley. Then pick up the A610 and then onto the A6 following signs for Matlock. About 2 miles along the A6 turn left onto the B5035 which will lead you directly to Wirksworth.

The Red Lion at Wirksworth is a delightful 18th-century coaching inn located in the heart of the historic town. An attractive building, the original arch through which the horse-drawn carriages once passed remains a striking feature and today leads to the car park. The inn offers excellent food, fine wines, real ale and comfortable accommodation throughout the year. The cosy interior retains a great deal of traditional charm with its open fires, wooden floors, oak panels and settle-style seating. The main bar has a pleasant atmosphere and

visitors and locals mingle happily while enjoying the fine offerings of the pumps. There is a guest ale kept on tap together with other popular draught beers and lagers. The place has been run by Simon and Sandra for the past 18 months and the local couple have proved themselves to be friendly and efficient hosts. Sandra is in charge of the kitchen and puts together a delicious menu of home-cooked dishes each lunchtime (except Wednesdays).

The accommodation comprises six individually designed and furnished guest rooms with gleaming bathrooms and quality all round. Four enjoy en-suite facilities and all are provided with remote control TV and tea and coffee making facilities. Evenings meals are available to residents on request.

- 🕐 Mon-Sat 11.00-23.00; Sun 12.00-22.30
- 🍴 Delicious home-made dishes. No food Wednesdays
- 🛏 6 triple rooms inc 4 en-suite
- Ⓟ Car park, patio garden
- 🎵 Pub quiz Tuesday nights, monthly comedy nights, occasional live music
- @ email: shfarrand@aol.com website: www.redlionwirksworth.co.uk
- ❓ Gullivers Kingdom Adventure Park 3 miles, Riber Castle Wildlife Park 4 miles, Matlock 5 miles, Carsington Water 2 miles, Peak District National Park 4 miles

THE ROYAL OAK

20 HIGH STREET, TIBSHELF, DERBYSHIRE DE55 5NY
TEL: 01773 872257

Derbyshire

> **Directions:** From junction 29 of the M1 take the A6175 towards North Wingfield. After a little over a mile, turn right onto the B6039 and you will reach Tibshelf after a further 3 miles

The Royal Oak is an historic inn which at one time was located directly on the main road through the village of Tibshelf, flanked on either side by two breweries. However, at the end of the second World War the building was knocked down and rebuilt in its present location, set back from the road, and no trace of the breweries remains. A large, spacious etablishment, it retains a traditional feel which is currently being updated and enhanced by the new owners, Steve and Sharon Bland. The couple, and their two young children, arrived here just six months ago and are gradually making their mark on the place.

🕐 Mon-Sat 11.00-23.00; Sun 12.00-22.30

🍴 Traditional home-cooked food

£ Visa, Mastercard, Delta, Switch, Amex, Diners

Ⓟ Children's playground, car parking

🎵 Live music every Saturday night

❓ Five Pit Trail, Hardwick Hall 3 miles, Denby Potteries 10 miles, Riber Castle Wildlife Park 9 miles, Gulliver's Kingdom 10 miles, Sherwood Forest 12 miles

Within the atmospheric surroundings you can a refreshing pint all day every day. The bar stocks a selection of real ales together with a popular range of lagers, ciders, beer and Guinness. There is also a superb choice of food with two chefs creating a menu of traditional, home-cooked dishes using Derbyshire meat and locally grown vegetables. The Sunday lunch is always popular, as are the home-cooked pies and fresh fish cooked in a lager batter. The specials board is updated weekly to make the most of seasonal produce, and if you have the chance we can recommend the Wexford Mushroom starter.

In warm weather, families with children can make the most of the family garden room where there is a great kiddies play area with plenty of benches for the mums and dads.

THE SEVEN OAKS INN AND RESTAURANT

LOWS LANE, STANTON-BY-DALE, ILKESTON, DERBYSHIRE DE7 4QU
TEL: 0115 932 3189

> **Directions:** Stanton-by-Dale lies in the lee of the M1. From junction 25 pick up the minor road which heads northwest and will lead you directly to The Old Stanton Ironworks

On the outskirts of the small village of Stanton-by-Dale visitors will find **The Seven Oaks Inn and Restaurant**. Dating back, in part, to the early-18th century it was originally built as a farmhouse. It later became an alehouse and the first landlord came from Sevenoaks in Kent, hence the rather unusual name. The superb premises sprawl between two buildings and provide a spacious environment in which to enjoy your food and drink.

The bar areas retain most of the olde worlde charm, with coal fires, a quarry

tiled floor and traditional furnishings. Here you can enjoy the offerings of the well-stocked bar with Black Sheep being the real ale kept on tap, together with other popular selections.

The owners, Margaret and David Meek have been in residence since 1994, and Margaret herself was actually born in the ironworks. The couple have firmly established the restaurant as a popular eating place and it is necessary to book for Friday and Saturday evenings and Sunday lunch. Margaret can take the credit for the fine food, with the emphasis placed firmly on using fresh ingredients to create delicious home-made dishes. The a la carte menu offers a wide choice, catering to all tastes and appetites, with vegetarian and gluten-free dishes clearly marked on the menu.

🕐 Mon-Thur 12.00-15.00, 18.00-23.00; Fri-Sat 12.00-23.00; Sun 12.00-15.00, 19.00-22.30

🍴 Superb home-cooked menu specialising in vegetarian and gluten-free dishes

💷 Visa, Mastercard, Delta, Switch

🅿 Beer garden, patio, car park

🎵 Live music each Saturday night, pool

@ dave.sevenoaks@barbox.net

❓ Derby 10 miles, Nottingham 9 miles, American Adventure Theme Park 5 miles, Shipley Country Park 6 miles, Donington Park Racetrack 11 miles, Kedleston Hall 13 miles

THE SWAN INN

49 MAIN STREET, MILTON, DERBYSHIRE DE65 6EF
TEL: 01283 703188

> **Directions:** From junction 24 of the M1, follow the A50 Uttoxeter road to the junction with the A38. At the roundabout here take the first exit, onto the A5008, which will lead you straight to Milton via Willington and Repton

The Swan Inn is a well proportioned red brick inn, painted white, with pretty shutters on the ground floor that give it an almost continental air. The hamlet of Milton sits in one of the most historic areas in the Midlands, close to the picturesque village of Repton, which is best known for its public school, and the area is well worth exploring. Stella and Roger Salt know the pub well, as they used to live just across the road and it was their local for over 30 years. They sadly watched it become run down before taking the plunge, almost three years ago, and taking it on themselves! It's the couple's

first venture into the licensed trade but through lots of hard work they have set it back on an even keel.

Inside is spick and span, with subdued wall lighting, white walls, and highly polished, comfortable furniture. It's a real village hostelry where children are welcome, popular with both locals and visitors, and Stella and Roger are determined to keep it that way. The bar has a railway theme, and three real ales are usually on offer – Marstons Pedigree and two guest ales - together with lager, Guinness, Dry Blackthorn and the usual wines and spirits. You will also find tea and coffee is available throughout the day. Traditional home-cooked food is served at most sessions, and Stella is always happy to rustle up a snack if requested, even when the kitchens are closed.

- 🕐 Mon 18.00-23.00; Tue-Sat 12.00-23.00; Sun 12.00-22.30
- 🍴 Traditional home-cooked food using mainly local produce
- 🅿 Car park, beer garden, children's play area,
- 🎵 Occasional live entertainment, darts, pool
- ❓ Sudbury Hall 11 miles, Tutbury Castle 7 miles, Derby 6 miles, Calke Abbey 6 miles, Donington Park Grand Prix Museum 9 miles, East Midlands Airport 12 miles Foremark Resevoir 1 mile.

THE WHITE COW

NOTTINGHAM ROAD, ILKESTON, DERBYSHIRE DE7 5NX

TEL: 01159 304825

Directions: From the M1 take the A610 west from junction 26. After about 2 miles Ilkeston is signposted south along the A6096 and is then a further 3 miles.

A short drive from the centre of Ilkeston along the Nottingham road will bring you to **The White Cow** public house. Dating to the early-19th century the property was formerly the private residence of a prosperous local businessman. However, more recent history records that the place was taken over by John and Carol Windmill and they have instigated an extensive refurbishment, both inside and out, with the result at first glance having the effect of a rather splendid garden centre.

Venturing inside, the large number of windows creates a superb, light and airy bar which has been designed with a great

deal of flair using only the highest quality materials throughout. The bar itself is well stocked and, as this is a free house, there is a good selection available with six real ales including Mallard Duckling which is produced by a local micro-brewery. The enthusiasm for real ale has resulted in The White Cow being voted CAMRA pub of the year for this area and there are at least two beer festivals held each year. The food is of an exceedingly high standard with the extensive menu served from midday until 8pm (until 9pm Friday and Saturday). The non-smoking restaurant area is superb and bookings are essential at weekends.

The high quality accommodation comprises seven letting rooms - one en-suite family room, one en-suite double and five further rooms.

- ⏰ Mon-Sat 11.00-23.00; Sun 12.00-22.30
- 🍴 Food served all day until 8pm daily
- 💷 Visa, Mastercard, Delta, Switch
- 🛏 1 family en-suite, 1 double en-suite, 5 further rooms
- Ⓟ Beer garden, car park
- 🎵 Folk night Wednesdays, Pub quiz Thursdays, occasional live entertainment Fridays, at least two beer festivals each year
- ❓ Nottingham Castle 7 miles, Holme Pierrepont National Watersports Centre 11 miles, American Adventure Theme Park 3 miles, Shipley Country Park 2 miles, Grand Prix Collection 13 miles

THE WHITE HART HOTEL

10 CHURCH STREET, ASHBOURNE, DERBYSHIRE DE6 1AE
TEL: 01335 344711

> **Directions:** The pretty spa town of Ashbourne lies midway between Stoke on Trent and Derby. The closest motorway is the M1 and the A52 will take you directly from junction 25, around Derby city centre, and onto Ashbourne.

Conveniently situated in the heart of Ashbourne is the delightfully traditional White Hart Hotel. The pretty black and white timbered building dates back to the early-18th century and by the turn of the century was a busy coaching inn lying on a route between Manchester and London. Today it caters to locals and travellers of a different kind, serving fine food and drink each day of the week. The menus are wide ranging, with a superb selection of snacks and tasty home-cooked dishes, all served at very reasonable prices. The fully stocked bar offers a range of traditional ales, with Marstons Pedigree always available, lagers, spirits and fine wines. However, the specialities of the house are almost

certainly the forty plus malt whiskies, the twenty or more vodkas, flavoured schnapps, brandy and gin selections. These are all presented on blackboards of their own, together with prices and details of the alcohol content. Perhaps you will be tempted to try a 20-year old malt whisky, a butterscotch schnapps or a mandarin-flavoured vodka?

If you think you might be struggling to find your way home after sampling everything the White Hart has to offer, then owners Mike and Sarah Rhodes can also provide B&B accommodation. There are five rooms, of varying sizes, ranging from a single to a family room, all comfortably furnished and provided with hot drinks tray and colour TV. The rooms either have en-suite facilities or the use of a private bathroom. Ring for details.

- 🕐 Mon-Sat 11.00-23.00; Sun 12.00-22.30
- 🍴 Good selection of hot and cold food each lunchtime and evening
- 🛏 1 single, 1 twin, 1 double and 2 family rooms
- 🅿 Car park
- 🎵 Pool, darts
- ❓ Ilam Park 4 miles, Carsington Water 7 miles, Gulliver's Kingdom 10 miles, Alton Towers 7 miles, Kedleston Hall 10 miles, Uttoxeter Racecourse 15 miles, Sudbury Hall 12 miles

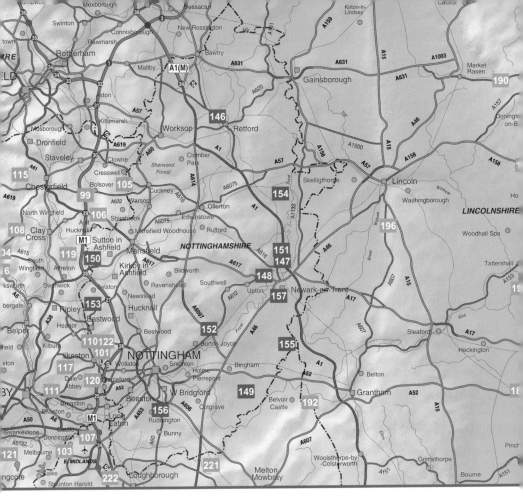

146   The Clinton Arms, Retford, Nottinghamshire

147   The Crown Inn, North Muskham, Newark-on-Trent, Nottinghamshire

148   The Kelham Fox, Kelham, Newark-on-Trent, Nottinghamshire

149   The Marquis of Granby, Granby, Vale of Belvoir, Nottinghamshire

150   The Miners Arms, Huthwaite, Sutton in Ashfield, Nottinghamshire

151   The Muskham Inn, North Muskham, Newark-on-Trent, Nottinghamshire

152   Railway Inn, Lowdham, Nottinghamshire

153   Royal Oak, Westwood, Nottinghamshire

154   The Square and Compass Inn, Normanton on Trent, Nottinghamshire

155   The Staunton Arms, Staunton in the Vale, Nottinghamshire

156   The Three Crowns, Ruddington, Nottinghamshire

157   The White Swan, Newark-on-Trent, Nottinghamshire

Please note all cross references refer to page numbers

NOTTINGHAMSHIRE

The county of Nottinghamshire lies mainly on the low ground basin of the River Trent between the peaks of Derbyshire and South Yorkshire and the lowlands of Lincolnshire. It is a county of contrasts, with plenty of industry

Sherwood Forest, Birklands

and also a rural heritage as well as the remains of the famous Forest of Sherwood.

When the Vikings arrived in England in 878, they recognised Nottingham's importance by making it one of the five boroughs of the 'Danelaw' - the area of Middle England they controlled. There was more significant development in Norman times when the famous Castle that features so prominently in the Robin Hood legends was built.

The glory of the central part of the county is Southwell Minster, a uniquely graceful building which is perhaps the least known cathedral in the country.

Southwell itself is small, with a population of less than 7,000, but is a delightful town with many fine buildings and a picturesque old coaching inn where Charles I spent his last night of freedom. Surrounding this appealing little town is a maze of country lanes and ancient villages.

With a historic castle, magnificent parish church and a host of fine buildings, Newark is an immensely likable place. In medieval times, the town thrived as a centre for the wool trade, benefiting from its position on

Trent Bridge, Nottingham

the Great North Road and beside the River Trent. The Civil War brought great suffering but, apart from the Castle, surprisingly little damage to the town's buildings. South of Newark lies the Vale of Belvoir, an unspoilt pastoral landscape dotted with the spires of village churches and overlooked by the mighty towers and turrets of Belvoir Castle, just across the border in Lincolnshire.

Sherwood Forest is known to old and young alike, all over the world, thanks to the tales of Robin Hood and the various stories, films, and television series made about this legendary hero of the people. Sherwood, the shire wood of Nottinghamshire, was once part of a great mass of forest land which covered much of central England. Now officially designated as 'Robin Hood Country', the tract of land running north from Nottingham is an attractive mix of woodland and rolling hills.

To the north of the forest is the area known as The Dukeries, which is scenically one of the most attractive parts of the county. Here, in the 18th century, no fewer than four different Dukes acquired huge estates: Rufford, Welbeck, Clumber, and Thoresby. All their great houses are now put to different uses but the glorious parks they created, especially at Clumber, make this a delightful area to visit.

The area around Mansfield was once the industrial heart of Nottinghamshire, its landscape dominated by pit-head wheels and chimneys, and the serried ranks of miners' terraced houses. This is Pilgrim Fathers' Country, since it was here that the unorthodox worship of Richard Clyfton inspired such men as William Brewster of Scrooby, and William Bradford of Austerfield, later Governor of New England. The best introduction to their story is to follow the Mayflower Trail, devised by Bassetlaw District Council, which follows a circular route starting from Worksop.

Nottingham Castle

Bestwood was a favourite hunting ground of Charles II, who often stayed here with Nell Gwynne. One local story tells of a wager the king struck with Nell, saying she could have all the land she could ride around before breakfast. Nell, not known for being an early riser, made an exception on this occasion. The next morning, she rose at dawn and rode around the countryside dropping handkerchiefs along the way. Arriving back before breakfast, Nell claimed her winnings and Charles kept his side of the bargain. Whether or not the story is true, the king certainly gave Nell substantial landholdings in the area.

Part of the old royal hunting park is now **Bestwood Country Park** whose 450 acres offer many differing landscapes. Here you'll also find the **Bestwood Pumping Station**, erected in the early 1870s. The Duke only gave his permission for it to be built after the architect solemnly promised that it would look nothing like a pumping station. With its 150ft tower, cooling pond disguised as an ornamental lake, and surrounded by beautifully maintained gardens, the station certainly lives up to the architect's promise.

BUNNY

This pretty village with a pretty name has a wealth of lovely architecture and owes much of its charm to the eccentricities of its one-time squire, Sir Thomas Parkyns (1663-1741). A man obsessed with the sport of wrestling, Sir Thomas employed two full time professionals to spar with him at Bunny Hall. He also organised an annual tournament in the village to promote local wrestling talent and this event continued for nearly 70 years after his death. In **St Mary's Church**, which was designed by Sir Thomas, his memorial graphically illustrates his commitment to the sport. It depicts the squire standing victorious over his defeated opponent on a wrestling mat, while Old Father Time stands by, perhaps as referee.

Another of Sir Thomas's hobbies was collecting stone coffins, which he provided free to those of his tenants in need of one. During his long lifetime he rebuilt much of the village to his own designs, provided a school, gave his tenants free medical and legal advice, and also found time to write a Latin Grammar and a book on wrestling, *Cornish Hugg Wrestling.*

CLUMBER PARK

Clumber Park (NT) was created in 1707 when the 3rd Duke of Newcastle was granted permission by Queen Anne to enclose part of the Forest of Sherwood as a hunting ground. Clumber House was built in the years after 1760 and was much altered in the early 19th century. After a devastating fire in 1879, the house was rebuilt in an Italianate style but, due to the vast expense of its upkeep, it was demolished in 1938. All that remains today are the foundations. However, any sense of disappointment is quickly dispelled by the charm of the other buildings in this lovely setting. The estate houses with their high-pitched gables and massive chimneys are most picturesque. The red-brick stables are particularly fine, as they are surmounted by a clocktower crowned by a domed cupola. The inset clock in the tower dates back to 1763 and the stables now house the café and visitor centre.

By far the most striking building on the estate, however, is the **Chapel of St Mary the Virgin,** built by GF Bodley in the 1880s. It was commissioned by the 7th Duke of Newcastle to commemorate his coming of age. A fervent Anglo-Catholic, he spent the then-colossal sum of £30,000 on its construction. The church has many elaborate features including some wonderful stone and woodwork.

The 4,000-acre Clumber Park is owned by the National Trust and attracts more than a million visitors each year. The man-made lake, crossed by a fine classical bridge, is particularly lovely. Five different roads enter the park and each entrance is marked by an impressive gateway. Most imposing of them all is the Apleyhead Gate, off the A614, which leads into the glorious Duke's Drive. Stretching for a distance of two miles, the drive is the longest double avenue of limes in Europe and contains almost 1,300 trees.

COTGRAVE

The discovery of an Anglo-Saxon burial ground on **Mill Hill,** Cotgrave's highest point, confirms that there has been a settlement here for many centuries.

Cotgrave is probably best known as the home of **Cotgrave Colliery,** which opened in 1964 and was a showplace mine for a number of years. The promise of work here for the next 100 years brought many miners from other coalfields to the village and also generated a huge expansion and building programme. Unfortunately, major geological faults made it impossible to mine the huge reserves and the colliery is now closed.

CUCKNEY

Five main roads converge on this sizeable village which in medieval times was a marshy island. A large mound in the churchyard is all that is left of Thomas de Cuckney's 12th century castle. Because the nearby church was built on the marshes it was necessary in the 1950s to shore it up by building a concrete platform underneath. In the course of this work the remains of hundreds of skeletons were uncovered. At first it was thought the bones were the grisly relics of some 12th century battle, but later research has revealed that the remains are much older. They have now been linked to the 7th century Battle of Heathfield between Edwin of Northumbria and Penda of Mercia.

An estate village to the country seat of the Dukes of Portland, Welbeck Abbey, Cuckney is made up of farm workers' cottages. Along with Clumber House, Thoresby Hall, and Rufford Abbey,

Welbeck Abbey makes up the four large estates in this area of Nottinghamshire, all owned by Dukes. Naturally, the area become known as The Dukeries. It was the 5th Duke of Portland who began, in 1854, an extensive building programme that turned Welbeck into what is seen today. The most impressive of his additions was the riding school, the second largest in the world, complete with a peat floor and gas jet lighting. The building is now owned by the Ministry of Defence and is used as an Army training college, though the abbey and the grounds have been maintained in perfect condition.

"I have always hated it" wrote DH Lawrence of the mining town where he was born in 1885. Reviling the *"ugliness of my native village"*, he wished it could be pulled down, *"to the last brick"*. Local people reciprocated his dislike: *"He were nowt but a big soft gel"* said one of his contemporaries many years later when the gawky lad whose mum insisted he should never go down the pit had become a writer and painter of international repute.

The Lawrence family home, a two up, two down, terrace house at 8a Victoria Street, is now the **DH Lawrence Birthplace Museum.** It has been furnished in a late 19th century style with which the Lawrence family would have been familiar. There are also some household items on display which belonged to the family and anyone visiting the museum will see that the house's front window is larger than others in the same street. This is where Mrs Lawrence displayed children's clothes and other linen items which she made and sold to supplement the fluctuating wages brought home by her miner husband.

In 1887, the Lawrence family moved to a larger, end-of-terrace house in Eastwood which today is known as the **Sons and Lovers Cottage,** since it featured as the Morels' house, The Bottoms, in Lawrence's novel. This house too is open to the public, though by

D. H. Lawrence Birthplace, Eastwood

appointment only, and is also laid out with furnishings and artefacts which are appropriate to the time. Young Lawrence attended the local school and was the first Eastwood boy to gain a scholarship to Nottingham High School, where he was a pupil until 1901. Lawrence started his working life as a clerk before undertaking a teacher training course and moving to teach in a school in Croydon.

Though Lawrence had already begun writing, his major novels were not written until after 1912, the year he eloped with his former professor's wife and left England. Drawing heavily on the influences of his upbringing in Eastwood, *Sons and Lovers*, first published in 1913, not only describes the countryside around Eastwood but also portrays many local personalities. The unflattering descriptions of, among others, Lawrence senior, caused a great deal of local resentment, a resentment that astonishingly persists to this day in the village. Lawrence and his wife, Frieda Weekley, returned to England during World War I but were unable to settle and at one point were detained as suspected German spies. They were soon on their travels once again.

In the early 1920s, Lawrence published *Women in Love* and, a few years later, was diagnosed with tuberculosis, the disease from which he died in 1930. It was while he was in Florence, trying unsuccessfully to find a cure for his crippling condition, that Lawrence wrote his most famous novel, *Lady Chatterley's Lover*. First published in 1928, the full text of the controversial story was not published until 1960 and, even then, it was the subject of a court case that is almost as famous as the book.

A place of pilgrimage for devotees of Lawrence, Eastwood also attracts those with an interest in railway history. It was at the Sun Inn in the **Market Place** that a group of 'Iron Masters and Coal Owners' gathered on 16th August 1832 to discuss the construction of a railway that would eventually become the mighty Midland Railway. A plaque on the wall of the inn commemorates the seminal meeting.

The railway was formed to compete with the **Erewash Canal,** completed in 1779 and effectively put out of business by the 1870s. Almost a century later, following years of neglect, the canal was cleared and made suitable for use by pleasure craft. The towpath was resurfaced and now provides a pleasant and interesting walk.

EDWINSTOWE

Lying at the heart of Sherwood Forest, the life of the village is still dominated by the forest, as it has been since the 7th century. Edwin, King of Northumbria, who gave the village its name, died in the Battle of Hatfield in 632. The village developed around the church built on the spot where he was slain. In 1912 a cross was erected by the Duke of Portland to mark the king's grave. From then on until the time of the Domesday Survey, Edwinstowe remained small. Following the Norman Conquest, the village found itself within the boundaries of the royal hunting forest of Sherwood and became subject to the stringent laws of the verderers. Dating from the 12th century, the **Church of St Mary** was the first stone building in Edwinstowe and according to legend it was here that the marriage took place between Robin

The Major Oak, Sherwood Forest

Hood and Maid Marian. Buried in the graveyard is Dr Cobham Brewer, whose *Dictionary of Phrase & Fable*, first published in 1870 and still in print, is one of the most readable reference books ever compiled.

A little way up the road leading northwards out of Edwinstowe is the **Sherwood Forest Visitor Centre**. Sherwood, the 'Shire Wood', was once a great woodland mass stretching from Nottingham to Worksop. Although only relatively small pockets of the original forest remain today, it is still possible to become lost among the trees. Whether or not Robin and his Merry Men ever did frolic in the greenshawe is debatable. Arguments still rage as to which particular historical figure gave rise to the legend of the famous outlaw. Records from the 12th century suggest a number of possible candidates, including the Earl of Huntingdon.

Tracing the stories of Robin Hood is a

difficult task as the tales, which have been told for over 600 years, were spoken rather than written since few local people could read and write. One of the earliest known stories of the outlaw's exploits can be found on a piece of parchment which dates from the mid-15th century but it was not until William Caxton set up his printing press in London in 1477 that cheaper books could be produced. From then on, the story of Robin Hood, his merry band of men, Guy of Gisborne, and the evil Sheriff of Nottingham has inspired countless books and at least a dozen major films.

Undeterred by the vague foundations upon which the legend is built, visitors still flock to see the great hollow tree which the outlaws purportedly used as a meeting place and as a cache for their supplies. The **Major Oak** is located about 10 minutes walk along the main track in the heart of the forest and presents a rather forlorn appearance. Its 30ft girth and branches 260ft in circumference are now supported by massive wooden crutches and iron corsets. There is no denying that the tree is at least 500 years old, and some sources claim its age to be nearer to 1,000 years. Despite its decayed appearance the tree is still alive thanks to careful preservation. Recent tests have established that some parts of the tree have successfully taken to grafting and there are hopes that at some stage a whole colony of minor oaks might be produced.

The Visitor Centre also houses a display of characters from the Robin Hood stories, with appropriate scenes of merrymaking. This theme has also been successfully translated to the city of Nottingham in the Tales of Robin Hood exhibition.

Another impressive attraction in Edwinstowe is the **Sherwood Forest Fun Park**, a family-run funfair containing a variety of popular fairground rides.

Not far from Edwinstowe, off the A6075, is the **Sherwood Pines Forest Farm Park,** a naturalist and animal lover's delight. Enjoying a peaceful setting in a secluded valley on the edge of Sherwood Forest, the Farm Park boasts no fewer than 30 rare and threatened species of farm animal and is beautifully laid out, with ornamental ponds and three wildfowl lakes.

A couple of miles south-east of Edwinstowe is **Vicar Water Country Park.** Open daily throughout the year, from dawn to dusk, the Park covers 80 hectares of attractive countryside, complete with a large lake, and provides excellent walking, fishing, cycling and horse-riding. Footpaths and bridleways link the Park to the Sherwood Pines Forest Farm Park; the Timberland Trail; the Maun Valley Way and the Robin Hood Way. The Visitor Centre has ample information about the area and also a café.

HOLME PIERREPONT

Although Holme has been in the hands of the Pierrepont family since 1284, the present **Holme Pierrepont Hall** dates from the early 1500s and is regarded as one of the best examples of a brick-built house in the county. Some of the ground floor rooms have been restored to their original state and are furnished in the style of the early 17th century, and the Upper Lodging still has superb ceiling timbers dating from the 1400s. There are two Victorian bedrooms with four-poster beds, one with its original William Morris fabrics. Refreshments are available in the Long Gallery with its walnut furniture and family portraits gazing down from the walls. Outside, the Charles II Grand Staircase leads down to a formal Courtyard Garden with an elaborate parterre, created around 1875, and in the park Jacob sheep graze peacefully.

These days, Holme Pierrepont is more widely known as the home of the **National Water Sports Centre**. Built to Olympic standards, the Centre boasts a full-size rowing course and a wild-water slalom course, all man-made from the pasture and quarries which once dominated the area.

HUCKNALL

A constant stream of visitors comes to this little industrial town to see **St Mary Magdalen Church,** not so much for its 14th century font or for the 27 attractive stained glass windows by Kempe, but to gaze at a simple marble slab set in the floor of the chancel. It bears the inscription: BYRON, *Born January 22nd, 1788, Died April 19th, 1824.*

The inscription is surmounted by a laurel wreath, in classical times the only award to winners in the original Olympic Games. The memorial was presented to the church in 1881 by the King of the Hellenes in appreciation of Byron's support for the Greeks against their imperial masters, the Turks.

Hucknall boasts another famous son. Eric Coates, the son of a local doctor, was born here on 27th August 1886. He displayed musical talent at an early age (he demanded and got his first violin at the age of 6), and became the most celebrated viola player of his generation. But Coates became even more famous as a composer of light music – his *Sleepy Lagoon* is immediately recognisable to millions as the signature music of BBC Radio's long-running programme *Desert Island Discs.*

MANSFIELD

The second largest town in the county, Mansfield stands at the heart of what were once the great North Nottinghamshire coalfields. That industry has now vanished but Mansfield still has the atmosphere of an industrial town although its economy is now based on a broader spread of varying business.

The most distinctive structure in Mansfield is undoubtedly the great **Railway Viaduct** that sweeps through and above the town, carried by 15 huge arches of rough-hewn stone. Built in 1875, it is one of the largest viaducts to be found in an English town and gives some dignity to a community which suffered badly from thoughtless development in the 1960s.

The old market place still hosts markets on Mondays, Thursdays, Fridays, and Saturdays with colourful stalls gathered around the impressive Gothic **Bentinck Monument**. This was erected in 1848 in memory of Lord George Bentinck, the younger son of the Duke of Portland. Bentinck was a long serving Member of Parliament for the town and a great friend of Disraeli. The memorial was raised by public subscription but unfortunately funds ran out before the finishing touch, a statue of Bentinck himself, could be placed in the central space.

Standing just to the northwest of the market place, **Mansfield Museum** concentrates its collections largely on local interest and includes a model of a Roman villa that once stood at nearby Mansfield Woodhouse. The collection spans the centuries from that early occupation right up to more recent times, with pictures and artefacts relating to the industry of the town and surrounding villages. The adjoining art gallery also carries a local theme and features works by artists of the area including the water-colourist AS Buxton, who is well known for his paintings of Mansfield.

MANSFIELD WOODHOUSE

Originally a settlement within Sherwood Forest, Mansfield Woodhouse is now virtually a suburb of Mansfield, but the core of the village remains remarkably intact and several interesting buildings have survived.

Opposite **The Cross**, in the heart of the town, stands one of these fine houses, the Georgian Burnaby House. Still retaining many of its original, elegant features the house was obviously built for a prosperous family and, during the mid-1800s, it was occupied by the Duke of Portland's land agent. On the other side of the road stands a stump which is all that remains of the Market Cross, erected here after a great fire in 1304. The village stocks also stood close by and were once used to detain George Fox, the Quaker Movement founder, after he had preached the gospel to the villagers.

At the bottom of the street stands the oldest building in Mansfield Woodhouse, **St Edmund's Church**. Most of the original church was lost, along with the parish records, when fire swept through the village in the early 14th century. The present church was built on the same site though it underwent some severe restoration in the 19th century. Standing not far from the church is a manor house known as **Woodhouse Castle** because of the battlements which were added to the building in the early 1800s. Dating from the 1600s, this was the home of the Digby family and, in particular, of General Sir John Digby, Sheriff of Nottingham, who distinguished himself during the Civil War.

Another building of note is the essentially 18th century **Wolfhunt House** found just off the High Street. The unusual name is derived from a local tale which suggests that the land on which the house is built once belonged to a man who was employed to frighten away the wolves in Sherwood Forest by blowing a hunting horn.

NEWARK-ON-TRENT

John Wesley considered Newark one of the most elegant towns in England; more recently the Council for British Archaeology included it in their list of the best 50 towns in the country; and in 1968 Newark town centre was designated as one of the first Conservation Areas. Its medieval street plan remains intact, complete with a fine market square which is still busy every day of the week, except Tuesdays, with a market of one kind or another - plus a Farmer's Market once a month.

The square is lined with handsome houses and inns. The most remarkable of them is the 14th century former **White Hart Inn** (now a bank), which has a magnificent frontage adorned with 24 plaster figures of angels and saints. Close by are the Saracen's Head where Sir Walter Scott often stayed, and the Clinton Arms, the preferred lodging of Gladstone during his 14 years as Newark's Member of Parliament.

Dominating one side of the square is the noble Georgian **Town Hall**, built in 1777 and now fully restored. It houses the town's civic plate and regalia, and an art gallery displaying works by Stanley Spencer, William Nicholson and notable local artists.

The grandest building of all is the **Church of St Mary Magdalene**, by common consent the finest parish church in the county. Its slender, elegant spire soars above the town and serves as a landmark for miles along the Trent Valley. The church dates back to the early 12th century though all that survives of that structure is the crypt, which now houses the treasury. Much of the building seen today dates from the 14th, 15th, and 16th centuries and its exterior is a fascinating blend of carvings and tracery. The interior is spacious and airy, and the treasures on display include a huge brass commemorating Alan Fleming, a Newark merchant who died in 1373; a dazzling Comper reredos of 1937; a splendid east window depicting Mary Magdalene; a Victorian mosaic reproducing Van Eyck's *Adoration of the Lamb*; and fragments of a painted 'Dance of Death' from around 1500.

Newark's recorded history goes back to Roman times when the legionaries established a base here to guard the first upstream crossing of the River Trent. One of their major arterial roads, **Fosse Way**, passes close by on its way to Lincoln. Saxons and Danes continued the settlement, the latter leaving a legacy of street names ending in 'gate', from *gata*, the Danish word for street.

When the Normans arrived, they replaced the wooden **Castle** with one of stone. The present building is mostly 12th century and for some 300 years it was owned by the powerful Bishops of Lincoln. Then in 1483, ownership of the castle was transferred to the Crown and leased out to a succession of noblemen.

The castle's most glorious days occurred during the Civil War. The people of Newark were fiercely loyal to Charles I and endured three separate sieges before finally surrendering to Cromwell's troops. Parliament ordered the 'slighting' of the castle, rendering it militarily useless, but left the demolition work to the townspeople. Understand-ably, they showed little enthusiasm for the task of demolishing the 8ft thick walls. As a result, the ruins are quite substantial, especially the mighty gateway that Pevsner called "the biggest and most elaborate of its period (1170-75) in England". It was here that King John, devastated by the loss of his treasure while crossing the Wash, came to die in 1216. The castle crypt and an intimidating beehive dungeon have also survived. Guided tours of the castle (and the town) are available and its history is colourfully interpreted at the **Gilstrap**

Centre. This lies within the Castle Grounds which, with its gardens and Victorian bandstand, is a popular venue for special events as well as a pleasant spot for a picnic.

Newark possesses several other reminders of the Civil War. As a defensive measure two small forts were built to guard this strategic crossing over the River Trent. The King's Sconce, to the northeast, has long since disappeared but its twin, the **Queen's Sconce,** still lies to the southeast. Named after Queen Henrietta Maria, who brought supplies into the town after the first siege in 1643, this square earthwork has a bastion in each corner and a hollow in the middle.

In the town centre, on Kirk Gate, are **Henrietta Maria's Lodgings**, where according to tradition the queen stayed in 1643. Travelling from Bridlington to the king's headquarters at Oxford, the queen was bringing with her men and arms from the continent. She had paid for them by selling off some of the Crown Jewels.

Nearby is the **Governor's House** where the governors of Newark lived during the Civil War and also the place where Charles I quarrelled with Prince Rupert after the prince had lost Bristol to Parliament. This wonderful timber framed building was restored in the late 19th century and during the work a medieval wall and some beam paintings were revealed along with graffiti dating from 1757. With such a wealth of history inside its boundaries, Newark naturally has its fair share of museums. **Newark Museum** is housed in a former school which dates back to 1529 and the history of the area is traced from the Stone Age to the 19th century. A large Anglo-Saxon cemetery, discovered in Millgate, is also on display.

Occupying a former riverside warehouse, the **Millgate Folk Museum** concentrates on everyday life in the 19th and 20th centuries. The exhibits include an interesting array of shops and shop fronts, and there is also a reconstruction of an early 20th century terraced house. The Mezzanine Gallery within the museum hosts temporary exhibitions featuring the work of local artists, designers and photographers.

On the outskirts of the town, at **Beacon Hill**, one of the greatest victories over the Roundheads took place, in 1644, when Prince Rupert arrived to lift the second of Newark's sieges.

Just east of the town, close to the A1, lies the **Newark Air Museum**, one of the largest privately managed collections in the country. Opened in the 1960s, the museum has more than 50 aircraft and cockpit sections on display. Visitors can see jet fighters, bombers, and helicopters which span the history of aviation as well as a great deal of aviation memorabilia, relics, and uniforms on display in the Exhibition Hall.

NEWSTEAD

A magnificent 13th century ruin attached to a Victorian reworking of a

Newstead Abbey Wood

proclaimed Queen of the Midlands, Nottingham is known worldwide because of the legendary Robin Hood and his persecutor, the villainous Sheriff of Nottingham. Others associate the city with Boots the Chemist, Players cigarettes (whose packets carry a picture of Nottingham Castle), Raleigh cycles and motor-cycles, and with the ice skaters Torvill and Dean - their world-beating performances led directly to the siting in Nottingham of the National Ice Centre.

A good place to begin exploring the city is in the **Old Market Square**, known to locals as Slab Square and believed to be largest market square in the country. Although no market has been held here since the 1920s, the vast expanse of the square still lies at the centre of Nottingham life. At its eastern end stands the dignified **Council House** with its porticoed frontage and a dome that is a replica of St Paul's in London. Part of the stately ground floor with its lofty ceilings and neo-classical architecture now houses some prestigious shops.

Until the Council House was built, the Market Square was the setting for the famous Nottingham **Goose Fair** which began in medieval times and gained its name from the large flocks of geese that were sold here around Michaelmas. Mentioned in a charter dated 1284, the Goose Fair still takes place in early October but has grown so much it is now held at Forest Fields on

Tudor mansion provides one of the county's most historic houses. **Newstead Abbey** was founded by Henry II around 1170 as part of his atonement for the murder of Thomas à Becket, and sold at the Dissolution of the Monasteries to Sir John Byron, who destroyed much of the Abbey and converted other buildings into a mansion. The Newstead estate remained in the Byron family for almost 300 years, its last owner being the celebrated poet, George Lord Byron.

NOTTINGHAM

A lively city of some 300,000 inhabitants, Nottingham offers a vast choice of shops, restaurants (more than 200 of them), cinemas, art galleries, two theatres, a world-class concert hall, and a host of other visitor attractions. The city also boasts a leading University, a major medical centre and a famous football team, Nottingham Forest. The self-the edge of the city.

A short walk from the Market Square, in the appropriately named Maid Marian Way, **The Tales of Robin Hood** tells the story of the celebrated outlaw through a series of historically accurate displays.

Nottingham Castle commands an imposing position on a rocky outcrop high above the city centre. Those looking for the famous castle which features so frequently in the tales of Robin Hood will be sorely disappointed as the present buildings date from after the English Civil War and precious little remains of the original medieval fortification.

Council House, Old Market

The original castle was built soon after the Battle of Hastings by William Peveril as part of William I's general fortification of many strategically important sites. Its heyday came in the 14th and 15th centuries, when not only was King David II of Scotland held prisoner here for a while around 1346 but, in the mid-1400s, Edward IV proclaimed himself king from Nottingham Castle. Later his brother, Richard III, rode out from here to the Battle of Bosworth field and his death.

For some reason, the Tudors shunned the castle, which gradually fell into disrepair until Charles I came to Nottingham in 1642 and raised his standard, marking the beginning of the Civil War. Unfortunately, the king found little support for his cause in the city

(only 30 citizens joined his troops) so he moved on to Shrewsbury, leaving Nottingham and its castle in the hands of the Parliamentarians. During the course of the war, the Royalists made several attempts to recapture the castle but Cromwell's supporters held out. After the fighting was over the castle building was rendered uninhabitable and was finally demolished in 1674 by the Duke of Newcastle who then built his own palace on the site.

Today, that palace is home to the **Castle Museum and Art Gallery**. Some remains of the original castle still stand, most notably the 13th century gatehouse and parts of the moat and outer bailey. The museum, when it was opened by the Prince of Wales in 1878, was the first municipal art gallery in the country outside London. Today, the gallery is particularly noted for its fine selection of Victorian paintings. The museum also has an outstanding collection of silver-ware and ceramics.

Alongside the Castle Museum is the **Sherwood Foresters Regimental Museum**, which continues the castle's connections with the military. The regiment was first raised in 1741 and among the many displays there is an area dedicated to the Nottingham flying ace of World War I, Captain Albert Ball, VC. He died in 1917, at the age of 20, having shot down 43 enemy aircraft. A statue erected to his memory stands in the castle grounds.

At the base of Castle Rock lies the famous **Trip to Jerusalem Inn** where crusaders are said to have stopped for a pint before setting off on their long journey to the Holy Land. Dating back to around 1189, it claims to be the oldest pub in England (a claim hotly contested by several other hostelries). Set back into the sandstone rock, the building was once the brewhouse for the castle and from here travellers to the Holy Land bought their ale.

Also at the base of Castle Rock and housed in a terrace of four 17th century cottages is the **Brewhouse Yard Museum**. Depicting the life of the people of the city up to the 1990s, the museum has accurately furnished rooms as well as a series of reconstructions that includes a Victorian kitchen and shop window displays of the 1920s.

Just around the corner, the **Museum of Costume and Textiles** in Castle Gate contains a fine collection of costumes from 1790 to the mid-20th century, all displayed in period rooms. Further down Castle Gate is **Newdigate House**, built in a refined fashion in 1680 and distinguished by a wrought iron screen and gates dating from the early 1700s. The house now forms part of the United Services Club but between 1705 and 1711 it was the home of Marshal Tallard, commander of the defeated French army at the Battle of Blenheim in 1704.

Nearby, in Castle Road, is a charming medieval building that is home to the **Lace Centre**. As well as holding lace-making demonstrations, the Centre stocks a vast selection of high quality lace available for purchase. Continuing the textiles theme, not far away and set in the heart of Nottingham's historic and recently revital-ized Lace Market, is the Lace Market Centre, occupying a restored chapel in High Pavement. Here the story of Nottingham's famous industry is told, from the days when it was a cottage craft through to

Trip to Jerusalem Inn

mechanisation and the days of the great textile factories. Across the road from the Museum, in the impressive Shire Hall, the **Galleries of Justice** provides an unusual and interesting insight into justice 19th century style. Also in High Pavement is Nottingham's largest parish church, St Mary's, which is probably also the city's oldest as it appears to have been founded in Saxon times.

Another short walk leads to the **Caves of Nottingham**, a popular attraction which lies beneath the Broadmarsh Centre, one of the city's major shopping precincts. The city is built on sandstone and throughout Nottingham's history the rock has been tunnelled to provide first shelter and then hiding places. More than 400 man-made caves run beneath the city streets, saved thanks to local voluntary groups for future generations. The most spectacular cave in the system, the Pillar Cave, was carved out back in 1250 and contains remnants of the country's only underground tannery.

RETFORD

Retford is actually two communities, East and West Retford, set on either side of the River Idle. West Retford is the older settlement; its twin grew up during the 1100s as a place where tolls could be collected from travellers making the river crossing. Retford has been a market town since 1246 and markets are still held here every Thursday and Saturday.

Retford received a major economic boost in 1766 when the Great North Road was diverted through the town.

That was when the Market Square was re-developed and some of the elegant Georgian buildings here, and in Grove Street, still survive from that time. The grand and rather chateau-like **Town Hall**, however, dates from 1868 and replaced the Georgian hall.

Cannon Square is home to one of Retford's more unusual attractions: a Russian cannon. Dating from 1855 and weighing over 2 tons, the cannon was captured by British soldiers at Sebastopol and brought to Retford at the end of the Crimean War. The townsfolk paid for its transportation and, in 1859, after arguments raged about its siting, the cannon was finally placed in the square and named the Earl of Aberdeen after the incumbent Prime Minister.

Not far from Cannon Square is, reputedly, the oldest chemist's shop in the country still on its original site. Opened in 1779, **Norths Chemists** first belonged to a local vet, Francis Clater, whose books on animal medicine and treatment were bestsellers for over 100 years.

While in Retford, it is well worth visiting the **Bassetlaw Museum** in Amcott House, Grove Street. This imposing late-18th century town house is noted for its finely executed internal plasterwork and elegant wrought iron staircase which the restoration has returned to their full Georgian splendour. The museum has a distinct local emphasis, with displays of local archaeology, civic, social and industrial history, and fine and applied art. Occupying the former service wing of the house, the **Percy Laws Memorial Gallery** has a permanent display of historic Retford civic plate and also hosts short term exhibitions.

RUDDINGTON

This historic village, whose name is derived from the Saxon word Rudda - meaning headman - was once the home of many hosiery workers and several of their cottages still remain. In 1829, a factory and frameworkers cottages were built around a courtyard in Chapel Street. Later, a school was built and this is now occupied by the **Ruddington Framework Knitters' Museum** which depicts community life through several reconstructed shops and an Edwardian schoolroom. Of the 25 hand frames seen here today, most are fully operational and there is an opportunity to buy samples made at the museum.

The industry reached its height in 1880, with the staggering number of 20,000 frames operating in Nottingham, Derbyshire, and Lincolnshire. As well as the knitting frames on show, the museum also has other machinery of specific importance to the village and to the hosiery industry. Regular demonstrations are given using the working exhibits. Visitors can try out their own weaving skills on one of the collection of circular sock machines.

Not far away is the **Ruddington Village Museum**, housed in the old village school building of 1852 and concentrating on the everyday life of the villagers.

RUFFORD

Rufford Abbey was founded in 1148 by Gilbert de Gant as a daughter house to Rievaulx Abbey. During the Dissolution it suffered the fate of many religious houses and came into the hands of the 6th Earl of Shrewsbury, fourth husband of the redoubtable Bess of Hardwick. The Earl pulled down most of the abbey and built a grand Elizabethan mansion. All that remains of the abbey is a vaulted crypt, said to be haunted by the ghost of a giant monk with a skull-like face. According to the parish register for Edwinstowe, a man died of fright after catching sight of this unholy visitor!

The abbey's stable block now houses an impressive craft centre while the restored 18th century Orangery hosts modern sculpture exhibitions.

The grounds of the abbey, now the **Rufford Country Park,** are well worth a visit. In addition to the nine formal gardens near the house, there are also some hides where birdwatchers can overlook a portion of the lake which has been designated a bird sanctuary. In the grounds too stands an 18th century corn mill, now home to a display of Nottinghamshire history, and two icehouses dating from the mid-1800s.

SHERWOOD FOREST

It seems likely that it was William the Conqueror who designated Sherwood as a Royal Forest, an administrative term for the private hunting ground of the king. The land was not only thickly wooded but also included areas of rough heathland as well as arable land, meadow land, small towns, and villages. The Norman kings were passionate about their hunting and, to guard their royal forests, there were a set of rigidly upheld laws, to conserve the game (known as the venison) and vegetation (known as the vert). No one, not even those with a private estate within the royal forest, was allowed to kill or hunt protected animals, graze domestic animals in the forest, fell trees, or make clearings within the boundaries without the express permission of the king or one of his chief foresters. It is little wonder then, with such strict rules imposed upon them, that the people turned to the likes of Robin Hood and others who defied the laws and lived off the king's deer.

Sherwood Forest

SNEINTON

Sneinton's main claim to fame is as the birthplace, in 1829, of William Booth, the founder of the Salvation Army. The small terraced house where he and his family lived until 1831 is still standing in Notintone Place, fronted now by a statue of the great man. The family home has become the **William Booth Birthplace Museum**: entry to the house is free but by appointment only.

In 1849, Booth left Nottingham for London where he became a Methodist minister. But, finding the church structures too constraining, he established in 1865 the Christian Missions which, in 1878, was renamed the Salvation Army. During the next 10 years, the movement spread to all corners of the world, including America, Australia, and South Africa. The Army is still mobilised, with more than 1,000 local corps in the UK involved in both social and evangelistic work. Its missing persons bureau traces anything up to 5,000 people each year.

SOUTHWELL

Southwell is undoubtedly one of England's most beguiling towns, miraculously preserved from developers and with scarcely an ugly building to be seen. From whichever direction you approach, it is the twin towers of **Southwell Minster** that first catch the eye. With their pyramidal 'Rhenish

Southwell

Canons' seats.

The Minster stands in a delightful precinct, surrounded by attractive buildings. To the south stand the ruins of the palace of the archbishops of York built in the 14th and 15th centuries. Parts of the old palace, closest to the minster's south doorway, have been incorporated into the present Bishop's Palace.

At the east end of the minster is **Vicar's Court,** a charming group of five Queen Anne houses built for the Vicars Choral around 1702. Just across the road from the Minster is a picturesque old coaching inn, the 16th century Saracen's Head. Charles I spent his last hours of freedom before his final surrender in this delightful half-timbered building. At that time the inn was known as the King's Head: the name was changed after Charles was beheaded.

Southwell is credited as the birthplace of the Bramley apple. The story goes that in the early 19th century, two ladies planted some apple pips in their cottage garden in the nearby village of Easthorpe. Nature took its course and one of the seedlings grew into a tree. By this time, Matthew Bramley owned the cottage and the quality of the tree's fruit began to excite public interest.

Mr Henry Merryweather, a local nurseryman, persuaded Bramley to let him take a cutting, which he consequently propagated with enormous success. Permission had been granted on the condition that the apples took Mr Bramley's name and not the two ladies'!

Caps', these towers are unique in this country although they would look perfectly in place anywhere in the Rhineland.

Perhaps the least well-known of English cathedrals, Southwell's history goes back to 956 when Oskytel, Archbishop of York, established a church here. The present building was erected in three phases. The nave, transept and western towers are the oldest part, completed around 1150; the east end was built around 1240, and the superb Chapter House around 1290.

Octagonal in design, the Chapter House has been hailed as the pinnacle of the Decorated period of architecture - "among chapter houses as the rose amongst flowers". The architectural historian, Nikolaus Pevsner devoted a whole book, *The Leaves of Southwell*, to the incredible wealth of stone carvings of foliage decorating the arcades above the

The **Bramley Apple Exhibition** in Halam Road explains the full history and development of this famous fruit.

The disused railway line from Southwell to Mansfield, opened in 1871, is now an attractive footpath known as the **Farnsfield to Southwell Trail**. As well as the varied plant and wildlife that can be found along the 4½ mile walk, there is also plenty of industrial archaeological interest including the **Farnsfield Waterworks** of 1910, a late 18th century cotton mill, and **Greet Lily Mill**, a corn mill on the banks of the River Greet.

UPTON

Upton boasts a couple of very good pubs and its nine-pinnacled church is also worthy of a visit. A famous son of the village was James Tenant, the man who cut the world-renowned Koh-I-Noor diamond. But perhaps the most impressive building here is **Upton Hall**, a stylish Grecian villa with a central dome and elegant colonnade, built in the early 1800s. The hall is now the headquarters of the British Horological Institute and, inside, visitors can see the **National Exhibition of Time** - a fascinating display of timepieces.

WOLLATON

Built in creamy white Ancaster stone, **Wollaton Hall** is one of the most attractive and elaborate Elizabethan mansions in the Midlands. Set in a spacious park, the house was built in the 1580s to the design of Robert Smythson, who also designed Hardwick Hall in Derbyshire. His client was Francis Willoughby, whose family had made a fortune from the local coal mines. The Elizabethan passion for symmetry is displayed on the magnificent front facade with its classical columns, busts of philosophers and mythological characters, and flamboyant gables.

The building also houses the **Natural History Museum,** based on the collection of another Willoughby, a noted naturalist of the mid-1600s, while some of the Hall's outbuildings have been transformed into the Nottingham Industrial Museum where the city's major industries are represented. The 525 acres surrounding the Hall are contained within a 7-mile long wall, providing security for the herds of deer that roam here as they have for more than 400 years.

WORKSOP

One of the major attractions of Worksop is the **Priory Gatehouse**, which is best approached from Potter Street where the full glory of the 14th century building can be seen. Its great niches house large and beautifully carved statues and the immense entrance is reminiscent of a cave opening. Originally the portal to a large Augustinian monastery, the gatehouse together with the Church of St Mary and St Cuthbert is all that remains. There is also a wayside shrine, making it a unique ecclesiastical attraction. Today, the upper floor of the gatehouse houses an art gallery.

The first canal to be built in Nottinghamshire was the **Chesterfield Canal**, running from Chesterfield in Derbyshire to the River Trent. Some 46 miles long, work on the canal was begun in 1771 and took 6 years to complete under the supervision of John Varley, the deputy of the canal engineer, James Brindley. In the mid-1800s, the canal was taken over by the Sheffield and Lincoln Junction Railway, which decided to cease maintaining it in 1863 and it was allowed to run down. The collapse of one of the canal's two tunnels, at Norwood in 1908, hastened its decline by cutting off Chesterfield from the rest of the waterway.

The National Trust's **Mr Straw's House** at 7 Blyth Grove, is well worth visiting. The house, together with an endowment of a million pounds, was left to the Trust by William Straw in his will. The Trust's surveyors were surprised to find upon inspection of the Edwardian semi-detached house that they were actually stepping back in time. Inside, everything had remained untouched since the death in 1932 of William Straw senior, a grocer and seed merchant in Worksop. His wife, who died seven years later, neither altered nor added anything. Nor did her two sons, William and Walter, who lived a bachelor existence at the house. Walter, who took on the family business, died in 1976; his brother, William, in 1990.

In all those years, virtually nothing had changed in the house. The parents' bedroom had been closed up and everything left as it was. A 1932 calendar was still hanging on the wall; William Senior's hats were still perched in the hall; his pipes and tobacco pouch lay ready by the fireside.

Worksop Museum, found in Memorial Avenue, is housed in a purpose-built gallery within the library and museum provided by the Carnegie United Kingdom Trust. It was opened in 1938 and has small exhibitions relating to the history of Worksop and the neighbouring area of landed estates known as the Dukeries, together with a larger display on the Pilgrim Fathers whose roots lay in north Nottinghamshire. Presiding over this exhibition is a life-size model of the Pilgrim Elder William Brewster, one of the leaders of the movement.

The Museum is also the start of the **Mayflower Trail** which guides visitors around the local sites connected with the Pilgrim Fathers, including William Brewster's Manor House at Scooby and Gainsborough Old Hall.

THE CLINTON ARMS

ALBERT ROAD, RETFORD, NOTTINGHAMSHIRE DN22 6JD
TEL: 01777 702703

Directions: From the M18 take the A619 east from junction 30 towards Worksop. Bypass to the south side of the town along the A57 and then head north on the A1. After a couple of miles turn right onto the A620 which will lead you straight to Retford.

For over 125 years, **The Clinton Arms** has been a popular town centre pub located just half a mile from Retford railway station. The neatly presented building boasts its own small car park and a pleasant beer garden, both located to one side. Venturing inside you will find a traditional bar furnished with wooden tables and chairs and upholstered benches combined with a décor that is bright and modern. There is a separate games room where you will find the pool table and there is a much larger room which is the venue for the busy

programme of live music. This is certainly one of the most lively pubs in town, with visiting bands, a resident DJ and a big screen TV showing all the major sporting events.

But the attraction isn't only the entertainments. The bar stocks a good selection of real ales, including Charles Wells Bombadier, Adnams and Greene King IPA, plus regular guest ales, and all sensibly priced too. There is also an excellent wine list with over 30 on offer, and again there are several that are not too pricey. There is also a good menu of bar food served until 7pm most days, and until 11.30pm Thursday to Saturday. The offerings range from burgers and jacket potatoes to home-made pies and chilli and you are sure to be spoiled for choice.

- 🕐 Mon-Wed 12.00-23.00; Thur-Fri 12.00-midnight; Sat 11.00-midnight; Sun 12.00-22.30
- 🍴 Great value food served all day
- 🅿 Beer garden, patio, car park, cashpoint
- 🎵 Live music several times a week, regular DJs, Big Screen TV
- @ email: clinton@bluesmusic.co.uk website: www.bluesmusic.co.uk/clinton
- ❓ Clumber Park 7 miles, Sundown Advertureland 8 miles, The World of Robin Hood Visitor Centre 7 miles, Sherwood Forest 12 miles, Doncaster 17 miles

THE CROWN INN

MAIN STREET, NORTH MUSKHAM, NEWARK-ON-TRENT,
NOTTINGHAMSHIRE NG23 6HQ
TEL: 01636 640316

Nottinghamshire

Directions: North Muskham lies just on the A1, a couple of miles north of
Newark-on-Trent

If you like cosy village pubs, with a homely, friendly feel, then you need look no further than the charming **Crown Inn** located in the heart of North Muskham. Dating back to the 17th century, it is believed to have always been a hostelry of some sort, with the spirit licence finally being granted in 1890. The current owners are Janet and her partner Paul, who have

been at the helm for just 18 months. Already they have made their mark, and are proving to be popular and lively hosts.

Venturing inside, the bar is made up of three 'snugs' and offers plenty of options for the real ale connoisseur, with John Smith's Cask, Greene King IPA and regular guest ales, together with other popular beers and lagers.

If you like a good pub quiz, you can pit your wits against the locals each Sunday night, and there are also occasional karaoke nights. If traditional pub games be your cup of tea, there is a covered skittle alley outside which is available to all.

- 🕐 Mon 12.00-15.00, 17.00-23.00, Tue-Thur 16.00-23.00; Fri 12.00-15.00, 17.00-23.00; Sat 12.00-23.00; Sun 12.00-22.30
- 🍴 Sandwiches
- 🅿 Car parking
- 🎵 Quiz Nights Sundays, outside covered skittle alley, darts, karaoke machine
- ❓ Newark Castle 3 miles, River Trent cruises 4 miles, Southwell Minster 3 miles, Southwell Racecourse 4 miles, Aircraft Musuem 3 miles, Lincoln Cathedral 13 miles

MAIN STREET, KELHAM, NEWARK-ON-TRENT, NOTTINGHAM NG23 5QP
TEL/FAX: 01636 679444

> **Directions:** From the A1, take the junction with A46 and head southwest. After just over a mile, bear right at a roundabout onto the A617 Mansfield road. Kelham is then just another couple of miles.

Richard and Jill Winter are waiting to welcome you to **The Kelham Fox**, where you can enjoy a wide range of home-cooked food and well kept beer throughout the day. The historic pub has been on the site since at least the 1800's when it would have started life as a coaching inn and with its location near to Kelham Bridge, a crossing point of the River Trent, it has always been a convenient stopping place for travellers.

There are three main bar areas and an adjoining restaurant. There is a spacious and characterful room in the older part of the pub with a full-sized pool table and a warm, cosy bar area, known as the Foxes Earth, with a wide open hearth and attractive wood-panelled bar. The open plan main bar has comfortable seating and a spacious airy feel, while the separate raised restaurant area provides quiet sanctuary for couples and groups wishing to eat in a relaxed atmosphere.

At The Fox they believe that you should never go away hungry, which is why Richard has introduced the *Mixed Grill Challenge*. If you can manage to eat two in quick succession, they'll give you the second one free! The rest of the menu offers an excellent choice of traditional dishes with the puddings playing a starring role, and there is also a good selection of snacks. Food is available all day Monday to Saturday and on Sundays a traditional roast is available from 12-4pm. The bar stocks a wide range of beers including Pedigree, John Smiths Cask, Chestnut Mild, Guinness Draft, Carling Black Label, Stella Artois, Fosters and a guest ale.

- 🕐 Mon-Sat 12.00-23.00; Sun 12.00-22.30
- 🍴 Wide ranging menu offering exceptional value
- Ⓟ Large Car park, Large Beer Garden, Long Skittle Alley, cash point
- 🎵 Occasional live entertainment
- @ email: enquiries@thekelhamfox.co.uk
  website: www.thekelhamfox.co.uk
- ❓ Kelham Hall, walking along the River Trent, Southwell Minster 3 miles, Southwell Racecourse 3 miles, Newark Castle 3 miles, Sherwood Forest 9 miles

THE MARQUIS OF GRANBY

DRAGON STREET, GRANBY, VALE OF BELVOIR,
NOTTINGHAMSHIRE NG13 9PN
TEL: 01949 850461

> **Directions:** From the M1, turn onto the A52 at junction 25 and follow it around Nottingham and on towards Grantham. About 2 miles after the junction with the A46, Granby will be signposted to the right.

The charming pub known as the **Marquis of Granby** can be found tucked away in the small village of the same name, in the delightful surroundings of the Vale of Belvoir. The rather grand title is shared with the first born son of the Duke of Rutland, whose ancestral home is nearby Belvoir Castle. Originally dating back to 1565, the inn was given to a general in 1744 as "post-war pension".

The resident hosts are Loz and Su, a local couple from nearby Burton Joyce, and who have been in charge for just a year. They have made their mark with some tasteful redecorating and the installation of an impressive bar top made from English yew. Su is in charge of the cooking and presents an all home-cooked menu of traditional English dishes, home-made cakes, toasted sandwiches, jacket potatoes and local pork pies and stilton. However, the real highlight is to be found behind the bar. Loz is enthusiastic about real ale and the Marquis of Granby claims to be one of the best real ale pubs in Notts -winning Vale of Belvoir CAMRA Pub of the Year in its first year. The emphasis is on locally-brewed ales from micro-breweries, with eight always available, and offering over 400 different ales in any one year! You can also enjoy Bass on the jug, guest ciders and fine wines sourced via a local merchant. It will also come as no surprise to learn that the pub hosts two beer festivals each year. Ring for details.

- 🕐 Mon-Fri 11.00-15.00, 17.30-23.00; Sat 12.00-23.00; Sun 12.00-22.30
- 🍴 Tasty home-cooked food
- 🎵 Occasional live music, speciality evenings, e.g. slide shows, two annual beer festivals, skittle alley, traditional pub games.
- ❓ Belvoir Castle 6 miles, Grantham 10 miles, Holme Pierrepont National Watersports Centre 11 miles, Belton House 13 miles, Southwell Minster 13 miles

THE MINERS ARMS

222 BLACKWELL ROAD, HUTHWAITE, SUTTON IN ASHFIELD,
NOTTINGHAMSHIRE NG17 2RF
TEL: 01623 550087

Directions: The village of Huthwaite lies on the eastern edge of Sutton in Ashfield. From the A1 take exit 28 and follow the A38 towards Mansfield. After about a mile turn left onto the B6027 which will take you straight to Huthwaite

Tucked away, almost in the shadow of the M1, you will find Huthwaite on the outskirts of Sutton in Ashfield, a town which grew around the mining industry. **The Miners Arms** is a legacy from the olden days when the local coal miners held their meetings here, collected their pay and were held to account for any misdemeanours. The building itself dates back to the late 1700's and is full of character, with lots of old beams and a wealth of bygone memorabilia - pewter mugs, bed warming pans and gleaming copper pieces. There is a resident ghost, believed to be Mrs Yates, the longest serving landlady of the establishment. She reputedly kept a mynah bird on the bar, who would inform her of new

arrivals, and was forced to retire at the ripe old age of 84!

Today's visitors will find a well laid out pub, with spacious bar areas and an attractive conservatory restaurant overlooking the garden. The menu offers a simple selection of popular dishes, together with a well priced carvery lunch on Sundays. All dishes are realistically priced, and there are special meal deals on steaks and most main dishes in the early evening.

Your hosts are Michelle and Dave and although they have only been at the Miners Arms for a relatively short time they have many years' experience in the trade. A friendly, outgoing couple, they have proved popular with the locals. A delightful feature of the pub is the attractive beer garden, with children's play area, which overlooks open countryside.

- 🕐 Mon-Sat 11.00-23.00; Sun 12.00-22.30
- 🍴 Good value, classic pub food
- 🅿 Beer garden, car park, children's play area
- 🎵 Karoake Friday nights, live music Saturdays, Folk music once a month
- ❓ Hardwick Hall 3 miles, Newstead Abbey 8 miles, Sherwood Forest 15 miles, Riber Castle Wildlife Park 13 miles, Peak District National Park 16 miles

THE MUSKHAM INN

GREAT NORTH ROAD, NORTH MUSKHAM, NEWARK-ON-TRENT,
NOTTINGHAMSHIRE NG23 6HN
TEL: 01636 704010 FAX: 01636 612746

Directions: North Muskham lies just off the M1, a couple of miles north of
Newark-on-Trent

The Muskham Inn is conveniently located on a roundabout adjoining the A1, making it ideal for those travelling through the area by car. The unprepossessing exterior belies the attractive interior which has been refurbished in recent years. There are two bars, their names making reference to the pub's previous incarnation as The Lord Nelson. Nelson's bar has a cosy atmosphere and is attractively furnished with light coloured wooden fixtures, while the more spacious Hamilton bar has a distinctly colonial feel with wicker chairs, tiled floor and lush green plants.

Here you can be sure of finding a good quality pint of ale with the bar stocking John Smiths Cask permanently, together with two weekly-changing guest ales. A good variety of other lagers, beers and cider as well as a comprehensive wine list, cater to other tastes. The seasonal menus are served each lunchtime and evening and all day Saturday and Sundays, with fresh fish usually available every Friday. The delicious dishes are far removed from the usual pub fayre, with only the best, locally sourced meat and poultry being used, together with seasonal, market fresh vegetables.

The accommodation here is housed within a separate block which was constructed just three years ago. There are ten guest rooms in all, each with its own front door and not disturbed by the comings and goings of the pub. Each of the spacious rooms is comfortably furnished and is complete with en-suite bathroom, colour TV, fridge and tea and coffee making facilities. Overnight guests can enjoy a full cooked English breakfast served with toast, fruit juice and tea and coffee.

- Mon-Sat 12.00-23.00; Sun 12.00-22.30
- Superb seasonal menu
- Visa, Mastercard, Delta, Switch
- 10 spacious guest rooms
- Large beer garden, car park
- Newark Castle 3 miles, River Trent cruises 4 miles, Southwell Minster 3 miles, Southwell Racecourse 4 miles, Aircraft Musuem 3 miles, Lincoln Cathedral 13 miles

Nottinghamshire

RAILWAY INN

STATION ROAD, LOWDHAM, NOTTINGHAMSHIRE NG14 7DU
TEL: 0115 966 3214 FAX: 0115 966 4878

Directions: Lowdham lies to the northeast of Nottingham. From the M1 take the A610 into Nottingham then pick up the ring road around the north side of the town and take the A612 towards Burton Joyce and up to the A6097. Turn left here and Lowdham will almost immediately be signposted to the left

The Railway Inn is a pretty pub located in a equally picturesque village not far from Nottingham and Sherwood Forest. The rural location can be enjoyed at its best from the sizeable beer garden where there are plenty of tables for you to enjoy your drinks on warm sunny days. The interior is charming and cosy, with décor and furnishings designed to give the place an intimate feel, and there are numerous little corners in which to tuck yourself away if you want a quiet drink. In keeping with the name, one part of the bar has a railway theme with lots of old

photos of Lowdham station and railway memorabilia on display.

The tenants, Jane and Shaun, have newly arrived at the Railway and this is their first venture into the trade, though early indications are that they are going to be popular hosts. They operate a well stocked bar which offers a good selection of draught offerings together with four real ales (Marstons Pedigree, Mansfield Bitter, Green Label and a guest ale). Shaun is in charge of the kitchens and prepares a lunchtime and evening menu of fresh bar meals and snacks. A non-smoking dining room seats to 32 diners and children are welcome.

- ⏰ Mon-Sat 11.00-23.00; Sun 12.00-22.30
- 🍴 Printed menu with daily specials
- 💷 Visa, Mastercard, Delta, Switch
- 🅿 Large beer garden, car park
- 🎵 Ring for details
- ❓ Nottingham 9 miles, Holme Pierrepont National Water Sports Centre 8 miles, Sherwood Forest 8 miles, Southwell Racecourse 7 miles

ROYAL OAK

29 PALMERSTON STREET, WESTWOOD,
NOTTINGHAMSHIRE NG16 5HY
TEL: 01773 602839

> **Directions:** From the M1, leave at junction 27 and follow the A608 west towards Eastwood. After a mile turn right onto the B600 and after Selston bear left onto the B6016. Westwood will then be signposted to the left

Tucked away within the small village of Westwood is the **Royal Oak**, a friendly hostelry owned and run by David and Tracy for the past three years. Much loved by locals, the 19th-century building is almost covered with ivy and adorned with colourful hanging baskets and flowering tubs in summer months. A small car park to one side makes this suitable for visitors to the area who are travelling by car.

It is clear that one of the main reasons

this place is so popular is the active programme of entertainment, with something going on most nights of the week. Friday night is kept free though, so if you prefer a quiet drink this could be night for you. The Royal Oak is a free house and the bar stocks a great selection of beers and lagers, including John Smiths Smooth, Theakstons Best, Chestnut Mild, Kronenburg and Guinness, with the real ales being Marstons Pedigree and a regularly updated guest ale. A selection of light snacks is available on request Friday to Sunday although there are plans to introduce a more extensive menu. Simply ring ahead for details.

- Mon-Thur 19.00-23.00; Fri-Sat11.00-23.00; Sun 12.00-22.30

- Light snacks on request with more extensive selection being introduced

- Beer garden, patio, outside bar, small car park

- Skittles every other Monday, darts and dominoes Tuesdays, quiz and bingo Wednesdays, pool Thursdays, live entertainment Saturdays, bingo Sundays

- Midland Steam Railway 1 mile, Denby Potteries 6 miles, Newstead Abbey 9 miles, Wingfield Manor 7 miles, Riber Castle Wildlife Park 11 miles, Peak District 15 miles

Nottinghamshire

THE SQUARE AND COMPASS

EASTGATE, NORMANTON ON TRENT, NR. NEWARK-ON-TRENT,
NOTTINGHAMSHIRE NG23 6RN
TEL: 01636 821439 FAX: 01636 822794

Directions: From the A1, you will need to turn off at Carlton-on-Trent, 5 miles
north of Newark. Immediately turn north on the B1164 which follows the route of
the A1. After a couple of miles, Normanton on Trent is signposted to the right.

The Square and Compass at
Normanton-on-Trent, owned by Ken
and Fran Munro, is at 500 years old the
oldest village pub in Nottinghamshire.
As a freehouse the pub stocks an ever-
changing range of guest ales, as well as
ales from its own Maypole Brewery, and
has a warm and friendly atmosphere. The
pub enjoys a beautiful rural setting and
has a well-equipped children's play area
and beer garden.

Within the comfortable surroundings
of the bars, with their low beamed
ceilings, open log fires and wooden
furnishings, you can sample superb ales
and the tasty bar snacks. Food is
available each lunchtime and evening
through the week and all day Saturday
and Sunday, with the wide ranging
menus providing excellent value for
money. Meals can be taken in the
lounge, bar, or in the light and airy
dining room. Ken bought the Maypole
brewery in 2001 and now produces nine
different beers supplying The Square
and Compass as well as a number of
other real ale pubs.

The recent addition of an
accommodation annexe enables you to
stay for just a night, or for a few days
whilst exploring the area. The three high
quality double rooms have colour TV
and video and the en-suite bathrooms
include a power shower. Rated 4
diamond by the English Tourist Board.

- 🕐 Mon-Sat 12.00-23.00; Sun 12.00-22.30
- 🍴 Excellent meals, good range of bar snacks, daily specials
- 💷 Visa, Mastercard, Delta, Switch
- 🛏 3 en-suite, double rooms
- Ⓟ Large children's play area, beer garden, car parking
- 🎵 Skittles, darts
- @ email: info@squareandcompass.co.uk website: www.squareandcompass.co.uk
- ❓ Sundown Adventureland 7 miles, Aircraft Museum 9 miles, The World of Robin Hood Visitor Centre 7 miles, Sherwood Forest 10 miles, Rufford Country Park 11 miles

THE STAUNTON ARMS

STAUNTON IN THE VALE, NR. NEWARK ON TRENT,
NOTTINGHAMSHIRE NG13 9PE
TEL: 01400 281062 FAX: 01400 282564

Nottinghamshire

Directions: Six miles north of Grantham North Services, turn east off the A1 for Long Bennington. Immediately there is a turning to the right which take you back over the A1 towards Normanton, and the village of Staunton will be signposted to the right after about a mile.

The Staunton Arms is a delightful country inn nestling within the Vale of Belvoir, to the east of Nottingham. History of an alehouse on this site goes back as far as the 10th century, although the present structure only dates from the late 17th century. The building is of a classic, traditional style and many original features, including the sash windows and beamed ceilings, have been retained.

The pub enjoys a fine reputation for the quality of its food and three chefs compile the mouth-watering menu. The lunchtime menus offer a choice of snacks and light meal options and in the evening there is more extensive a la carte selection. The freshest available produce is used throughout and there is always a fine range of fish and seafood dishes. Meals can be taken in the charming restaurant, which is decorated and furnished with a fresh, blue theme, while light meals and snacks can be enjoyed in the bar and lounge. The pub prides itself on being a member of CAMRA, and the bar can offer plenty of choice to the real ale lover. There are also a number of popular lagers, other beers and fine wines available too. There is a friendly atmosphere to the Staunton Arms, due in the main to Trevor Walker and his lovely family who run the place. They provide friendly service and fine food and look forward to welcoming you.

- 🕐 Mon-Sat 12.00-15.00, 18.00-23.00; Sun 12.00-22.30 Longer opening hours in summer
- 🍴 Good selection of meals and snacks at every session
- Ⓟ Car parking, patio garen
- 🎵 Monthly jazz nights
- @ email: trevorwalker@stralyns.fsnet.co.uk website: www.stauntonarms.co.uk
- ❓ Southwell Racecourse 8 miles, Belton House 9 miles, Belvoir Castle 8 miles, Nottingham 17 miles, Sherwood Forest 20 miles, Woolsthorpe Manor 15 miles

THE THREE CROWNS

23 EASTHORPE STREET, RUDDINGTON, NR. NOTTINGHAM NG11 6LB
TEL: 0115 921 3226 FAX: 0115 984 4363

Directions: At junction 25 of the M1, head east into the centre of Nottingham along the A52. A couple of miles from the city centre take the ring road south ftowards Melton Mowbray. After a couple of miles, Ruddington will be to the right.

The Three Crowns is housed within an unusual, very tall building, which dates back to 1852 and was a pub and piggery. The new management has just completed an extensive programme of rebuilding and refurbishment and the pub is now reopened with a fresh new look. Much of the original character has been retained, with the bar having a mellow, traditional feel and keeping the pitch pine and slate floors and beautiful bay window to the front.

Here you can enjoy fine ales, beer and tasty bar snacks in convivial surroundings. This is a free house and the bar stocks at least five real ales, including Timothy Taylor's Landlord, and regular guest beers such as Everard's Tiger. There is also a fine list of quality wines from across the world. At the back, in a separate extension, is the 'Luk Pra Tor' Restaurant, where an acclaimed Thai chef recreates the tastes of his homeland in an exciting international and Thai menu. Both the restaurant and bar lounges have a laid back style and affordable prices for you to enjoy the varied tastes of the east and west, combined with attentive service in contrasts of tradition. The owners, although not Thai themselves, are actively involved in Thai boxing in Nottingham, and also own a tradition Thai tuk tuk which may often be seen pootling around Ruddington. The restaurant is available for party bookings, receptions, business meetings and private lunches by arrangement.

🕐 Mon-Fri 12.00-15.00, 17.00-23.00; Sat 12.00-23.00; Sun 12.00-22.30

🍴 Separate Thai and International restaurant

£ Visa, Mastercard, Delta, Switch

🎵 Live music each week

@ email: threecrowns@nottinghamthai.co.uk website: www.nottinghamthai.co.uk

❓ Nottingham Castle 5 miles, Holme Pierrepont National Watersports Centre 5 miles, Nottingham Steam Heritage Museum 1 mile, National Frameknitters Museum ¼ mile, Donington Park Racetrack 10 miles

THE WHITE SWAN

50 NORTHGATE, NEWARK-ON-TRENT, NOTTINGHAMSHIRE NG24 1HF
TEL: 01636 704700

Directions: The inn sits near the heart of Newark-on-Trent which lies just off the A1, southwest of Lincoln

---

The White Swan has all the appeal and charm of a period inn, and sits on a prominent corner site near the centre of the town of Newark-on-Trent and just 500 metres from the castle. Dating from the 18th century it has been finished in a mock Tudor style, resulting in a pretty, picture book pub. This is a typical English hostelry with a comfortable, old fashioned interior. The ceilings are low and dark-beamed, the lounge bars are large and airy, there is a dining room and in the sports bar you will find a darts board and games machines.

Offering a choice of fourteen main

- 🕐 Mon to Sat 12.00-23.00; Sun 12.00-22.30
- 🍴 Restaurant open Thursday to Sunday nights
- Ⓟ Beer garden, car park, children's play area
- ♪ Regular race nights, occasional live music, quiz nights
- ❓ Newark Castle, Southwell Racecourse 7 miles, Lincoln15 miles, Vina Cooke Museum of Dolls and Bygone Childhood 5 miles, Nottinghamshire Showground 3 miles, River Trent

dishes, the restaurant is open Thursday to Sunday evenings with other nights by prior booking only. Sunday lunch is a must, with two roast joints served together with a vegetarian option. Private parties can be catered for. To complement your meal there are wines and liqueurs available. The bar stocks Mansfield Beers with two real ales and regular guest ales. There are also lagers and cider, sherry and champagne, cognac and coffee to choose from.

Patrick Harkin is the present licensee – he has many years experience in the food and drinks business and is a member of the British Institute of Innkeepers. Ray Carmichael is the manager and gives the pub the benefit of his Dublin training in food and drink. All in all a well-kept pub run by people who know the hospitality business.

Please note all cross references refer to page numbers

LINCOLNSHIRE

Known to the Romans as Lindum Colonia, Lincoln stood at the junction of two major Imperial thoroughfares, Fosse Way and Ermine Street. By the time of the Domesday Book, it had grown into a settlement of around 1,000 households. William the Conqueror won few friends here by peremptorily ordering 166 of these houses to be destroyed to make way for an imposing castle. Around the same time, he authorised the building of a cathedral and made Lincoln the ecclesiastical centre of a vast bishopric that extended from the Humber to the Thames.

The city reached its peak of prosperity during the Middle Ages but when Henry VIII visited in 1541 the town fathers were reduced to begging relief from taxation or *"they would be compelled in short time to forsake the city, to its utter desolation"*. Henry rejected their plea. When Daniel Defoe passed through Lincoln in the 1770s he found *"an ancient, ragged, decayed and still decaying city"*. Half a century later, another traveller dismissed the historic city as *"an overgrown village"*.

Happily, improvements in roads and canals, and the arrival of the railway in the 1840s, returned the city to prosperity and Lincoln became a major centre for heavy engineering, steam engines, agricultural machinery, excavators, motor cars and other heavy duty items. But you only have to climb the hill to the old town to enter the serenity of the cathedral close, a tranquil enclave lying in the shadow of the noblest and most

Babbling Brook, South Lincolnshire

majestic of all English cathedrals.

The south bank of the River Humber is indeed Lincolnshire's most industrial area but that is only part of the story. Rural north Lincolnshire is as peaceful and unspoilt as anywhere in the county, with scenery that ranges from the northern tip of the Wolds in the east, to the level plains of the Isle of Axholme in the west. The area also includes the largest town in the county, Grimsby, once one of the busiest fishing ports in the world and now an important centre of the food processing industry. A striking reminder of Grimsby's days of glory is the magnificent Dock Tower rising high above the town. A few miles up-river and even more imposing is the colossal Humber Bridge, the largest single span suspension bridge in Europe.

Stretching from Wainfleet and Skegness in the south to Cleethorpes and the mouth of the Humber to the north, the Lindsey Coastal Plain runs for about 40 miles, north to south, and extends between five and ten miles wide, east to west. The Plain offers a good range of animal sanctuaries and nature reserves, and there are some interesting connections with the Poet Laureate Tennyson and with Captain John Smith, founder of the State of Virginia, whose name is inextricably linked with that of the Indian princess Pocahontas.

The area's other main attraction, the splendid sandy beaches running virtually the whole length of the coast, didn't come into their own until the railways arrived in the mid-1800s. The coastal villages of Skegness, Mablethorpe and Cleethorpes have grown steadily to become popular resorts for East Midlanders, each one offering a wide range of family entertainment.

The Elizabethan writer Michael Drayton must have deterred many of his contemporaries from visiting southeast Lincolnshire by his vivid word picture of the "foggy fens". It was, he wrote, *a land of foul, woosy marsh...with a vast queachy soil and hosts of wallowing waves*. It can't have been quite that bad - the Romans farmed extensively here, for example. Since Drayton's day, various drainage schemes, from the 16th century onwards, have reclaimed many thousands of waterlogged acres. Spalding is known around the world for its annual Tulip and Spring Flower Festival when a procession of floats, adorned with millions of tulip heads, progresses through the town.

The landscape of this southwestern corner of the county divides into two distinct areas. Grantham and Stamford lie in the gently rolling hills that form the continuation of the Leicestershire Wolds; while to the east, Bourne and the Deepings stand on the edge of the Fens. Historically, this has always been one of

Nettleton, North Wolds

the more prosperous parts of the county, a wealth reflected in the outstanding churches at Stamford, Grantham and Corby Glen.

The Great North Road, now the A1, brought Grantham and Stamford a constant stream of travellers and trade, a traffic whose legacy includes some fine old coaching inns. One visitor during the early 1800s regarded this as *the only gentrified region* of Lincolnshire: indeed, Belton House, Belvoir Castle, Grimsthorpe Castle and the breathtaking Elizabethan Burghley House are four of the grandest stately homes in England.

ABY

Claythorpe Watermill & Wildfowl Gardens are a major draw for visitors of all ages to this small village on the edge of the Wolds. A beautiful 18th century watermill provides the central feature, surrounded by attractive woodlands inhabited by hundreds of waterfowl and other animals. Built in 1721, the mill is no longer working but it provides a handsome setting for a restaurant, gift shop and Country Fayre shop.

ALFORD

Often described as Lincolnshire's Craft Centre, Alford is a flourishing little town with markets that were first established in 1238 still taking place on Tuesdays and Fridays. These are supplemented by a regular Craft Market every Friday throughout the summer.

Small though it is, Alford boasts some outstanding buildings. **Alford Manor House**, built around 1660, claims the distinction of being the largest thatched manor house in England. It's an attractive building with brick gabling and a beautifully maintained thatched roof. It serves now as a folk museum where visitors are invited to step back into the past and take a look at local life through time-warp shops, an old-fashioned veterinary surgery and a Victorian schoolroom. Reaching even further back into the past, the History Room contains a collection of interesting Roman finds and also displays from the salt works that once prospered in this part of the county.

Another exhibit explores the still-flourishing connections between Alford and the USA.

An even more tangible link with the past is provided by **The Five Sailed Windmill** on the eastern side of the town. It was built by a local millwright, Sam Oxley, in 1813. Standing a majestic six floors high, it has five sails and four sets of grinding stones. This sturdy old mill came perilously close to total destruction in 1955. Thanks to the efforts of local enthusiasts it is now back in full commercial operation, complete with a vintage oven producing bakery items with the full flavour that only the old-fashioned methods seem able to produce.

Alford's handsome medieval **Church of St Wilfrid** dates from the 14th century and among its treasures are a curiously carved Jacobean pulpit, the marble tomb of the former Manor House residents (the Christopher family), and an amazing collection of tapestry kneelers. With so many parish churches nowadays locked for most of the time, it's good to know that St Wilfrid's is open daily from 9am to 4pm. In August, St Wilfrid's hosts a Flower Festival, part of the **Alford Festival**, which began in 1974 and over the years has attracted a growing variety of craftspeople, joined nowadays by dancers, singers, poets and actors.

BARTON-UPON-HUMBER

Today, Barton is dominated by the colossal south tower of the **Humber**

Humber Bridge

The surrounding park has a picnic area, play area and various recreational facilities.

Just to the north of Barton, on the banks of the Humber, is an observation area for viewing the mighty Humber Bridge. Opened in 1981, this is Europe's longest single-span suspension bridge with an overall length of 2,428yds (2,220m). This means that for more than a third of a mile only four concrete pillars, two on each bank, are preserving you from a watery death. From these huge pylons, 510ft (155m) high, gossamer cables of thin-wired steel support a gently curving roadway. Both sets of pylons rise vertically, but because of the curvature of the earth they actually lean away from each other by several inches. The bridge is particularly striking at night when the vast structure is floodlit.

Around the bridge are important nature reserves. **Barton Clay Pits** cover a five-mile area along the river bank and offer a haven for wildlife and recreation for sporty humans. **Far Ings,** with hides and waymarked trails, is home to more than 230 species of wild flowers, 50 nesting bird species and hundreds of different sorts of moths.

Bridge, connecting Lincolnshire with East Yorkshire. This has been a major crossing point for more than a thousand years. The Domesday Book recorded a ferry here and the community was then the largest town in north Lincolnshire. In the 1770s, Daniel Defoe gave a vivid description of his passage across the Humber *"in an open boat in which we had about fifteen horses, and ten or twelve cows, mingled with about seventeen or eighteen passengers, we were about four hours tossing about on the Humber before we could get into the harbour at Hull"*. (The river at this point is only about 2½ miles wide.)

The heart of the town still has some pleasant streets - Fleetgate, Bargate, Beck Hill and Priestgate - all distinguished by mainly Georgian and early Victorian buildings. **Baysgarth House**, now a museum, is an 18th century mansion with a collection of 18th and 19th century English and Oriental pottery, a section on country crafts and an industrial museum in the stable block.

BELTON

"An English country-house at its proudest and most serene", **Belton**

House stands in 1,000 acres of parkland surrounded by a boundary wall 5 miles long. Built in 1685 of honey-coloured Ancaster stone and in the then fashionable Anglo-Dutch style, Belton was the home of the Brownlow family for just under 300 years before being given to the National Trust in 1983. The Trust also acquired the important collections of pictures, porcelain, books and furniture accumulated by 12 generations of Brownlows. With its Dutch and Italian gardens, orangery, deer park, woodland adventure playground and indoor activity room, Belton provides a satisfying day out for the whole family.

BOSTON

An important inland port on the River Witham, Boston's fortunes reached their peak during the Middle Ages when the town was second only to London in the amount of taxes it paid. Today, it's a prosperous market town and the administrative centre for the region. The market, more than 450 years old now and the largest open air market in Lincolnshire, takes place every Wednesday and Saturday.

The town's most famous landmark is St Botolph's Church, much better known as the **Boston Stump.** Stump is a real misnomer since the tower soars 272ft into the sky and is visible for 30 miles or more from land and sea. Building of the tower began around 1425 and was not completed for a hundred years. The body of the church is older still - it dates back to 1309 and is built mainly in the

Boston Huildhall Museum

graceful Decorated style of architecture. St Botolph's is the largest parish church in England and its spacious interior is wonderfully light and airy. The church is noted for its abundance of often bizarre medieval carvings in wood and stone - a bear playing an organ, a man lassooing a lion, a fox in a bishop's cope taking a jug of water from a baboon.

One of Boston's most striking secular buildings is the 15th century **Guildhall**, which for 300 years served as the Town Hall and now houses the town museum. The most popular attraction here is connected with the Pilgrim Fathers. In 1607 this famous band of brothers tried to escape to the religious tolerance of the Netherlands but were betrayed by the captain of their ship, arrested and thrown into the Guildhall cells. The bleak cells in which they were detained can still be seen, along with the old town stocks.

Another impressive building is the **Maud Foster Windmill** (1819), the tallest working windmill in Britain and unusual in having five sails, or sweeps. Visitors can climb to the top of the mill, see the machinery and millstones in action, and enjoy some fine views from the outside balcony. There's a tea room and a Mill Shop that sells the mill's own stone-ground organic flour as well as local books and souvenirs.

If you enjoy seeking out architectural curiosities, then there's a splendid one in a quiet back street of the town. The frontage of the **Freemason's Hall** represents a miniature Egyptian temple, complete with columns crowned by papyrus fronds. Half a century earlier, following Napoleon's Egyptian campaign there had been a spate of such monumental buildings, but Boston's temple, built in the 1860s, presents a very late flowering of the style.

BOURNE

An attractive little town, Bourne has a fine church, an impressive **Town Hall** of 1821 with an unusual staircase entry, delightful **Memorial Gardens**, and a variety of family shops, craft and antiques emporia, as well as modern shopping precincts. A colourful market takes place every Thursday and Saturday.

It was the springs of clear water that enticed the Romans to settle here.

Today, the springs flow into St Peter's Pool from which a small stream known as the **Bourne Eau** runs into the town and Memorial Gardens. Here, willow trees border the crystal clear water, home to fish, wildfowl and small roosting houses. En route, the Bourne Eau passes Baldocks Mill which functioned between 1800 and the 1920s, and now houses the **Bourne Heritage Centre.**

A mile west of the town, beside the A151, stands **Bourne Wood,** 400 acres of long-established woodland with an abundant and varied plant and animal life.

About 4 miles south of Bourne, near the village of Witham on the Hill, stands the **Bowthorpe Oak**, which is believed to be larger in terms of its girth than any other tree in Britain. When last measured, the oak was just over 39ft around. The tree is hollow and it's claimed that on one occasion 39 people stood inside it.

BRIGG

King John was not universally liked but one of his more popular deeds was the granting of a charter (in 1205) which permitted this modest little town to hold an annual festivity on the 5th day of August. **Brigg Fair**, along with Widdecombe and Scarborough, has joined the trio of 'Best Known Fairs in England', its celebrity enhanced by a traditional song and a haunting tone poem composed by Frederick Delius in 1907. Almost 800 years later, the fair still attracts horse traders from around the country, along with all the usual fun of the fair.

King John's son, Henry III, also showed favour to the town. He granted the loyal burghers of Brigg the right to hold a weekly market on Thursdays, a right they still exercise to the full.

Many visitors to Brigg, including the architecture guru Nikolaus Pevsner, have commented that some of the town's most interesting buildings are its pubs. Pevsner picked out for special mention the Lord Nelson, with its broad Regency bow window, the Dying Gladiator, remarkable for the *"gory realism"* of its pub sign, and the Black Bull which boasts *"a vigorous Edwardian pub front"*.

BURGH LE MARSH

Pronounced *"Borough"*, this small town was once the terminus of a Roman road from Lincoln. Although Burgh is now several miles inland, it was from here, centuries ago, that travellers boarded a ferry to cross The Wash and join the **Peddars Way** in Norfolk.

About 3 miles northwest of Burgh, **Gunby Hall** (National Trust) is reputed to be the setting Tennyson had in mind when he wrote of:

"an English home – gray twilight pour'd
On dewy pastures, dewy trees
Softer than sleep – all things in order stored,
A haunt of ancient peace".

Built in 1700 and extended in the 1870s, Gunby Hall is a delightful William & Mary house of plum-coloured brick surrounded by sweeping lawns and flower gardens.

CLEETHORPES

One of the town's claims to fame is that it stands on zero longitude, i.e. on the Greenwich Meridian line. A signpost on the coastal path marks the Meridian line and points the way to London, the North Pole and other prominent places, an essential snap for the family album.

Just south of Grimsby and almost merged with it, Cleethorpes grew from a little village into a holiday resort when the railway line was built in the 1860s. The Manchester, Sheffield & Lincolnshire Railway Company developed much of the town and also built the splendid promenade, a mile long and 65ft wide, below the cliff. Above the promenade they built the sham ruin known as **Ross Castle**, named after the railway's general secretary, Edward Ross. Swathed in ivy, the folly marked the highest point of the cliffs which the promenade now protects from erosion.

The railway company also funded the construction of a **Pier**. This was opened on August Bank Holiday Monday 1873, when nearly 3,000 people paid the then princely sum of sixpence (2½p) for admission. The toll was reduced the next day to a much more reasonable penny (½p), and it is recorded that in the first five weeks 37,000 people visited. The pier, like many others, was breached during the Second World War as a defence measure to discourage enemy landings, and it was never restored to its full length. The pier now measures 355ft compared to its original 1,200ft but the

Edwardian pavilion of 1906 is still in place and is currently the largest nightclub in the area.

The town also boasts the last surviving seaside steam railway, the **Cleethorpes Coast Light Railway.** This narrow-gauge steam railway runs along the foreshore and lakeside every day from Easter to September, and on weekends throughout the year. In the **Cleethorpes Humber Estuary Discovery Centre**, visitors can become time travellers, discover extinct creatures and submerged forests, and work off their aggression by participating in a Viking raid. The Lincolnshire clockmaker, John Harrison, who solved the problem of finding longitude is celebrated in one of the many exhibits and the complex also offers refreshments in the Boaters Tea Room.

CONINGSBY

The centre of this large village, which started life as a Danish settlement, is dominated by the church tower of **St Michael**, notable for its enormous single-handed clock; at over 16ft in diameter, this 17th century clock claims to be the largest working example of its kind. South of the village is RAF Coningsby, a major Tornado base and also home to the **Battle of Britain Memorial Flight**. Created in memory of the gallant airmen who flew in that crucial battle, the Flight operates a Lancaster (one of only two in the world still flying), five Spitfires, two Hurricanes and a Dakota. These historic World War II aircraft are not just museum pieces - they are all still flying and can be seen at a variety of air shows during the summer months.

CROWLAND

It was in 699AD that a young Mercian nobleman named Guthlac became disillusioned with the world and took to a small boat. He rowed off into the fens until he came to a remote muddy island, (which is what the name Crowland means). Here he built himself a hut and a small chapel. Guthlac's reputation as a wise and holy man attracted a host of visitors in search of spiritual guidance He died in 714 and shortly afterwards his kinsman, King Ethelbald of Mercia, founded the monastery that became known as **Crowland Abbey.**

Crowland Abbey

The abbey buildings have suffered an unusually troubled history. Nothing but some oak foundations remain of the first abbey - the rest was destroyed by Danish invaders. The monastery was rebuilt in Saxon style in about 950 when the community began to live according to the rule of St Benedict. That abbey was also destroyed, on this occasion by a great fire in 1091. An earthquake in 1117 interrupted the rebuilding. Some 50 years later, the third abbey was completed, in the Norman style. Parts of this splendid building can still be seen, notably in the dog-tooth west arch of the central tower. Another fire caused massive damage in 1143 and the restoration that followed provides most of the substantial ruins that remain.

Crowland is also noted for its extraordinary 'Bridge without a River', also known locally as the 'Three Ways to Nowhere Bridge'. When it was built in the 1300s, **Trinity Bridge** provided a dry crossing over the confluence of three small streams - hence its unique triangular shape. But the streams dried up and the bridge now serves no purpose apart from being extremely decorative.

THE DEEPINGS

There are four Deepings in all and they lie alongside the River Welland which here forms the county boundary with Cambridgeshire. The largest is **Market Deeping**, which was once an important stop on the London to Lincoln coaching route. The triangular town centre has some imposing Georgian buildings, a large antique and craft centre, and a church dating back to 1240.

Today, Deeping St James merges imperceptibly with its larger neighbour. The old village sits on the banks of the Welland which at this point is controlled by two locks. The **Priory Church of St James** is an impressively large structure and was originally built as a satellite cell of Thorney Abbey. Among its possessions is a hude - a small shelter rather like a sentry box which was designed to keep the Vicar dry when conducting burial services in the rain. Another interesting curiosity is the small square building in the centre of the village. It was originally the Market Cross but was converted into a lock-up in 1819 to contain village drunks and other troublemakers.

DONINGTON-ON-BAIN

Country roads lead westward into wonderful walking country at Donington-on-Bain, a peaceful Wolds village on the **Viking Way**. This well-trodden route, which was established in 1976 by Lincolnshire County Council, runs 147 miles from the Humber Bridge to Oakham in Rutland and is waymarked by Viking helmet symbols. While in Donington, have a look at the grand old water mill and the 13th century church. There is a story that it was usual at weddings for old ladies to throw hassocks at the bride as she walked up the aisle. This boisterous custom was ended in

The Viking Way

1780 by the rector after he was hit by a badly aimed hassock!

To the east of Donington and south of Goulceby is the celebrated **Red Hill Nature Reserve.** The hill itself is an outcrop bearing a vein of spectacular red chalk that is rich in fossil finds, and the small reserve is home to several species of butterflies and moths, the meadow pipit, common lizard and grass snake. From the clifftop there are some wonderful views across the Wolds. The hill also provides the setting for a Good Friday procession when the vicar of Asterby and three parishioners carrying crosses climb the steep lane. The three crosses are erected above a chalk pit and a short service takes place with music provided by the Horncastle Brass band.

GAINSBOROUGH

Britain's most inland port, Gainsborough is located at the highest navigable point on the River Trent for seagoing vessels. The town's most famous building is the enchanting **Gainsborough Old Hall,**

one of the most striking architectural gems in the county. The Hall was built in the 1470s by Sir Thomas Burgh, a Yorkist supporter in the Wars of the Roses. Sir Thomas later entertained Richard III in the Great Hall with its vast arched roof. The kitchens also remain virtually unchanged since those days. A century or so later, around 1597, a London merchant, William Hickman, extended the building in Elizabethan style. The Hall is generally considered one of the best preserved medieval manor houses in the country.

Gainsborough also boasts an outstanding church. Beautifully set in its own grounds in the centre of the town, **All Saints** is a magnificent example of a Georgian classical 'city' church. The interior, with its massive columns, box pews and gallery, is richly decorated in gold and turquoise. Another notable building is **Marshall's Britannia Works** in Beaumont Street, a proud reminder of Gainsborough's once thriving engineering industry. Built around 1850, the long frontage bears an impressive figure of Britannia herself.

Gainsborough is believed to have provided material for George Eliot's *The Mill on the Floss*. The now-demolished Ashcroft Mill on the River Trent was the model for Tulliver's mill and the eagre, or tidal bore, that precipitates the tragic climax of the novel is clearly based on the surge that happens at Gainsborough. This usually takes place about 50 minutes after high tide at Grimsby and the bore can be anything between 8 feet and 13 feet high.

GRANTHAM

A lively market town set beside the River Witham, with a pleasing core of old buildings in its centre. These cluster around the town's famous church, **St Wulfram's,** whose soaring spire, 282 feet high, has been described as *"the finest steeple in England"*. When completed in 1300, it was the loftiest in England and is still the sixth highest. St Wulfram's interior is not quite so inspirational, dominated as it is by uncharacteristically drab Victorian stained glass, but the rare 16th century chained library of 150 volumes is occasionally open to the public and well worth seeing.

Just across from the church, **Grantham House** in Castlegate is a charming National Trust property, parts of which date back to around 1380. The house stands in 25 acres of garden and grounds sloping down to the River Witham and although the house itself is not open to the public there is a right of way through the meadows on the opposite bank of the river. Also in Castlegate, look out for the only living pub sign in the country. In a lime tree outside the **Beehive Inn** is a genuine beehive whose bees produce some 30lbs of honey each year. This unique advertisement for the pub has been in place

since at least 1830.

After St Wulfram's Church, Grantham's most venerable building is that of the **Angel and Royal Hotel** in High Street. The attractive 15th century facade still bears the weather-beaten sculptured heads of Edward III and Queen Philippa over its central archway. King John held his court here and it was in one of the inn's rooms that Richard III signed the death warrant of the 2nd

Sir Isaac Newton

Duke of Buckingham in 1483.

A hundred yards or so from the inn stands an unusual Grantham landmark. The **Conduit** is a miniature tower built by the Corporation in 1597 as the receiving point for the fresh water supply that flowed from springs in the nearby village of Barrowby. At the southern end of the High Street stands a monument to **Sir Isaac Newton**, who was born nearby and educated at the town's King's School. It's an impressive memorial, cast in bronze from a Russian cannon captured during the Crimean War. Behind the statue is the ornate Victorian Guildhall (1869), which now houses the **Guildhall Arts Centre.** Originally, the building incorporated the town's prison cells but these now serve as a box office for the Arts Centre.

Just round the corner, the **Grantham Museum** provides a fascinating in-depth look at local history - social, agricultural, industrial, and has special exhibits devoted to Sir Isaac Newton, and to Lady Thatcher, the town's most famous daughter. When elevated to the peerage she adopted the title Baroness Thatcher of Kesteven - the local authority area in which Grantham is located. She still retains close links with the town and once declared *"From this town I learned so much and am proud to be one of its citizens"*.

There is another connection with the former Prime Minister in **Finkin Street Methodist Church,** just off the High Street. Inside this imposing building with its pillared entrance and spacious balcony is a lectern dedicated to Alderman Alfred Roberts, a Methodist preacher, grocer, and father of Margaret Thatcher.

The local delicacy is **Grantham Gingerbread**, created in 1740 by a local baker who mistakenly added the wrong ingredient to his gingerbread mix. The unusual result was a white crumbly biscuit, completely unlike the regular dark brown gingerbread. Traditionally, the sweetmeat was baked in walnut-size balls and until the 1990s was always available at Catlin's Bakery and Restaurant, whose baker possessed the secret recipe. Sadly, Catlin's is now closed and Grantham Gingerbread is no longer easy to find.

GRIMSBY

According to tradition it was a Dane called Grim who founded Grimsby. He had been ordered to drown the young Prince Havelock after the boy's father had been killed in battle. Grim could not bring himself to murder the child so he set sail for England. After a tempestuous crossing of the North Sea, Grim and the boy arrived at the Humber estuary, where he used the timbers of their boat to build a house on the shore. They lived by selling fish and salt, thus establishing the foundations of an industry for which Grimsby would become known the world over.

But until 1848, Grimsby didn't even rank among Lincolnshire's ten largest towns. That was the year the railway arrived, making it possible for fish to be swiftly transported to major centres of population inland. Only four years later, the town's most famous landmark, the elegant, Italianate **Dock Tower,** was built, soaring more than 300 feet above the busy docks. The Tower now enjoys Grade I listed building status, ranking it alongside such national treasures as

Buckingham Palace and Chatsworth House. The tower's original function was purely utilitarian, the storage of 33,000 gallons of water to operate the hydraulic system that worked the lock gates. But shortly after it was built in 1852 it was discovered that water in a pressurised tube worked just as well so the tower became redundant. On open days, visitors can undertake the gruelling climb up the inside of the tower to enjoy the breathtaking views from the top.

The Tower stands beside Alexandra Dock, which enjoyed its heyday during the 1950s when Grimsby was the world's largest fishing port. The story of those boom days is told in vivid detail in the **National Fishing Heritage Centre** in Alexandra Dock, where visitors are challenged to navigate the icy waters of the Arctic, experience freezing winds, black ice, and lashing rain as the trawler decks, literally, heave and moan beneath your feet. A popular all-in arrangement is **The Fishy Tour**. This begins with an early morning visit to the fish auction, (white coats and wellies provided), followed by a traditional haddock and poached egg breakfast. Then on to the fish filleting and smoking houses, after which there's a guided tour of the Heritage Centre and an exploration of the *Ross Tiger*, a classic fishing trawler from the 1950s. A fish and chip lunch rounds off the trip.

The Time Trap, housed deep in old prison cells of the Town Hall, recreates the seamier side of life on dry land, and has proved a very popular annexe to the Heritage Centre. Visitors pass through dark, twisting corridors, explore mysterious nooks and crannies, discovering en route some unexpected facets of the town. The **Town Hall** itself, built in 1863, is a dignified building whose frontage has a series of busts depicting Queen Victoria, Prince Albert, local man John Whitgift, later Archbishop of Canterbury, Edward III (who granted the land around here to the Freemen of Grimsby), the Earl of Yarborough (local landowner and High Steward of the borough at that time), and the historian Gervase Holles, who was Mayor of Grimsby in 1640.

Many Victorian buildings were destroyed during World War II but a surviving legacy from that era is the **People's Park** where the facilities include a heart-shaped lake, children's play area, bowling greens, croquet lawn, ornamental gardens and plenty of open space. Away from the centre, by the banks of the River Freshney, is **Freshney Park Way,** 300 acres of open space that attracts walkers, cyclists, anglers and birdwatchers as well as picnickers.

A final note for football fans. Be prepared for the question: Why does Grimsby Town Football Club play all its games away? Answer: Because the Mariners' ground is actually in Cleethorpes, a resort which has spread northwards to meet up with Grimsby itself.

GRIMSTHORPE

Grimsthorpe Castle is definitely two-faced. Seen from the north, it's a stately 18th century demi-palace. Viewed from the south, it's a homely Tudor dwelling. The Tudor part of the house was built at incredible speed in order to provide a convenient lodging place in Lincolnshire for Henry VIII on his way north to meet James V of Scotland in York. The royal visit to Grimsthorpe Castle duly took place in 1541 but the honour of the royal

Grimsthorpe Castle Gardens

presence was tarnished by the adultery that allegedly took place here between Henry's fourth wife, Katherine Howard, and an attractive young courtier, Thomas Culpepper. In Tudor times, royal misbehaviour of this nature constituted an act of high treason. The errant Queen and her ardent courtier paid a fatal price for their nights of passion at Grimsthorpe Castle. Both were condemned to the executioner's axe.

The imposing Georgian part of Grimsthorpe Castle was built in the early 1700s. The 16th Baron Grimsthorpe had just been elevated by George I to the topmost rank of the peerage as Duke of Ancaster. It was only natural that the new Duke should wish to improve his rather modest ancestral home. He commissioned Sir John Vanbrugh, the celebrated architect of Blenheim Palace and Castle Howard, to completely redesign the building. As it happened, only the north front and the courtyard were completed to Vanbrugh's designs, which is why the castle presents two such different faces.

The grounds of Grimsthorpe Castle were landscaped by Capability Brown, who in return for a fee of £105 (perhaps £100,000 in today's money) miraculously transformed the flat fields of south Lincolnshire into an Arcadian landscape of gently rolling hills, complete with an artificial lake and a sham bridge.

HECKINGTON

There's plenty of variety and interest here, in particular the tall Church of St Andrew, the Victorian almshouses and the magnificent eight-sailed **Heckington Windmill** by the railway station. When built in 1830 the mill's sails numbered a modest five, but after storms damaged the mill in 1890, eight sails were removed from another mill nearby and installed here. The only surviving eight-sailed mill in Britain rises to five floors and was in use up until 1942. It is now owned by Lincolnshire County Council and can be visited on weekend afternoons, Thursday and Friday afternoons in the season, and at other times by appointment. A few steps away, the **Pearoom** is a contemporary craft centre housed in an old mill building four storeys high.

Heckington's other major attraction is its early-14th century **Church of St Andrew**, which is famous for the wealth of stone carvings on its tower. Inside, there's an outstanding Easter Sepulchre on which medieval master masons depicted the events of Christ's Crucifixion and Resurrection. The same masons were also responsible for the nearby sedilia (stone seats), beautifully carved with scenes from village life and figures of saints.

HORNCASTLE

"Few towns of Horncastle's size can have so many Regency bow-windows", noted Nikolaus Pevsner. These attractive features, and the houses that went with them, were a direct result of the town's increased prosperity and the building boom that followed the opening of the **Horncastle Navigation Canal** in 1802. The town also has an unusual number of hotels for its population, currently about 4,500. The hostelries were built to accommodate visitors to the annual Horse Fair which started some time in the 1200s and continued until 1948. Its modern successor is the **Horncastle Town & Country Fayre**, a popular event

that takes place each June.

St Mary's Church has some interesting features. Outside the north porch is the ground level tombstone of a 19th century local doctor. This is an unconsecrated quarter of the churchyard, but the doctor insisted on being buried here. It was his personal gesture of solidarity with suicides to whom, at that time and until very recently, the Church of England refused interment in hallowed ground. Inside the church there's a brass portrait of Lionel Dymoke, dated 1519. The Dymokes were the hereditary King's Champions who, at the coronation feast of medieval monarchs, challenged anyone who disputed the validity of the king's succession to mortal combat. Above an arch in the south aisle hang 13 scythe blades. These agricultural tools were the only arms available to the local people who took part in the Pilgrimage of Grace of 1536, a mostly northern protest against Henry VIII's policy of closing down every monastery in the country. Their rebellion failed. The king graciously pardoned those who had taken part and the rebels returned peacefully to their homes. Once the crisis had been defused, Henry ordered the summary execution of the most prominent leaders and supporters of the uprising.

IMMINGHAM

A small village until the early 1900s, Immingham's breakthrough came when a new port on the south bank of the Humber was proposed. Grimsby naturally thought that the honour should be hers but consultants favoured Immingham because the deep water channel of the river runs close to the shore here. The new Docks were opened by King George V in 1912 and rapidly grew in importance, especially when the Great Central Railway switched its passenger liner service from Grimsby. The Docks expanded further when the Humber was

Lincoln Cathedral

dredged in the late 1960s to accommodate the new generation of giant tankers and a huge refinery now stands to the west of the town.

The **Immingham Museum** traces the links between the Docks and the railways and there's also an exhibit about the group of Puritans who set sail in 1607 from Immingham to the Netherlands. A memorial to this event, the **Pilgrim Father Monument**, was erected by the Anglo-American Society in 1925. It originally stood near the point of embarkation but is now located near the church. Most of the 20ft-high column is made from local granite but near the top is a block of hewn from Plymouth Rock in New England, where these religious refugees first landed.

LINCOLN

Apart from Durham, **Lincoln Cathedral** is the only one in England to occupy a magnificent hilltop location, its towers soaring high above the Lincolnshire lowlands and visible for miles around. William the Conqueror ordered the first cathedral to be built here but that was almost entirely destroyed by an earthquake on April 15th 1185. The rebuilding that followed, under the energetic direction of Bishop Hugh of Avalon, resulted in the creation of one the country's most inspiring churches. Among its many superb features are the magnificent open nave, stained-glass windows incorporating the 14th century Bishop's Eye and Dean's Eye, and the glorious Angel Choir, whose carvings include the Lincoln Imp, the unofficial symbol of the city.

The imposing ruins of the **Bishops Old Palace** in the shadow of the Cathedral reveal the sumptuous lifestyle of the wealthy medieval bishops, whose authority stretched from the Humber to the Thames. Visitors can wander through splendid apartments, banqueting halls and offices, explore the dramatic undercroft, gaze at the views from inside the Roman city walls, relax in the peaceful Contemporary Heritage Garden and see one of Europe's most northerly

Steep Hill, Lincoln

vineyards.

A good way to explore the city is to follow the **Lincoln Heritage Trail** which takes in the city's 'Magnificent Seven' tourist attractions. The Cathedral naturally takes pride of place but close by is **Lincoln Castle** which dates from 1068. Visitors can climb to the ramparts, which include Observatory Tower, to savour some fine views of the city.

Interesting features abound, notably the keep, known as Lucy Tower, Cobb Hall, where the public gallows were located, and the Victorian prison whose chapel has separate pews like upright coffins. The building also houses an original version of Magna Carta.

There are some fine Norman buildings on a lesser scale in Steep Hill and the Strait. **Jews House**, which dates from about 1170, is thought to be the oldest domestic building in England to survive intact. Its neighbour is Jews Court, a reminder of the time when there was a thriving Jewish community in Lincoln. Medieval splendour lives on in the black and white half-timbered houses on High Bridge, and in the old city Gateways, while the residences in the Cathedral Close and Castle Square are models of Georgian elegance.

The most impressive survival of the old town walls is **The Stonebow**, which spans the High Street pedestrianised shopping mall. The 3-storey building houses the city's Guildhall, its Civic Insignia, royal Charters and other historic artefacts. The Mote Bell on the roof, dated 1371, is still rung to summon the City Fathers to council meetings.

Another place of interest is the

Greyfriars Exhibition Centre, housed in a beautiful 13th century building. The Centre hosts themed exhibitions focused on the collections of the City and County Museum which range from prehistoric times to 1750.

The Lawn, originally built in 1820 as a lunatic asylum and set in eight acres of beautiful grounds and gardens, is an elegant porticoed building whose attractions include an archaeology centre, a tropical conservatory with a display dedicated to the botanist Sir Joseph Banks, an aquarium, a specialist shopping mall and a fully licensed pub and restaurant.

Lincolnshire's largest social history museum is the **Museum of Lincolnshire Life**, which occupies an extensive barracks built for the Royal North Lincoln Militia in 1857. It is now a listed building and houses a fascinating series of displays depicting the many aspects of Lincolnshire life.

Set in beautiful landscaped gardens, **The Usher Gallery** was built in 1927 with funds bequeathed by a Lincoln jeweller, James Ward Usher. It is a major centre for the arts, with collections of porcelain, glass, clocks and coins, and a display of memorabilia connected with the Lincolnshire-born Poet Laureate, Alfred Lord Tennyson. The gallery also houses an important collection of works by Peter de Wint and paintings by Turner, Lowry, Piper, Sickert and Ruskin Spear.

Ellis Mill is the last survivor of a line of windmills that once ran along the Lincoln Edge, a limestone ridge stretching some 70 miles from Winteringham by the Humber to Stamford on the county's southern border. This tower mill dates back to 1798 and is in full working order.

Lincoln stages several major annual events, including a flower festival in the Cathedral, the Lincolnshire Show at the Showground just north of the city, and the Jolly Water Carnival on Brayford Pool in the centre of the city.

Just southeast of the city are the popular open spaces of **Hartsholme Country Park** and **Swanholme Lakes Local Nature Reserve**, 200 acres of woodland, lakes and meadows. A little way further south is **Whisby Nature Park,** set on either side of the Lincoln-Newark railway line and home to great crested grebes, teal and tufted duck. Also on the southern outskirts of the city is the **Lincolnshire Road Transport Museum**, where 40 vintage cars, commercial vehicles and buses span more than 70 years of road transport history.

About 5 miles west of Lincoln, **Doddington Hall** is a very grand Elizabethan mansion completed in 1600 by the architect Robert Smythson, and standing now exactly as then, with wonderful formal gardens, a gatehouse and a family church. The interior contains a fascinating collection of pictures, textiles, porcelain and furniture that reflect four centuries of unbroken family occupation.

LONG SUTTON

Long Sutton is a very appropriate name for this straggling village. **St Mary's Church** has an unusual 2-storeyed porch, the upper floor of which was once used as a school, and a rare, lead-covered spire 160ft high.

The surrounding area borders The Wash and is a favourite place with walkers and naturalists, especially bird-watchers. One of the most popular routes is the **Peter Scott Walk** – during the 1930s the celebrated naturalist lived in one of the two lighthouses on the River Nene nearby. Another route, **King John's Lost Jewels Trail**, covers 23 miles of quiet country roads and is suitable for cyclists and motorists. It starts at Long Sutton market place and passes Sutton Bridge where the unfortunate King is believed to have lost all his treasure in the marsh. Sutton Bridge itself is notable for the swing bridge over the River Nene. Built in 1897 for the Midland and Great Northern Railway, it is one of very few examples still surviving of a working swing bridge.

LOUTH

One of the county's most appealing towns, Louth is set beside the River Lud on the eastern edge of the Wolds in an Area of Outstanding Natural Beauty. Louth can make the unusual boast that it stands in both the eastern and western hemispheres since the Greenwich Meridian line passes through the centre of the town.

The town is a pleasure to wander around, its narrow winding streets and alleys crammed with attractive architecture and bearing intriguing names such as Pawnshop Passage. Westgate in particular is distinguished by its Georgian houses and a 16th century inn. A plaque in nearby **Westgate Place** marks the house where Tennyson lodged with his grandmother while attending the King Edward VI School. Founded in the 1200s, the school is still operating and among its other famous old boys are Sir John Franklin and Captain John Smith of Pocahontas fame. Broadbank, which now houses the **Louth Museum,** is an attractive little building with some interesting artifacts including some amazing locally woven carpets that were displayed at the 1867 Paris Exhibition. And Tennyson fans will surely want to visit the shop in the market square that published *Poems by Two Brothers* and is still selling books.

But the town's pre-eminent architectural glory is the vast **Church of St James**, which boasts the tallest spire of any parish church in England. Nearly 300 feet high and built in gleaming Ancaster stone, this masterly example of the mason's art was constructed between 1501 and 1515. The interior is noted for its glorious starburst tower vault, beautifully restored Georgian pine roof, a wonderful collection of Decorated sedilia, and a fascinating array of old chests.

The **Louth Art Trail** links commissioned works of art, each with some significant connection with the town's history.

MABLETHORPE

Mablethorpe is the northernmost and most 'senior' of the three Lincolnshire holiday resorts that almost form a chain along this stretch of fragile coast which has frequently been threatened by the waves, and whose contours have changed visibly over the years. Much of the original village of Mablethorpe has disappeared into the sea, including the medieval Church of St Peter. In the great North Sea flood of January 31st 1953, seven Mablethorpe residents were drowned.

Long popular with day trippers and holidaymakers, Mablethorpe offers all that could be asked of a traditional seaside town, and a little more. One of the most popular attractions is the **Animal Gardens, Nature Centre & Seal Trust** at North End. This complex houses creatures of all kinds, with special wildcat and barn owl features, and includes a seal and seabird hospital, as well as a nature centre with many fascinating displays. The lynx caves are particularly interesting, displaying 3-dimensional scenes of Mablethorpe as it was 9,000 and 20,000 years ago, along with prehistoric tools and fossils.

A unique collection is on view at **Ye Olde Curiosity Museum** where Graham and Sue Allen have amassed an astonishing collection of more than 18,000 curios. One of the oddest is an 1890 'fat remover', which looks like a rolling pin with suction pads and was used in massage parlours. Almost everything in the museum is on sale - apart from Graham's beloved Morris Minor!

MARKET RASEN

This pleasing little market town stands between the great plain that spreads north of Lincoln and the sheltering Wolds to the east. Now happily bypassed, the town still has a market on Tuesdays and throughout the year there are regular National Hunt meetings at the **Market Rasen Racecourse.**

Taking its name from the little River Rase, Market Rasen was once described by Charles Dickens as being *"the sleepiest town in England"*. Much of the central part is a conservation area.

NORMANBY

Normanby Hall was built in 1825 for the Sheffield family and extended in 1906. The interior is decorated in Regency style, and displays include eight rooms that reflect the changes made down the years, as well as two costume galleries. The 300-acre Park has plenty to see and enjoy, including a deer park, duck ponds, an ice house in the middle of the miniature railway circuit, a Victorian laundry and a walled garden. The **Normanby Hall Farming Museum** majors on rural life in the age of the heavy horse, and among the exhibits illuminating the workings of a 19th century country estate are traditional agricultural equipment and transport, and country crafts.

A mile or so northwest of the Hall, St Andrew's Church in the agreeable village of Burton-on-Stather contains an impressive range of memorials to the Sheffield family, the oldest of which dates back to the 1300s.

OLD BOLINGBROKE

Old Bolingbroke is the site of **Bolingbroke Castle**, now in the care of English Heritage. Originally built in the reign of William I, it later became the property of John of Gaunt whose son, afterwards Henry IV, was born at the castle in 1367. During the Civil War, Bolingbroke Castle was besieged by Parliamentary forces in 1643, fell into disuse soon after and very little now remains.

SCUNTHORPE

Up until the 1850s the main activity around Scunthorpe was the maintaining of rabbit warrens - the local breed with their silvery coats being much in demand with furriers. Then a local landowner, Rowland Winn, discovered that the poor local soil lightly covered vast deposits of ironstone. Scunthorpe's rapid rise to becoming a major steel town was under way.

More of Scunthorpe's industrial and social heritage is on display at the **North Lincolnshire Museum & Art Gallery,** with exhibits that include an ironmonger's cottage. The town has also created a Heritage Trail which takes visitors through three of the parks created by Victorian benefactors - Scunthorpe is proud of its parks and gardens and has claimed the title of 'The Industrial Garden Town of rural North Lincolnshire'.

SKEGNESS

In the early 1800s, when the Tennyson family used to visit Skegness with the future Poet Laureate, Alfred, in tow, it was still a tiny fishing village but already famous for its miles of firm sandy beaches and its "oh-so-bracing" sea air. As late as 1871, the resident population of Skegness was only 239 but two years later the railway arrived and three years after that the local landowner, the Earl of Scarborough, built a new town to the north of the railway station.

A huge **Pier**, 1,843 feet long, was erected. This survived for almost 100 years before a gale on the night of January 11th, 1978 left it sadly truncated. Other amenities provided by the Earl of Scarborough for visitors included the Lumley Hotel, St Matthew's Church and a grand promenade. The **Jubilee Clock Tower** on the seafront was added in 1899, and in 1908 the town fathers amazed even themselves by a stroke of advertising genius – their adoption of the Jolly Fisherman as the town's mascot. **The Jolly Fisherman** has an interesting story behind him. In 1908 the Great Northern Railway purchased an oil painting of the plump and prancing fisherman for £12. After adding the famous slogan 'Skegness is so Bracing', they used the painting as a poster to advertise trips from London to Skegness (fare 3/-, 15p). Almost a century later the same Jolly Fisherman is still busy promoting Skegness as a holiday resort. There are two statues of him in town, one at the railway station, another in Compass Gardens, and during the summer months he can also be seen strolling around the town.

Naturally, the town is well-provided with funfairs – Bottons, Fantasy Island, and **Butlin's**, the latter two of which are actually in the contiguous town of Ingoldmells. It was in 1936 that Billy Butlin opened his very first holiday camp with the slogan 'A Week's Holiday for a Week's Wage' – about £2.50 in those days. The price included accommodation, meals and entertainment and the holidays were understandably popular with workers – a new law had just guaranteed them a statutory week's leave with pay. Just three years later, World War II erupted and the holiday market imploded. But Billy Butlin still prospered. The government bought his camps to use as army barracks, appointed him Director-General of Hostels, and at the end of the war sold the camps back to him at a knock-down price.

Alongside the obvious attractions of the beach and all the traditional seaside entertainment, Skegness and Ingoldmells have other places of special interest. **Church Farm Museum,** a former farmhouse, is home to a collection of old farm implements and machinery, re-created village workshops, a paddock of Lincoln Longwool sheep and a fine example of a Lincolnshire 'mud and stud' thatched cottage brought here from the nearby village of Withern. Craft demonstrations can be viewed on most Sunday afternoons and a programme of special events - sheep shearing, steam threshing and so on - continues throughout the season.

Natureland Seal Sanctuary on North Parade provides interest and fun for all the family with its seals and baby seal rescue centre; aquarium; tropical house with crocodiles, snakes and tarantulas; a pets corner and Floral Palace; and a large greenhouse teeming with plant, insect and bird life, including butterflies and flamingoes.

Serious birdwatchers should head south along the coast to **Gibraltar Point National Nature Reserve**, a field station among the salt marshes and dunes with hides, waymarked routes and guided tours.

SLEAFORD

The history of this busy market town stretches back to the Iron Age. In Roman times there was a massive mint here (730 coins were discovered in one dig), and when a railway was being constructed in Victorian times a vast Anglo-Roman cemetery was uncovered. Later, the Normans built a sizeable castle of which only a small portion of a wall remains, but much of their other major contribution to the town, the **Church of St Denys**, still survives. Its tower, 144ft high and dating from around 1200, stands separate from the main body of the church, and is among the oldest stone-built towers in England. The interior is notable for the superb 14th century tracery in the north window, two magnificent monuments to the local Carre family, some stained glass by William Morris, and a striking rood loft restored by Ninian Comper in 1918.

Collectors of old inn signs will be interested in the **Bull and Dog** pub in Southgate. Set in the wall above its ground floor is a stone bearing the date 1689 and depicting a bull being baited by dogs. The scene is thought to be unique in the country and the stone itself the oldest surviving pub sign in England.

Sleaford also boasts one of the most unusual locations for a Tourist Information Centre. It is housed in **Money's Mill**, a 70ft high, 8-storeyed building erected in 1796 when the Slea Navigation canal allowed large quantities of corn to be brought by barge and offloaded right outside the door. On the eastern edge of the town, **Cogglesford Mill** has been restored to working order and is open to the public. Probably built around 1750, the Mill contains an exhibition detailing its history.

SOMERSBY

For pilgrims on the Tennyson trail, a visit to Somersby is essential. The poet's father, Dr George Clayton Tennyson, was Rector of the village and the adjoining parish of Bag Enderby. Alfred was born here in 1809 and for most of the first 30 of his life Somersby Rectory was his

home. Many of his poems reflect his delight in the surrounding scenery of the Wolds, Fens and coast.

The Rectory, now **Somersby House** (private), still stands, complete with the

Tennyson Memorabilia,
St Margaret's Church

many additions Dr Tennyson made to accommodate his family of 10 children. He is buried in the graveyard of the small church where he had been minister for more than 20 years and which now contains a fine bust of his famous son. Also in the graveyard, where a simple tombstone marks the Doctor's burial place, stands a remarkably well-preserved medieval cross.

The nearby village of **Bag Enderby** is associated with another celebrated figure, John Wesley. He preached here on the village green beneath a noble elm tree. The hollow trunk still stands. The church also has a special treasure in the shape of a beautifully carved 15th century font. The carvings include a tender Pietà, a hart licking the leaves of a tree growing from its back, and a seated figure playing what appears to be a lute.

SPALDING

This small market town is known around the world for its annual **Flower Parade** which attracts half a million visitors each year. Established in 1959, the Festival is held in early May when marching bands lead a succession of colourful floats, each adorned with thousands of tulip heads and spring flowers, through the town. The floats are then displayed at **Springfield Gardens** whose 30 landscaped acres include marvellous show gardens, a carp lake and a sub-tropical palm house.

The two weeks around the Flower Parade coincide with the South Holland Arts Festival featuring open air concerts, workshops, exhibitions and a host of other activities and performances. The festival is based on the South Holland Centre, a stylish venue which is active throughout the year and also has a café-bar on the first floor overlooking the

Market Place.

Spalding itself is an interesting place to stroll around, with Georgian terraces lining the River Welland and with many of the buildings revealing Dutch architectural influences.

The jewel in Spalding's crown is undoubtedly **Ayscoughfee Hall Museum and Gardens,** a well-preserved medieval mansion standing in attractive gardens by the river and with some venerable Yew tree walks. Located in the lovely grounds of the Hall is Spalding's War

Tulip Fields, Spalding

Memorial, standing at one end of an ornamental pool which in winters past would freeze over. Blocks of ice were hewn from it and stored in the icehouse which still survives, tucked away in a corner of the garden walls.

Connoisseurs of odd buildings should

make their way down a lane off Cowbit Road to a red brick building that belongs to no recognisable school of architecture. Known as the **Tower House**, it was built in Victorian times but no one has any idea who built it, why or exactly when. It's a bizarre medley of medieval towers and crenellations, a random obelisk, Georgian-style windows and other bits and pieces. One writer described it as being " *like a giant Lego construction*". It is now a private house but the exterior can be enjoyed from the lane.

A couple of miles south of Spalding, the **Gordon Boswell Romany Museum** has a colourful collection of Romany Vardos (caravans), carts and harnesses along with an extensive display of Romany photographs and sketches covering the last 150 years.

SPILSBY

A pleasant little market town with a population of about 2,000, Spilsby sits near the southern edge of the Wolds. Market day is Monday (with an open air auction as part of the fun), and there's an annual May Day Carnival with dancing round the may pole in the market square. The **Church of St James** has many interesting features, most notably the incredible array of tombs and memorials of the Willoughby family from the 1300s to the early 1600s.

About 2 miles east of Spilsby, on the B1195, the **Northcote Heavy Horses Centre** offers a unique hands-on experience with these gentle giants.

STAMFORD

Proclaimed as *"the finest stone town in England"*, Stamford was declared the country's first Conservation Area in 1967. Later, *"England's most attractive town"* (John Betjeman's words), became familiar to millions of TV viewers when its wonderfully unspoilt Georgian streets and squares provided an authentic backdrop for the BBC's dramatisation of George Eliot's *Middlemarch*. Stamford is a thriving little town with a wide variety of small shops (including a goodly number of antiques shops) and a bustling street market on Fridays.

What gives the present town its enchanting character is the handsome Georgian architecture, evidenced everywhere in private houses and elegant public buildings such as the **Town Hall**, the **Assembly Rooms**, the theatre and the well-known George Hotel whose gallows sign spans the main street.

Stamford's most ancient ecclesiastical building is **St Leonard's Priory**, founded by the Benedictines in the 11th century and a fine example of Norman architecture with an ornate west front and north side arcade.

Secular buildings of note include Browne's Hospital in Broad Street which was founded in 1494 by the same Browne brothers mentioned above. It now houses the **Museum of Almshouse Life** - the ground floor presenting aspects of almshouse life, the upper hosting various exhibitions.

The town is well-provided with

museums. The **Stamford Museum** includes an exhibit celebrating one of the town's most famous visitors. Daniel Lambert earned a precarious living by exhibiting himself as the world's heaviest man. As an additional source of income he would challenge people to race along a course of his choosing. Daniel would then set off along the corridors of the inn, filling them wall to wall and preventing any challenger from passing. When he died at Stamford in 1809 he body was found to weigh almost 59 stones. He had been staying at the Waggon & Horses Inn and the wall of his bedroom had to be demolished in order to remove the body (how did he get in?).

Railway buffs will want to pay a visit to the **Stamford East Railway Station**. The station was built in 1855-6 for the branch line of the Great North Railway. Because the land was owned by the Marquess of Exeter, of nearby Burghley House, the architect William Hurst was obliged to build in the classical style using the local honey-coloured stone. The result is surely one of the most elegant small stations in the country.

A rather more specialised museum is the **Stamford Steam Brewery Museum** which has a collection of original 19th century brewing equipment. The museum is housed in the malt house and brewery, which was established by William Burn in 1825 and continued brewing right up until 1974.

Two more of Stamford's famous residents should be mentioned. Buried in the town cemetery is Sir Malcolm Sargent, the 'pin-up' conductor of the Henry Wood Promenade Concerts in the 1960s and 1970s. The cross on his grave is inscribed with the Promenaders' Prayer. And in St Martin's Church is the splendid tomb of William Cecil, 1st Lord Burghley, who was Elizabeth I's Chief Secretary of State from her accession until his death in 1598. Cecil's magnificent residence, Burghley House, lies a mile south of the town.

"The largest and grandest house of the Elizabethan Age", **Burghley House** presents a dazzling spectacle with its domed towers, walls of cream coloured stone, and acres of windows. Clear glass was still ruinously expensive in the 1560s so Elizabethan grandees like Cecil flaunted their wealth by having windows that stretched almost from floor to ceiling. Burghley House also displays the Elizabethan obsession with symmetry - every tower, dome, pilaster and pinnacle has a corresponding partner.

Cecil commissioned the most celebrated interior decorator of the age, Antonio Verrio, to create rooms of unparalleled splendour. In his 'Heaven Room', Verrio excelled even himself, populating the lofty walls and ceiling with a dynamic gallery of mythological figures.

In the 18th century, Cecil's descendants commissioned the ubiquitous Capability Brown to landscape the 160 acres of parkland surrounding the house. These enchanting grounds are open to visitors and are also home to a large herd of fallow deer which was first established in Cecil's time.

Throughout the summer season, Burghley hosts a series of events of which the best known, the Burghley Horse Trials, takes place at the end of August.

TATTERSHALL

Tattershall lies on the opposite bank of the River Bain from Coningsby and is known all over the world for the astonishing keep of **Tattershall Castle.** Its six storeys rise 110 feet, a huge rectangular slab built in local red brick. In the 1400s it must have appeared even more formidable than it does now. Construction began around 1445 on the orders of the Lord Chancellor, Ralph Cromwell, and it was clearly designed more as a statement of his power and wealth rather than for defence. Military fashion had moved on from such huge keeps and in any case the peaceful heart of 15th century Lincolnshire had no need for fortifications on this scale. Originally, the keep was surrounded by a large complex of other buildings but these have almost entirely disappeared and the tower stands menacingly alone. Despite its magnificence, Tattershall had fallen into near ruin by the early 1900s. There was a very real possibility that it would be dismantled brick by brick, transported to the United States and re-erected there. Happily, the tower was rescued by Lord Curzon, who bequeathed it to the National Trust on his death in 1925.

In the shadow of the castle is **Tattershall Country Park**, set in 365 acres of woods, parks and lakes and offering all sorts of sporting facilities.

As well as this superb castle, Tattershall boasts one of the county's finest churches. **Holy Trinity** was also commissioned by Ralph Lord Cromwell. That was in 1440: the church was finally completed in 1480, long after Ralph's death. Constructed of Ancaster stone, this 'glasshouse church' is dazzlingly light and airy inside; among the items of note is a striking brass of Ralph himself, but sadly his image is headless.

WAINFLEET

Formerly a thriving port, Wainfleet now finds itself several miles from the sea. Narrow roads lead off the market place with its medieval stone cross, making this a place to explore on foot. The most striking building in the town is the former **Magdalen College School**, built in dark red brick in 1484 for William of Wayneflete, Bishop of Winchester and Lord Chancellor to Henry VI. William first founded Magdalen College, Oxford and later established the college school in the town of his birth. It continued as a school until 1933 but now houses the public library, a small museum, a tea room and a walled tea garden.

This attractive little town has a Friday market, held in the unspoilt Market Place with its **Buttercross** and **Clock Tower**.

A curious feature lies about a mile south of the town, on the western side of the A52. Rows and rows of small, rounded mounds are all that remain of an important industry that flourished here from the Iron Age to the 1600s - the extraction of salt from sea water. Throughout these long centuries, salt was an expensive, but absolutely vital, commodity, both as a preservative and a condiment. During the Roman occupation of Britain, part of an Imperial soldier's remuneration was a pouch of salt, his *salarium* or salary. When the mounds at Wainfleet were excavated in the 1950s they were found to contain *salterns* - low hearths surrounded by brick in which fires were lit to evaporate pans of sea water and leave behind the precious salt.

WILLOUGHBY

Willoughby is best known as the birthplace of **Captain John Smith**, founder of what is now the State of Virginia in the USA. A farmer's son, Smith was born in the village in 1580 and educated in nearby Louth. He left England as a young man and, after a spell as a mercenary in Europe, set sail with other optimistic colonists for Chesapeake Bay in 1607. A forceful character, Smith was elected Governor of the new settlement but his diplomatic skills proved unequal to the task of pacifying the local Red Indians. They took him captive and were intent on killing him until one of the chieftain's daughters, Pocahontas, interceded and saved his life. Pocahontas later married one of Smith's fellow colonists, John Rolfe, and

returned with him to England. Beautiful and intelligent, the dark-skinned Pocahontas was welcomed as an exotic celebrity. King James I graciously allowed her to be presented at his Court but within a few months the lovely Indian princess died "of a fever". Four hundred years later, the romantic tale continues to furnish the material for songs, stories, plays and musicals.

Willoughby village celebrates its most famous son with a fine memorial window in the church (a gift from American citizens), and in the Willoughby Arms pub, where a portrait is painted on an outside wall and, inside, accounts of his adventures may be seen.

WOODHALL SPA

Woodhall Spa is something of an anomaly – a chunk of the Home Counties transplanted to the heart of Lincolnshire. Surrounded by pine and birch woods, spacious Victorian and Edwardian villas are set back from tree-lined avenues and it's said that not a single house in the town is older than the 1830s. Woodhall became a spa town by accident when a shaft sunk in search of coal found not coal but mineral-rich water. In 1838 a pump room and baths were built, to be joined later by hydro hotels. Here, real or imagined invalids soaked themselves in 'hypertonic saline waters' heated to 40oC (102o F). The arrival of the railway in 1855 accelerated Woodhall's popularity, but by the early 1900s the spa had fallen out of favour and the associated buildings disappeared one by one. But this beautifully maintained village has retained its decorous spa atmosphere, pleasantly relaxed and peaceful, and also boasting a Championship golf course.

One interesting survivor of the good old days is a former tennis pavilion, now the **Kinema in the Woods**. When it was converted to a cinema during World War II, it inevitably became known as the "Flicks in the Sticks". It's one of very few back projection cinemas in the country and the entertainment on offer includes performances on an original Compton Organ. The **Cottage Museum** on Iddsleigh Road, also the Tourist Information Centre, tells the story of the establishment of the town as a spa resort.

Woodhall Spa had close connections with 617 Squadron, the Dambusters, during World War II. **The Petwood House Hotel** was used as the officers' mess. Memorabilia of those days are displayed in the hotel's Squadron Bar, and in Royal Square a memorial to those intrepid airmen takes the form of a 20ft long model of a breached dam.

At **Kirkstead**, off the B1191, stands a towering piece of brickwork, the only visible remains of a 12th century Cistercian Abbey. Close by is the fine 13th century **Church of St Leonard**, *"a gem of Early Gothic…with an interior like a cathedral aisle"*, according to Simon Jenkins. Originally built as a *"chapel outside the gates"* for visitors to the abbey, St Leonard's was closed in 1877, but restored in 1914 by the Society for the Protection of Ancient Buildings. Miraculously, its beautifully carved chancel screen has survived intact. Dating back to the 13th century, it is believed to be the second oldest such screen in England.

WOOLSTHORPE BY COLSTERWORTH

Isaac Newton was born in 1642 in the modest Jacobean farmhouse, **Woolsthorpe Manor,** which has scarcely changed since he lived here. It was at Woolsthorpe that the 'Father of Modern Science' later made some of his greatest inventions and discoveries. The Manor is now owned by the National Trust, which has furnished the rooms to reflect life of the period and has converted a 17th century barn into a Science Discovery Centre, which helps explain the achievements of one of the country's most famous men. Almost as famous is the legendary apple tree which helped clear Newton's thinking about the laws of gravity: the apple tree in the garden here is said to have been grafted from the original tree beneath which Newton was sitting when the apple fell on to his head.

A rather strange memento of the young Newton is preserved in the church at nearby Colsterworth. It's a sundial crafted by Newton when he was 9 years old. It seems odd to place a sundial *inside* a church and even odder to install it upside down.

THE BLACK BULL

MARKET PLACE, DONINGTON, NR. SPALDING,
LINCOLNSHIRE PE11 4ST
TEL: 01775 820960

Lincolnshire

> **Directions:** Donington lies 10 miles north of Spalding. It can be reached from the A1 by taking the Grantham turning and following the A52 for 20 miles. Then bear right onto the A152 you will immediately find yourself in Donington.

The Black Bull is conveniently located just off the A52 Grantham to Boston road, and is well worth making at stop at if you are passing through the area. This historic former coaching inn is a listed building and much of the character of the original structure has been retained both inside and out. There is certainly a cosy, traditional feel when you venture into the bar with the low beamed ceilings, inglenook fireplace and old wooden settles adding to the atmosphere. A lively atmosphere can be enjoyed throughout the weekends, with regular cabaret nights, live music of varying styles and a friendly

pub quiz too. Ring ahead for full details.

The bar stocks Charles Wells IPA Eagle, which is always a popular choice with real ale fans, together with a range of other beers and lagers. However, it is the superb food that attracts the majority of customers here. There is a good bar menu which is available all day every day and can be enjoyed throughout the bar areas. Here you will find all the popular choices of filled baguettes, jacket potatoes, burgers and the like. The restaurant opens each evening from 6pm until 10.30pm and the a la carte menu offers an outstanding selection of superb dishes. The finest meats are supplied by a local butcher and the vegetables are always the freshest that are available. Everything is cooked to order and is sure not to disappoint.

- 🕐 Mon-Sat 11.00-23.00; Sun 12.00-22.30
- 🍴 Bar snacks and outstanding a la carte restaurant
- 💷 Visa, Mastercard, Delta, Switch
- 🅿 Parking, small beer garden
- 🎵 Live music on Saturdays, Quiz night Sunday, cabaret night Friday, darts, pool
- ❓ Boston 10 miles, The Haven RSPB Reserve 11 miles, Springfield Gardens 10 miles, Belton House 20 miles, Butterfly and Falconry Park 24 miles

THE BLACK HORSE INN

Lincolnshire

MAGNA MILE, LUDFORD, NR. MARKET RASEN,
LINCOLNSHIRE LN8 6AJ
TEL: 01507 313645

> **Directions:** From the A1(M) take junction 34 and follow the A614 into Bawtry.
> Here pick up the A631 east through Gainsborough, on to Market Rasen and
> continue on towards Louth. About 6 miles beyond Market Rasen you will find the
> village of Ludford

The Black Horse Inn lies on the main road between Market Rasen and Louth and offers a friendly welcome to locals and visitors to the area. Popular with walkers, bikers and ramblers there is an RAF theme running throughout, with lots of mementos and photos relating to Bomber Command and Lancasters. Dating back to 1730 this is one of the highest points on the Lincolnshire Wolds and there are fabulous views across the surrounding countryside in all directions.

Yours hosts are Arnie and Julie Daniels, a friendly popular couple who are originally from Minehead in Somerset, and a long way from home!

Julie is the culinary queen, and presents a varied menu of home-made dishes Tuesday to Sunday lunchtimes and every evening. The superb selection ranges from salads and fish dishes, to chargrilled steaks which are cooked on the indoor barbecue every Friday and Saturday evening. There are also some delicious desserts, a children's menu and a good vegetarian selection, while on Sunday there is a carvery.

The bar stocks a choice of three real ales, including John Smiths, Batemans and Charles Wells Bombadier, together with other popular beers and lagers. There is also a selection of fine wines. For those who like to while away the hours there is a full sized snooker table as well as pool and darts. Ideal for a wet Sunday afternoon.

- 🕐 Mon-Sat 12.00-15.00, 19.00-23.00; Sun 12.00-15.00, 19.00-22.30
- 🍴 Outstanding choice of home-made dishes
- 💷 Visa, Mastercard, Delta, Switch
- 🅿 Car park, outside tables
- 🎵 Weekly pub quiz, snooker and pool
- ❓ Market Rasen Racecourse 5 miles, Cadwell Park Motor Racing 13 miles, Lincoln 22 miles, Grimsby 16 miles, Humberside Airport 16 miles

THE CASTLE INN

HIGH STREET, CASTLE BYTHAM, NR. STAMFORD,
LINCOLNSHIRE NG33 4RX
TEL: 01780 410504

Lincolnshire

Directions: Castle Bytham lies 9 miles north of Stamford. It can be easily reached from the A1 by turning right onto an unmarked road, about 9 miles north of the junction for Stamford and the A606

The Castle Inn is a pretty village pub built of creamy stone that is over 300 years old. Such is its age, and inextricable links with the village's history, that it is believed to have a ghost and a tunnel linking it to the church, both dating back to centuries past. Today's visitors will find a cosy establishment with a welcoming feel and a décor which retains the original exposed stone walls, open fires and low beamed ceilings. There are two snugs, where you can tuck yourself away for a quiet drink, and there is also an elegant restaurant where you can enjoy the

superb food.

The place is run by Barbara Cooper, who originally hails from Epsom in Surrey, and yet in her one year here has become very settled in this pretty village and come to love the area very much. Barbara does all her own cooking and uses fresh local produce to prepare the varied menu of traditional English and more innovative dishes. Fish is something of speciality, often using locally-caught trout or fish fresh from Grimsby. You are advised to leave a little room for the delicious desserts too, with ever popular favourites such as apple crumble and bread and butter pudding featuring regularly. Bookings for the restaurant are advisable at weekends. The bar stocks a good choice of wines, to accompanying your delicious meal, and of course real ales, lager and other beers.

- 🕐 Tue-Thurs 12.00-14.30, 18.30-23.00, Fri-Sat 12.00-14.30, 18.00-23.00; Sun 12.00-14.30, 19.00-22.30
- 🍴 Excellent home-cooked food using local produce
- 💷 Visa, Mastercard, Delta, Switch
- 🅿 Patio garden
- 🎵 Monthly jazz evenings
- @ labyb@one.uk
- ❓ Grimsthorpe Castle 6 miles, Burghley House 11 miles, Rutland Water 10 miles, Woolsthorpe Manor 7 miles, Stamford 9 miles, Bourne Wood 8 miles

THE CHEQUERS INN

WOOLSTHORPE BY BELVOIR, NR. GRANTHAM,
LINCOLNSHIRE NG32 1LU
TEL: 01476 870701 FAX: 01476 870085

Directions: Woolsthorpe lies 5 miles due west of Grantham on the Leicestershire/ Lincolnshire border. It can be reached from the A1 by taking the A607 southwest for 3 miles before turning right onto minor roads and following signs for Belvoir Castle.

Hidden in the shadow of Belvoir Castle, **The Chequers Inn** is located within its own grounds surrounded by country fields, overlooking a private cricket pitch and a beautiful summer garden. The A1 is easily accessible, being only a few miles away, and yet you feel as if you are in one of the remotest corners of the country. Originally a 17th-century village farmhouse, later becoming a coaching inn, the pub is full of nooks and crannies. Six open fires are an attraction in the winter, helping to keep the whole place warm and welcoming, and in summer you can take your drinks to one of the outside tables at the front or to the small garden at the back. Inside there is a cosy lounge furnished with comfortable sofas, which has a great deal of olde worlde charm.

The bakehouse, with its stone walls and original baker's oven, is the oldest part of the property and this is now a non-smoking dining area, while the main restaurant has French doors opening on to the gardens. The cuisine is excellent with the pub having been rated in the Michelin guide for the high standard it maintains. The fine food has been admired by many, including the film star Uma Thurman, who was a regular guest at the restaurant while filming The Golden Bowl at Belvoir Castle. Guests staying overnight are accommodated in four charming en-suite bedrooms with beautiful views over the countryside.

🕐 Mon-Sat 12.00-15.00, 17.00-23.00; Sun 12.00-15.00, 17.00-22.30

🍴 Superb a la carte restaurant

£ Visa, Mastercard, Delta, Switch

🛏 4 en-suite rooms

Ⓟ Beer garden, outside tables, petanque court

@ email: info@chequers-inn.net website: www.chequers-inn.net

❓ Belvoir Castle 1 mile, Nottingham 19 miles, Belton House 9 miles, Woolsthorpe Manor 9 miles, Melton Mowbray 12 miles, Holme Pierrepont National Watersports Centre 17 miles

THE CROWN LODGE AND RESTAURANT

CHAPEL HILL, NR. TATTERSHALL, LINCOLNSHIRE LN4 4PX
TEL/FAX: 01526 342262

> **Directions:** The village is most easily reached by taking the A17 Newark turning from the A1. When you reach Sleaford take the A153 northeast towards Skegness. After about 11 miles, Chapel Hill will be signposted to the right.

A warm welcome awaits all visitors to **The Crown Lodge & Restaurant**. This attractive roadside inn is just a mile or so off the Skegness road and would be ideal for a break from driving to enjoy a quick drink or a bite to eat. The place has been immaculately kept and efficiently run by Barry and Corrine for the past four years and the couple brought with them many years of experience in the trade.

Venturing inside, you will find a mainly open plan bar and restaurant area

- Mon-Sat 12.00-14.30, 18.00-23.00; Sun 12.00-17.00, 19.00-22.30; closed during the day Tuesday and Thursday
- A la carte and tasty bar menu served each lunchtime and evening
- 2 twins, 1 double, 1 family room
- Beer garden, car park, cash point
- Pool table
- email: barryharrington@hotmail.com website: www.smoothhound.co.uk/ hotels/crownlodge
- Battle of Britain Memorial Flight Museum 2 miles, Woodhall Spa Golf Course 6 miles, Skegness 25 miles, Horncastle 10 miles, Lincoln 24 miles, Cadwell Park Motor Racing 19 miles

with the pleasant lounge area having comfortable sofas in which to truly relax. There is seating for 24 diners in the restaurant, although meals can be taken throughout the bar areas too. The delicious bar menu offers a selection of sandwiches and light meals, with children having a meal option as well. The a la carte menu offers a wider range of starters and main dishes with the variety sure to cater to every taste and appetite. On the menu when we visited was the intriguingly-named Grunt Gobble Zoom Coo Pie, which comprised wild boar, turkey, hare and pigeon, though there are plenty of less exotic dishes available too.

The Crown Lodge is an ideal base for exploring the area and you will find four guest bedrooms available, all with en-suite facilities, hot drinks tray and TV.

Lincolnshire

MAIN STREET, BONBY, NR. BRIGG, NORTH LINCOLNSHIRE DN20 0PW
TEL: 01652 618793 FAX: 01652 618157

Directions: Bonby lies about 8 miles northeast of Scunthorpe. It is best reached from the end of the M180. From junction 5 follow the A15 north towards Barton-upon-Humber. After a little over three miles, at the junction with the B1206, head west into Bonby

You could be forgiven for driving right past the **Haymaker** and not realising that it was a pub, because at a quick glance from the road it looks very much like a private house. However it is worth keeping an eye out and taking the trouble to stop as you will find a friendly establishment that is open all day every day where you can enjoy a refreshing pint of real ale and a tasty meal. Families will particularly enjoy the children's play area and in warm weather you can also take your drinks outside on the patio.

Your hosts are Roy and Rose who

- 🕐 Mon-Sat 12.00-23.00; Sun 12.00-22.30
- 🍴 Home-cooked menu of bar meals and snacks
- 💷 Visa, Mastercard, Delta, Switch
- 🅿 Parking, children's play area, patio garden
- 🎵 Live music each Saturday night, pool table
- ❓ Elsham Country Park 3 miles Barton Clay Pits Nature Reserve 6 miles, Humber Bridge 6 miles, Normanby Hall 12 miles, Humberside Airport 6 miles

moved here after 20 years in the trade in Warwick, choosing to make the move to their own pub in this delightful village not so long ago. The modern building lends itself to a spacious bar area with plenty of room for a pool table, with the elegantly-furnished restaurant housed within a new extension to the rear. With food available each lunchtime and evening Monday to Saturday, the menu offers a varied selection of snacks and popular bar meals, such as steaks, scampi and pies together with vegetarian options. The Sunday lunches are served until 5pm and prove to be exceedingly popular with the regulars. Everything is home-cooked and offers great value for money.

SLUICE ROAD, SOUTH FERRIBY, NORTH LINCOLNSHIRE DN18 6JQ
TEL: 01652 635242

Directions: South Ferriby is easily located on the Humber estuary. From the end of the M180 take the A15 towards the Humber Bridge. At the large roundabout take the slip road to Barton-upon-Humber. Turn left onto the A1077 which will after 2 miles lead you directly to the Hope and Anchor.

The Hope and Anchor enjoys an unparalleled location on the banks of the River Humber, where the River Ancholme joins it, and offers views across the wildlife and bird sanctuary towards Read's Island. Avocet, seals and porpoises can often be seen here. Outside there is seating and a viewing point to get even closer to the wildlife, when the weather permits.

Taken over less than a year ago by local couple Marion and Bob Lowrie, the inn has been completely transformed, with extensive refurbishment both in the public areas and behind the scenes in the kitchens. Together with their head chef, Stephanie, they are establishing a far reaching reputation for fine cuisine served in delightful surroundings. The bar menu alone is impressive and offers all the popular favourites at reasonable prices all day every day. The bar is spacious and traditionally styled to create a cosy atmosphere and stocks an excellent selection of real ales, fine wines and malt whiskies.

The Riverview Restaurant enjoys the best views and the elegant surroundings are enhanced with fine table linen and polished cutlery. The a la carte menu shows off the chefs' talents and great pride is taken in the superb scallops and other seafood which is flown in daily from the Western Isles. The restaurant is open Mon to Sun lunch time and evenings, with Sunday lunch a special family treat. Booking is recommended.

- Mon-Sat 10.00-23.00; Sun 12.00-22.30
- Superb menu prepared by three chefs
- Visa, Mastercard, Delta, Switch
- Riverside gardens, car park
- Live performers each Friday night
- email: info@thehopeandanchor.com website: www.thehopeandanchor.com
- Clay Pits Nature Reserve 1 mile, Humber Bridge 3 miles, Normanby Hall 7 miles, Humberside Airport 13 miles, Hull 12 miles, Grimsby 25 miles

Lincolnshire

THE HORSE AND JOCKEY

HIGH STREET, WADDINGTON, NR. LINCOLN LN5 9RF
TEL: 01522 720224 FAX: 01522 722551

Directions: The town of Waddington lies 4 miles due south of Lincoln. It can be reached from the A1 by following the A46 into Lincoln. From the centre of town take the A15 Sleaford road before bearing right onto the A607 which will lead you directly to Waddington

The Horse and Jockey is a traditional 16th-century coaching inn located within the quaint village of Waddington just four miles from Lincoln. The pub has always had close ties with RAF Waddington dating back to the time of the bomber squadrons in the Second World War that were based there. A Grade One listed building, the pub has been carefully refurbished to retain much of its original character and has now taken on a horse racing theme, in keeping with its name, and is decorated with horse racing memorabilia.

The spacious, mainly open-plan

interior can seat up to 125 customers, and great pride is taken in serving good quality food at lunchtime and in the evening, seven days a week. Meanwhile, the bar can boast a wide range of cast conditioned ales, including Old Specked Hen, John Smiths and Marstons Pedigree, and a fine selection of new world wines.

Ascot, Goodwood, Sandown and Aintree are not only famous racecourses, but also the names of the finely furnished en-suite accommodation. There are two twin rooms, a family room, and a four poster room, all tastefully decorated and fitted with good quality, locally-made, pine furnishings. The provision of tea and coffee making facilities, complimentary toiletries and a colour TV help to make each of these rooms a pleasure to stay in.

- Mon-Sat 11.00-23.00; Sun 12.00-22.30
- Outstanding menu prepared by three chefs
- Visa, Mastercard, Delta, Switch
- 2 twin room, 1 family room, 1 four poster room
- Car park
- Pool table
- RAF Waddington, Lincoln Cathedral 4 miles, Lincolnshire Museum 8 miles, Battle of Britain Memorial Flight Museum 17 miles, Southwell Racecourse 16 miles

211 EASTGATE, LOUTH, LINCOLNSHIRE LN11 8DD
TEL: 01507 603657

Directions: From the A1 take the A46 exit and head for Lincoln. Follow the bypass around the town and pick up the A158 signposted for Skegness. After 11 miles turn left onto the A157 which will take you the 15 miles directly to Louth

The Lincolnshire Poacher is an elegant Georgian building, originally a privately-owned country house. Charles William Tindall, founder of the Lincoln Red Cattle Society lived here, and Winston Churchill stayed overnight during the Second World War. In fact, the mother of the current owner, Jan Milson, was a chambermaid at the time, and even prepared his room.

After the war, in 1950, the house was converted into a country inn, and today it is run by Jan and her family. The main bar area was created in 1993 and you would be hard pushed to find more

elegant surroundings, with many of the original architectural features having been retained. The well stocked bar has recently been awarded the Cask Marque award in recognition of the fine quality of its ales. The cosy restaurant has been refurbished in soft shades of green and lilac, creating stylish surroundings in which to enjoy your meal. Food is available each lunchtime and evening with the menu offering traditional home-made fayre using local produce. The Lincolnshire sausages are always popular, as is the fresh fish which comes from Grimsby and the Saltfleet crabs.

If you are looking for somewhere to stay in this delightful part of the country, then the Lincolnshire Poacher can provide six spacious, en-suite guest rooms. All are comfortably furnished and have tea and coffee making facilities and a colour TV.

🕐 Mon-Sat 11.00-15.00, 17.00-23.00; Sun 12.00-15.00, 19.00-22.30

🍴 Bar meals with restaurant open in evenings

🛏 6 en-suite rooms of varying sizes

🅿 Spacious car park, beer garden

🎵 Live entertainers and karaoke Saturday nights, pool, darts

@ email: jan@milson211.freeserve.co.uk
website: www.lincolnshirepoacher.com

❓ Cadwell Park Racetrack 5 miles, Viking Way Walk, Covenham Reservoir 7 miles, Mablethorpe Nature Centre & Seal Trust 13 miles, Skegness 22 miles

THE RED LION INN

LINCOLN ROAD, BAUMBER, NR. HORNCASTLE,
LINCOLNSHIRE LN9 5ND
TEL: 01507 578287

Lincolnshire

Directions: From the A1 take the A46 exit and head for Lincoln. Follow the bypass around the town and then turn onto the A158 which is signposted for Skegness. Baumber will be found about 17 miles from Lincoln

The village of Baumber lies directly on the A158 Skegness road which makes **The Red Lion Inn** an ideal stopping off place for those heading for the coast. With a good sized car park, and a children's play area planned, it is perfect for families. Venturing inside you will find a cosy, traditional pub with plenty of tables and chairs, and an lovely open fire for taking the chill off the air in cooler weather.

At the moment meals can be taken throughout the bar, or at the tables at the front, or in the beer garden at the back, however during 2003 there are plans to open a new conservatory restaurant which will seat up to 60 diners. Clearly the food is a popular attraction here and it's not very hard to see why. The menu is made up of traditional English dishes, all home-cooked by the owners mum, Marlene. With many years' experience working in a restaurant in Spain, it is clear that she knows what people like – delicious food, served in good sized portions, and at a reasonable price. There is a three-course meal option, priced at just £4.95, while at Sunday lunch there is a superb carvery.

If real ale is your thing, then the bar will not disappoint. Here they stock John Smiths Cask and Smoothflow, Theakstons and Chestnut Mild together with regular guest ales. Lager and wine drinkers will also find a good selection.

- 🕐 Mon-Sat 11.00-23.00; Sun 12.00-22.30; restricted opening hours in winter
- 🍴 Traditional English dishes
- 🅿 Car park, beer garden, children's play area planned
- 🎵 Live music planned for Saturday night
- ❓ Horncastle Antiques Centre 4 miles, Cadwell Park Motor Racing 9 miles, Battle of Britain Memorial flight Museum 13 miles, Skegness 25 miles

THE TURKS HEAD

MAIN ROAD, MALTBY LE MARSH, NR. MABLETHORPE,
LINCOLNSHIRE LN13 0JP
TEL: 01507 450084

> **Directions:** From the A1 take the A46 exit for Lincoln and then pick up the A158
> which is signposted for Skegness. At Parney, turn left onto the A16 and at the
> junction with A1028 continue straight ahead onto the A1104. Stay on this road,
> following signs to Mablethorpe, and you will reach Maltby le Marsh after 8 miles

The Turks Head is an attractive white-washed inn on the main road through Maltby le Marsh. Venturing inside visitors find a striking interior with white walls and black-painted beams throughout. The bar extends to three sides and is well stocked with a selection of real ales, including Courage, Directors and Pedigree, together with regular guest ales too. There are also many other popular choices, including Guinness, Strongbow Cider, Kronenbourg and Fosters, as well as wines by the glass and a fine range of malt whiskies.

- Mon-Sat 11.00-15.00, 19.00-23.00; Sun 12.00-15.00, 19.00-22.30; Easter to September open all day
- Home-cooked menu offering excellent value
- Visa, Mastercard, Delta, Switch
- 5 pitch caravan site
- Children's play area, beer garden, car park
- Live bands one Saturday a month, pub quiz Mondays, darts, pool
- Nature Reserve & Seal Sanctuary 3 miles, 9-hole golf course 3 miles, Claythorpe Watermill & Wildfowl Gardens 5 miles, Alford 4 miles, Cadwell Park Racetrack 20 miles

The Turks Head has a good reputation for serving tasty home-cooked food which offers excellent value for money. The menu offers jacket potatoes and burgers, home-made pies, steaks and other pub favourites. The Sunday lunch is always popular with a three-course lunch costing just £5.95. Meals can be taken throughout the bar area or outside in the spacious beer garden where families can make the most of the new children's play area.

Paul and Sharon Darling are members of the Caravanning Club and can offer five pitches for tourers and caravans. The site is fully equipped with electric and water hook ups and there are toilet and shower facilities too.

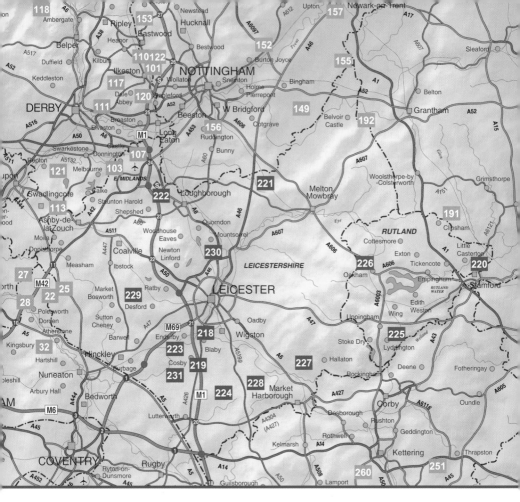

218 The Black Horse, Blaby, Leicestershire

219 The Bulls Head, Cosby, Leicestershire

220 The Crown Inn, Great Casterton, Stamford, Rutland

221 The Crown Inn, Old Dalby, Melton Mowbray, Leicestershire

222 The Falcon Inn, Long Whatton, Leicestershire

223 The Heathcote Arms, Croft, Leicestershire

224 The Joiners Arms, Bruntingthorpe, Lutterworth, Leicestershire

225 Marquess of Exeter, Lyddington, Uppingham, Rutland

226 The Odd House Tavern, Oakham, Rutland

227 The Old Barn Inn and Restaurant, Glooston, Leicestershire

228 The Staff of Life, Mowsley, Market Harborough, Leicestershire

229 The Windmill Inn, Brascote, Newbold Verdon, Leicestershire

230 The Woodmans Stroke, Rothley, Leicestershire

231 Ye Olde Bulls Head, Broughton Astley, Leicestershire

Please note all cross references refer to page numbers

LEICESTERSHIRE & RUTLAND

Leicestershire is generally dismissed by those who have merely driven through it as flat and pretty well covered with redbrick towns and villages. Its most attractive features are shy and quiet and have to be sought out, but they amply reward the explorer. The county is divided into two almost equal parts by the River Soar, which flows northward into the Trent. It separates the east and west by a broad valley, flowing like a silver ribbon through historic Leicester in the very heart of the county. This capital town was thriving in Roman days and is one of the oldest towns in England. It has managed to retain outstanding monuments of almost every age of English history. Red Leicester cheese was made in the southern part of the county in the 1700s, but now the only genuine product is made at Melton Mowbray, which also makes Stilton and, of course, the superlative pork pies. And every schoolchild knows the name of Bosworth Field, one of the momentous battles which changed the course of English history.

Leicestershire is a pleasant county of fields and woods, ancient earthworks, picturesque villages and some marvellous churches. The towns of Ashby, Coalville, Loughborough, Hinckley, Market Harborough and Melton Mowbray all have great history and character, and the county capital

Poppy Fields, Leicestershire

Leicester offers the best of several worlds, with a rich industrial and architectural heritage, a wealth of history, an abundance of open spaces, a firm commitment to environmental issues and an eye to the future with the opening of The National Space Centre.

Just 20 miles across and covering a mere 150 square miles, Rutland delights in its status as England's smallest county. Its inhabitants were incensed when the Local Government changes of 1974 stripped the county of its identity and merged it with neighbouring Leicestershire. It took more than 20 years of ceaseless campaigning before bureaucracy relented and Rutland was re-instated as a county in its own right once again. Rutland has villages of thatch and ironstone, clustered around their churches and the countryside is rich in pasture where once deer were hunted. Its central feature is Rutland Water, its 3,100 acres making it one of the largest man-made lakes in northern Europe. Started in 1971 to supply water to the East Midlands towns, it was created by damming the valley near Empingham. Among the lovely villages are the larger towns such as Uppingham and Oakham, offering their own diversions, sights and sounds for the visitor.

Belvoir Castle

ASHBY-DE-LA-ZOUCH

A historic market town whose name comes from the Saxon Aesc (ash) and Byr (habitation); the ending de la Zouch was added in 1160 when a Norman nobleman Alain de Parrhoet la Zouch became lord of the manor by marriage. In the 15th century Edward IV granted

Ashby Castle

Ashby Manor to his favourite counsellor, Lord Hastings, who converted the manor house into a castle and rebuilt the nearby St Helen's Church. During the Civil War **Ashby Castle** was besieged for over a year by the Parliamentarian Army until the Royalists surrendered in 1646. After the war the castle was partly destroyed to prevent its further use as a centre of resistance and almost wholly forgotten until the publication of Sir Walter Scott's *Ivanhoe* in 1820. He used the castle as the setting for the archery competition which Robin Hood won by splitting the shaft of his opponent's arrow in the bull's eye. The most striking feature of the imposing ruins is the Hastings Tower of 1464, which visitors

can still climb to enjoy the view. The earliest parts predate the conversion and include parts of the hall, buttery and pantry of the 12th century manor house.

Hard by the castle ruins stands **St Helen's Church**, built by Lord Hastings in the 1400s on the site of an 11th century church. Restored and enlarged in 1880, it contains much of interest, including some exceptionally fine stained glass depicting the life of Christ, several monuments to the Hastings family and an unusual relic in the shape of a finger pillory used to punish parishioners misbehaving in church. Ashby de la Zouch Museum contains a permanent display of Ashby history, the highlight being a model of the castle during the Civil War siege.

Ashby was for a while in the 19th century promoted as a spa town; the **Ivanhoe Baths** were designed in 1822 by Robert Chaplin in Grecian style and had a 150ft colonnaded front with 32 Doric columns. Nearby Georgian terraces, also by Chaplin, stand as testimony to the seriousness of the spa project, but a period of decline set in and the baths closed in the 1880s; the buildings were demolished in 1962. Yet another Chaplin building, the grand railway station, ceased to function as a station when the Leicester-Burton line was axed in the 1960s but was restored in the 1980s for use as offices.

BELVOIR CASTLE

The Leicestershire home of the Duke of Rutland is an imposing mock-medieval

Jousting at Belvoir Castle

building in an equally imposing setting overlooking the pastoral Vale of Belvoir. The present Belvoir Castle was completed in the early 19th century after previous buildings had been destroyed during the Wars of the Roses, the Civil War and major fire in 1816. In the stunning interior are notable collections of furniture and porcelain, silks and tapestries, sculptures and paintings. There are works by Van Dyck, Reynolds, Hogarth and, most familiar of all, Holbein's imposing portrait of Henry VIII. Also within the castle is the **Queen's Royal Lancers Museum**. The grounds are as splendid as the castle and are used for medieval jousting tournaments on certain days in the summer.

BURBAGE

The village was originally called Burbach, a name that came from the burr thistles that grew in profusion in the fields. The 9th Earl of Kent was an early incumbent, being rector here for 50 years at the Church of St Catherine, whose spire is a landmark for miles around. **Burbage Woods** are nationally important because of the spectacular ground flora, and Burbage Common is one the largest areas of natural grassland in the locality. For the visitor there's a network of footpaths, a bird observation hide, picnic tables and a visitor centre.

CASTLE DONINGTON

Originally just 'Donington' – the 'Castle' was added when the Norman castle was built to defend the River Trent crossing. It was demolished by King John to punish the owner for supporting Magna Carta and was rebuilt in 1278.

The **Donington Grand Prix Collection**, in Donington Park, is the world's largest collection of single-seater racing cars.

COALVILLE

Originally called Long Lane, the town sprang up on a bleak common when Whitwick Colliery was opened in 1824. The big name in the early days was George Stephenson, who not only established the railway here (in 1832) but also built the churches.

At Ashby Road, Coalville, **Snibston Discovery Park** is built on the 100-acre site of the former Snibston Colliery. Visitors can explore a unique mixture of nature, history, science and technology: topics covered include the industrial heritage of Leicestershire, and former miners conduct a lively surface tour of the colliery. There are rides behind a diesel locomotive on the newly restored colliery line and the Science Alive Gallery allows visitors to play with lightning, walk through a tornado or cycle with a skeleton. You can test your strength against a pulley system in the Engineering Gallery; see the clothes of days gone by in the Textile and Fashion Gallery; or relax in the Grange Nature Reserve and Victorian arboretum.

HALLATON

On the village green of this picturesque village in the rich grazing lands of the Welland Valley stands an unusual conical **Buttercross**. Every Easter Monday the cross is the setting for the crowning ceremony of the **Hare-Pie Scrambling & Bottle-Kicking** contest. The captain of the winning team is lifted to the top of the conical monument and there he broaches a bottle of ale. The contest is a free-for-all struggle between the neighbouring villages of Hallaton and Medbourne to get two out of three bottles (actually small oak casks) of ale across the village boundary by whatever means possible. As many as 400 players

may be milling around in the scrum and the battle has been known to continue for eight or nine hours. The day's events begin with a procession to Hare Pie Bank where pieces of a huge hare pie are thrown to the crowd. The antiquarian Charles Bilson believed the custom was a relic of a time when the hare was worshipped as a divine animal, but he has no explanation for the origins of the bottle-kicking contest. A display of this curious event is on show in the **Hallaton Village Museum**, along with relics from the motte and bailey castle and some unusual agricultural items.

HINCKLEY

Many of the old timbered houses still stand in the town of Hinckley, whose Fair is mentioned in Shakespeare's *Henry IV*. The turning point in its fortunes came in 1640 when the first stocking frame was set up, initiating the hosiery and knitwear industry that has made the town known internationally. A surviving example of framework knitters' cottages still stand in Lower Bond Street. This terrace of restored 17th century thatched cottages is home to **Hinckley & District Museum** whose displays depict aspects of the history of Hinckley and district and include amongst the hosiery exhibits a stocking frame of 1740.

It was in Hinckley that Joseph Hansom produced the first hansom cab, which he drove at full gallop along Regent Street to prove that it could not be overturned.

LEICESTER

When the Romans built a town here in the 1st century AD they called it Ratae Corielauvorum, and when they left 300 years later it survived in some form. It was the seat of a Christian bishop in the 7th century, and in the 9th century was conquered and settled by the Vikings along with Lincoln, Nottingham, Derby and Stamford. The city flourished in the Middle Ages when the cloth and wool trades became important, and the coming of the canals and the railways brought further prosperity. The development of road transport changed the face of the city, and modern Leicester is a thriving industrial and commercial city with superb shopping and recreational facilities and a mixture of cultures and communities as rich and diverse as any in the land.

At the heart of Leicester's heritage is **Castle Park**, the old town, an area of gardens, churches, museums and other fine buildings. Here are concentrated many of the city's main visitor attractions. **Castle Gardens** was just an area of marshland by the River Soar until it was drained and opened as gardens to the public in 1926. In the gardens is a statue of Richard III who on a sunny August day in 1485 rode out from the

city to his death at the Battle of Bosworth Field. Adjacent to the gardens is the **Church of St Mary de Castro**, founded in 1107 and still in use. The chancel, stained glass, carvings and tombstones are all well worth taking time to examine. Geoffrey Chaucer was

Town Hall Gardens, Leicester

married here and Henry VI was knighted in the church in 1426. Next to the church is the Great Hall of Leicester Castle. The Hall was built in the 12th century by Robert le Bossu and used by successive Earls of Leicester as their administrative headquarters; it is open to the public on special event days. Also in the same space is **Newarke Houses Museum**, a museum of social and domestic history contained in two 16th century houses. Displays include clocks, toys, furniture, a 1940s village grocer's shop and a reconstructed Victorian street scene. Leicester's diverse cultural heritage is represented by the **Jain Centre** and the **Guru Nanak Gurdwara**, a Sikh temple and museum. Across the road from the Jain Centre is the **Jewry**

Wall and Museum. The museum chronicles the history and archaeology of the city and the county from Roman times to 1485. The Church of St Martin, which was in existence before 1086, was extended in the 14th and 15th centuries, restored in the 19th century and hallowed as the Cathedral of Leicester in 1927. Stained glass and carvings are impressive, and the memorial to Richard III is a highlight.

Across the road from the Cathedral is Wygston's House, a part-timber-framed building, one of the oldest in the city, which now houses displays of fashion, textiles and crafts from around the world, along with a reconstruction of a 1920s draper's shop.

Leicester City Museums also include The New Walk Museum and Art Gallery, with displays including natural history, geology, ancient Egyptian mummies, a dinosaur skeleton more than 175 million years old, and a fine German

Leicester Guildhall

Expressionist collection; Belgrave Hall and Gardens, a Queen Anne house

whose rooms reflect Edwardian elegance and Victorian cosiness; and the Abbey Pumping Station, an 1891 station with massive beam engines and several exhibitions.

The city's most recent major attraction is the National Space Centre, opened in 2001 as part of the new millennium celebrations. This multi-million pound project offers real rockets and satellites, interactive challenges and the most advanced space theatre in the world, transporting the audience on an awe-inspiring journey through the universe and beyond.

In Western Park, Ecohouse is an environment-friendly show home featuring energy efficiency, sustainable living and an organic garden.

LOUGHBOROUGH

In Loughborough's Market Place is a statue of a seated man admiring his sock. Titled The Sock, this whimsical piece by sculptor Shona Kinlock celebrates the town's premier industry in times past, beginning with wool, then woollen stockings and progressing to knitwear and hosiery machinery and engineering.

Another major industry since mid-Victorian times is represented by the lofty Carillon in Queen's Park which was built as an imaginative War Memorial to the dead of the First World

War. The 151ft high carillon tower, the first to be built in Britain, contains a unique carillon of 47 bells, covering four chromatic octaves, under the care of the borough carilloner. Loughborough's connection with bells began in 1858 when the bell foundry of John Taylor moved here from Oxford. It is still producing and restoring bells for customers all over the world. Situated alongside the working factory, the **John Taylor Bell Foundry Museum** covers all aspects of bell-founding from early times and show the craft techniques of moulding, casting, tuning and fitting up of bells.

The **Charnwood Museum** displays the natural and local history of Charnwood, the district around Loughborough that includes the majestic Charnwood Forest.

For many visitors to Loughborough, the most irresistible attraction is the **Great Central Railway**, Britain's only main line steam railway. Its headquarters are at Loughborough Central Station, where there is a museum, a working signal box and a collection of historic steam locomotives. The station, with its ornate canopy over the island platform, is worth a visit in its own right, and is in regular demand from film companies. The line runs eight miles to Quorn and Birstall, crossing the Swithland Reservoir viaduct.

Loughborough Market is one of the finest street markets in the country. Full of tradition and atmosphere, it is held in the market place and adjacent streets every Thursday and Saturday. November sees the annual Loughborough Fair, with stalls, shows, rides and other attractions.

LUTTERWORTH

John Wycliffe was rector here under the tutelage of John of Gaunt. His instigation of an English translation of the Bible into English caused huge dissent. He died in 1384 and was buried in the church here, but when he was excommunicated in 1428 his body was exhumed and burned and his ashes scattered in the River Swift. Close to the church, **Lutterworth Museum and Historical Society** contains a wealth of local history from Roman times to World War II.

About 3 miles southeast of Lutterworth and set in meadows beside the River Avon, **Stanford Hall** is a pleasantly-proportioned, dignified and serene house with many interesting features.

MARKET BOSWORTH

Market Bosworth has been a Britain in Bloom winner for the years 1995 to 1998. This market town is of course most famous as the battle site for the turning point in the Wars of the Roses – Richard III (Duke of York, the 'White Rose' county) was routed here by 'Red Rose' forces (Henry Bolingbroke, later Henry IV, of Lancaster) and killed in 1485. **Market Bosworth Country Park** is one of many beautiful open spaces in the area. Another is **Bosworth Water Trust's Leisure and Water Park** on the B585 west of town. This is a 50-acre leisure park with 20 acres of lakes for dinghy sailing, boardsailing and fishing. At nearby Cadeby is the unusual combination that is the **Cadeby Light Railway & Brass Rubbing Centre**, comprising a narrow-gauge steam railway, model and miniature railways, a steam road engine and a brass rubbing centre in the church. More railway nostalgia awaits at Shackerstone, 3 miles northwest of Market Bosworth, where the **Battlefield Railway** offers a steam-hauled nine-mile round trip from Shackerstone to Shenton through the delightful scenery of southwest Leicestershire. At Shackerstone is an impressive museum of railway memorabilia, locomotives and rolling stock.

Old Grammar School, Market Harborough

MARKET HARBOROUGH

Halfway between Leicester and Northampton at a crossing point of the River Welland, Market Harborough was created as a planned market town in the mid-12th century. The booths that filled its market place were gradually replaced by permanent buildings, and many of these, along with the courts that led off the High Street, still stand. The development of turnpike roads - the motorways of their day – led to prosperity and the establishment of coaching inns in the town, many of them still in business. The canals and the railways transformed communications and manufacturing industry became established, the most notable company being RW & H Symington, creators of the Liberty Bodice.

The town trail takes in the major buildings, including the 14th century parish **Church of St Dionysius** with its superb limestone broach. The **Old Grammar School** is a timber-framed building with an open ground floor; built in 1614 to serve the weekly butter market and "to keepe the market people drye in time of fowle weather", it later became a school, a role which it sustained until 1892. The factory of the Symington Company, which grew from a cottage industry of staymakers to a considerable economic force in the town, now houses the Council offices, the library, the information centre and the **Harborough Museum,** which incorporates the Symington Collection of Corsetry.

Among the town's distinguished past residents is Thomas Cook, who spent ten years of his life here and was married in the town. While travelling one day by road to Leicester he conceived the idea of an outing using the then newly opened railway. He organised the excursion from Leicester to Loughborough on July 7 1841; the fare of a shilling (5p) included afternoon tea. Cook later moved to Leicester, where he is buried at Welford Road cemetery.

MELTON MOWBRAY

The very name of this bustling market town makes the mouth water, being home to the pork pie, one of the most traditional of English delicacies. The Melton Hunt Cake, a rich fruit cake spiced with Jamaican rum, is another local speciality, and Stilton, 'king of English cheeses', is also made here. The cheese has the longest history, dating back possibly as far as the 14th century. It is only manufactured in Leicestershire, Nottinghamshire and Derbyshire. Of the six producers, four are in the Vale of Belvoir and one in Melton itself. The noble cheese became nationally popular in the 1740s when Frances Pawlett of Wymondham came to an arrangement with the landlord of The Bell Inn at Stilton to market the cheese. The inn was a coaching stop on the Great North Road and travellers who sampled the noble cheese soon spread its fame.

Hand-raised pork pies have been made here since 1831 and since 1851 in the oldest surviving bakery, **Ye Olde Pork Pie Shoppe**, where visitors can watch the traditional hand-raising techniques

and taste the pies and the Hunt Cake. Markets have long been a feature of life in Melton Mowbray, and the Domesday Book of 1086 records the town's market as the only one in Leicestershire. **St Mary's Church,** considered the largest and stateliest parish church in the whole county, dates from 1170. It has a particularly imposing tower and impressive stained glass windows.

MOIRA

Contrasting attractions here. The **National Forest** is a truly accessible, multipurpose forest for the nation that is transforming 200 square miles in the Heart of England. Spanning parts of Derbyshire and Staffordshire as well as Leicestershire, the forest provides a full range of environmental, recreational and social benefits for current and future generations. **Conkers**, the visitor centre for the forest located off the B5003 Ashby-Overseal road, features interactive displays, 120 acres of themed trails, demonstrations, two licensed lakeside restaurants, shop, garden and plants centre, amphitheatre and a number of craft workshops. The site adjoins **Sarah's Wood**, a 25-acre farmland site transformed into a woodland and wildlife haven, with trails and paths suitable for wheelchairs, and a children's play area.

Near Donisthope, 2 miles south of Ashby, **Willesley Wood** was one of the first National Forest planting sites and is now an attractive 100-acre area of mature woodland, a lake and meadows.

The industrial heritage of the region is remembered in the **Moira Furnace**, an impressive, perfectly preserved blast furnace built in 1804 by the Earl of Moira.

NEWTON LINFORD

A picturesque village of thatched dwellings and timbered style buildings, Newton Linford lies alongside the River Lin, which flows through the village and into **Bradgate Country Park**. This is the largest and most popular park in the county with well over a million visitors every year exploring its 850 acres. The park was created from Charnwood Forest 700 years ago as a hunting and deer park, and the scene is probably little changed since, a mixture of heath, bracken, grassy slopes, rocky outcrops and woodland – and the deer are still there. Man-made features of the park include a well-known folly called **Old John Tower**.

Also here are the ruins of **Bradgate House**, built of brick at the beginning of the 16th century. This was the home of the Grey family and it was here that Lady Jane Grey was born in 1537.

STAUNTON HAROLD

The craft centre here has 16 craft workshops within a magnificent Georgian courtyard. Crafts at **The Ferrers Centre** include contemporary furniture, ceramics, copper-smithing and forge, picture framing and sign studio, designer clothing and textiles, automata, stained glass, china restoration, stone carving and silver jewellery. Gift shop, gallery and tea room on site. Staunton Harold Hall and Holy Trinity Church are surrounded by the beautiful parkland and lakes of the Staunton Estate. The Palladian-style hall is not open to the public, but the church is open for afternoon visits April to September daily except Thursday and Friday. In the care of the National Trust, the church is one of the few to have been built during the Commonwealth period in 1653 and retains the original pews, cushions and hangings, together with fine panelling and a painted ceiling.

Staunton Harold Reservoir, covering over 200 acres, has two nature reserves, fishing, sailing and a visitor centre with exhibitions and 3-D models.

SUTTON CHENEY

Bosworth Battlefield is the historic site of the Battle of Bosworth in 1485, where King Richard III was defeated by the future King Henry VII. The Visitor Centre gives a detailed insight into medieval times with the aid of models, replicas and a film theatre, and also on site are a picnic area, a country park and a battle trail, a self-guided trail of 1¾ miles which takes the visitor round the field of battle, passing the command posts of Richard and Henry. Huge flags are frequently flown from these sites, adding colour and poignancy to the scene. Visitors can see the well where Richard drank during the battle, and pause at the memorial stone on the spot where Richard died. A fascinating addition to the site is a display of weapons from the Tudor period, found on the *Mary Rose*, one of Henry VIII's warships, which sank in Portsmouth Harbour in 1545.

The Battlefield is on the route of the **Ashley Canal**, whose towpath offers delightful walks through beautiful countryside. It connects Hinckley, Bosworth Battlefield, Market Bosworth, Battlefield Railway, Measham Museum and Moira Furnace.

WOODHOUSE EAVES

The oldest house in this attractive village is Long Close, which is thought to have once been a royal hunting lodge. Secluded behind a high wall, the five acres of **Long Close Gardens** have become known as the Secret Garden. They've also been described as 'A Cornish Garden in Leicestershire' because of the rare and interesting plants that flourish here.

Woodhouse Eaves takes its name from being on the edges, or eaves, of Charnwood Forest. The views are superb, especially from the summit of **Beacon Hill Country Park**, one of the highest points in Leicestershire at 818 feet.

RUTLAND

The motto of the county is, appropriately, 'multum in parvo' ('much in little'). It has two delightful market towns, Oakham and Uppingham, and 52 small, unspoilt villages of thatch and ironstone cottages clustered round their churches. The county's central feature is **Rutland Water** which extends over 3,300 acres and is the largest man-made reservoir in Europe. Started in 1971 to supply water to East Midlands towns, it was created by damming the valley near Empingham. There's good walking around its 26-mile shoreline, some great bird-watching (including wild ospreys), excellent trout and pike fishing, and a wide variety of watersports. The county boasts two leading public schools, Oakham and Uppingham; one of the most striking and best-preserved Norman churches in the country, at Tickencote; a

Rutland Water

grand 12th century Great Hall and the home of the original 'Tom Thumb', both in Oakham.

Curiously for such a pastoral, peaceful county, it was Rutland men who were prime movers in two of the most dangerous conspiracies in England's history. In a room over the porch of Stoke Dry church, the Gunpowder Plot was hatched with the local lord of the manor, Sir Everard Digby, as one of the ringleaders. Some 75 years later, Titus Oates and his fellow conspirators hatched the anti-Catholic 'Popish Plot' at his home in Oakham.

CLIPSHAM

Just to the east of this small village is one of the most extraordinary sights in the county, **Yew Tree Avenue**. In the 1870s Amos Alexander, head forester to the Clipsham Hall Estate, began clipping the yew trees around his lodge into chimerical shapes – a fantastic parade of animals, chess pieces and abstract forms. The Squire of Clipsham admired them greatly and gave Amos a free hand with the 150 yew trees lining the approach to the hall. Along the 700-yard avenue appeared a dream-like succession of figures, some commemorating local or national events, others recording family events.

Amos died in the early 1900s and the trees were left untended until in 1955 the Forestry Commission assumed responsibility for the avenue and renewed the topiary tradition. Each of the trees is between 15 and 20 feet high, and each is shaped individually. An elephant looks across to a ballerina; a Spitfire takes off towards a battleship, Diddy-men cavort

near a windmill – there's even a Big Mac hamburger in there somewhere!

COTTESMORE

The **Rutland Railway Museum** is the big attraction here. The working steam/ diesel museum is based on local quarry and industrial railways. A little further along the B668 is the village of Greetham on the Viking Way, one of the three long-distance walks that converge on Oakham.

EDITH WESTON

This village takes its name from Edith, wife and then widow of King Edward the Confessor (1042-66), who gave her this part of the county as a gift. A peaceful spot in the heart of really lovely countryside on the south shore of Rutland Water. Near the village, off the A606 and A6121, stands Rutland's best-known landmark. **Normanton Church**, on the very edge of Rutland Water, was formerly part of the Normanton Estate and now houses a display dedicated to

Normanton Church

the construction of the reservoir by Anglian Water and a history of the area. The estate was the property of the big local landowner Sir Gilbert Heathcote, sometime Lord Mayor of London, who pulled down the village of Normanton to enlarge his park and moved the villagers to nearby Empingham.

EMPINGHAM

This pleasant little town is dominated by the tower and spire of St Peter's Church, whose interior features include fragments of ancient glass. In a field just outside the village stands a well-preserved **Dovecote** containing 700 nests. It could have been in this very field that one of the bloodiest slaughters of the Wars of the Roses took place, on 12 March 1470 – in all, some 10,000 men were killed. This gory clash of arms became known as the **Battle of Losecoat Field** because the defeated Lancastrians shed their uniforms as they fled in the hope of avoiding recognition, capture and certain death.

At Sykes Lane, North Shore is the Rutland Water **Butterfly Farm & Aquatic Centre**, with 5,000 square feet of walk-through jungle that is home to free-flying butterflies and tropical birds. Other creatures at the centre include koi carp, terrapins, iguanas, tarantulas, tropical insects and monitor lizards.

EXTON

A charming village in one of the largest ironstone extraction areas in the country

with a church set in delightful parkland. The **Church of St Peter & St Paul** is remarkable for its wealth of fine monuments, a sumptuous series commemorating members of the Noel and Harington families interred here from the early 1500s to the late 1700s. This imposing collection is dominated by a colossal memorial to Baptist Noel, 3rd Viscount Campden, who died in 1683. Sculpted in black and white marble by Grinling Gibbons, it stands 22ft high and 14ft wide, almost filling one wall of the north transept.

LITTLE CASTERTON

Tolethorpe Hall, just off the A1 and close to the Lincolnshire border, is best known as the home of the Stamford Shakespeare Company, which each summer performs three different plays on an open-air stage in an idyllic woodland setting facing a 600-seat covered auditorium. The old manor house was the birthplace in 1550 of Robert Browne, one of the earliest 'congregationalists'. His radical views led to his arrest and it was only through the intervention of his kinsman Lord Burghley that he was released. Browne's religious views mellowed with the passing of the years – his fiery temper did not. At the age of 80 Browne was consigned to Northampton for an assault on a constable and it was there that he died in 1633.

LYDDINGTON

A quiet village where English Heritage

oversees the **Bede House,** one of the finest examples of Tudor domestic architecture in the country. This house of prayer was once part of a retreat for the Bishops of Lincoln and was later converted to a hospital (bede house) for 12 poor men, 2 women and a warden. It remained in use right up until 1930. The fine 16th century rooms can be visited daily from April to October. The small gardens contain a notable herb garden with over 60 herbs, both culinary and medicinal, and just outside the grounds lie the fish ponds that used to supply the bishop's kitchen.

OAKHAM

Oakham is one of England's most appealing county towns, a friendly place with many old hostelries, a regular weekly market, a wide variety of family-owned shops, a fine church and a major public school.

Just off the Market Place with its charming market cross and stocks is **Rutland Castle**, a romantic, evocative fortified manor house built between 1180 and 1190, with the earliest surviving example of an aisled stone hall in the country. A unique feature is a collection of over 200 horseshoes hanging all around the walls of the hall. For centuries, any peer of the realm passing through the town has been required to present a horseshoe to the castle. When this custom began isn't clear although one plausible story says that it began in the days of William the Conqueror when his farrier lived here. This unusual tax is

still being imposed – among the hundreds of horseshoes of every size, some ornately gilded, others rusty, is one presented by Queen Elizabeth II.

All Saints Church is the spiritual centre of town, a fine parish church with a 14th century tower. On the capitals in the nave are striking carvings of traditional subjects, including dragons, the Green Man, Adam and Eve, and Reynard the Fox.

Rutland County Museum, housed in a splendid 18th century riding school in Catmose Street, has displays of farm equipment, machinery and wagons, domestic collections and local archaeology. The riding school belonged to the Rutland Fencibles, a volunteer cavalry regiment raised in 1794 and now remembered in a gallery in the museum.

Oakham's Tourist Information Centre is in **Flore's House**, one of the oldest buildings in the town. It dates from the late 1300s and was built by William Flore and his son Roger, who was a wealthy merchant and four times Speaker of the House of Commons.

Notable natives of Oakham include the infamous conspirator Titus Oates, who was born here in 1649 and lived in Mill Street. A minor cleric, he played the leading role in fabricating the 'Popish Plot' of 1678. Oates claimed to have uncovered a secret Jesuit plot to assassinate Charles II and return the Catholic church to power. Many innocent Catholics were killed as a result of this alarm, but Oates, when the truth was discovered, did not escape lightly.

He was sentenced to yearly whippings and was not freed until 1688; he died in obscurity in 1705.

Oakham School was founded in 1584 by Archdeacon Robert Johnson, who also founded Uppingham School. As at Uppingham, the original single room school building still stands, its walls inscribed with Hebrew, Latin and Greek quotations. Both schools expanded greatly in the 19th century but while the school buildings at Uppingham dominate the little town, at Oakham they are spread across the town centre, partly hidden away off the attractive market place where the ancient Butter Cross still provides shelter for the town stocks. Now co-educational, Oakham School has around 1,000 pupils.

On the outskirts of town, the road to Uppingham crosses **Swooning Bridge,** where condemned felons going on their last journey from the town jail first saw, on top of a small rise called Mount Pleasant, the gallows from which they were about to hang.

STOKE DRY

There are some striking monuments in the church at Stoke Dry to the Digby family, particularly an engraved alabaster slab to Jaquetta Digby who died in 1496. One of her descendants, Sir Everard Digby, was to bring great shame on the family. He was born in the village in 1578 but when the Protestant James I ascended the throne, Sir Everard and his Catholic friends became involved in the conspiracy now known as the Gunpowder Plot. It was in the priest's room over the porch of St Andrew's Church that the conspirators met. After his conviction in 1609 Sir Everard endured the gruesome ordeal of death by hanging, drawing and quartering. The porch where the plotters met has another macabre story attached to it – it's said that one vicar locked a witch in the room and left her to die by starvation.

Stoke Dry overlooks **Eyebrook Reservoir,** a 300-acre trout fishery in an idyllic location in the Welland Valley, by the border with Leicestershire and Northamptonshire.

TICKENCOTE

Apart from Canterbury Cathedral there is nothing in England to compare with the astonishing Norman sexpartite vaulting over the chancel of the parish **Church of St Peter** in the tiny village of Tickencote. Equally breathtaking is the chancel arch, a mighty six-layered portal leading to a minuscule nave beyond. Built around 1140, each of the overlapping six arches is carved with a different design – foliage, chevrons, double zig-zags, beak-head ornament or just plain round mouldings. In addition to these masterpieces of Norman architecture, St Peter's also contains a remarkably fine 13th century font and an unusual wooden life-size effigy of a 14th century knight.

UPPINGHAM

This picturesque stone-built town is the

Uppingham

gentry. Then, in 1853, the Rev Edward Thring was appointed headmaster. During his 43-year tenure the sleepy little school was transformed.

Dr Thring wrote extensively on educational matters, championed education for girls and founded the Headmasters Conference. When he retired in 1897 he could look back with pride on the creation of one of the country's most successful public schools, both academically and financially. The old school, the 18th century studies, the Victorian chapel and schoolrooms, and the 20th century great hall, all Grade I or Grade II listed, can be visited on a guided tour on Saturday afternoons in summer.

major community in the south part of the county. It has a long, handsome high street and a fine market place where traders have hawked their wares every Friday since 1280. The town is known for its bookshops and art galleries, but whereas other places are dominated by castles or cathedrals, in Uppingham it's the impressive **Uppingham School** that gives the town its special character. The school was founded in 1584 by Robert Johnson, Archdeacon of Leicester, who also founded Rutland's other celebrated public school at Oakham. For more than 250 years, Uppingham was just one of many such small grammar schools, giving rigorous instruction in classical languages to a couple of dozen sons of the local

WING

The little village of Wing is best known for a Maze in which it's impossible to get lost. The medieval **Turf Maze** is made of foot-high turf banks and measuring 40 feet across. Its design is identical to the mosaic patterns in the floors of Chartres Cathedral and other French cathedrals. An old tradition asserts that penitents were required to crawl around the maze on their knees, stopping at various points to say prayers. Once a fairly common sight, only eight such turf mazes are known to still exist in England. They were already falling into disfavour by Shakespeare's time. In A *Midsummer Night's Dream* he wrote:

And the quaint mazes in the wanton green
For lack of tread, are indistinguishable.

THE BLACK HORSE

SYCAMORE STREET, BLABY, LEICESTERSHIRE LE8 4FJ
TEL: 01162 771209

> **Directions:** Blaby lies on the southern side of the city of Leicester. From the M1 take junction 21 and head east on the A563. After a mile turn south on the A426 and this will bring you directly to Blaby.

Dating back to late 19th century, **The Black Horse** is an impressive town pub enjoying a prominent corner site. Its green roof makes it hard to miss and if you are travelling by car you will find the car park located to the rear. Venturing inside visitors will find a tasteful snug, bar and spacious, air-conditioned dining area which can seat up to 60 diners. In the restaurant there is an a la carte selection served lunchtimes and evenings Monday to Saturday and from midday until 6pm on Sundays. There is also a bar menu of

hot meals and snacks. With two top chefs working here you can be sure of finding only the best quality food, with imaginative dishes, on the menu.

There is a good selection of liquid refreshments stocked at the bar with the fine real ales including Greenalls and Pedigree. There are also a number of other popular beers and lagers. In fine weather your drinks can be enjoyed on the small patio which is a delightful little suntrap. Your host, John Maguire, has been at The Black Horse for 14 years and has established a loyal following drawn from the surrounding area. The new restaurant has led to further acclaim with many regulars coming to enjoy the fine cuisine. Another attraction is the live music each weekend which features mainly local talent.

- Mon-Sat 11.00-23.00; Sun 12.00-22.30
- Full a la carte menu and carvery
- Visa, Mastercard, Delta, Switch
- Car park
- Live music, mainly local artists, each weekend, darts, pool
- Leicester 5 miles, Leicester Racecourse 4 miles, Mallory Park Motor Racing 8 miles, Stanford Hall 13 miles, Brocks Hill Country Park 5 miles, Tropical Birdland 8 miles

THE BULLS HEAD

THE NOOK, COSBY, LEICESTERSHIRE LE9 1RQ
TEL: 01162 863368

> **Directions:** From the M1 turn east onto the A563 at Leicester. After a mile turn right onto the A426. After a couple of miles, just as you pass Blaby, turn right onto a minor road following signs for Cosby.

The Bulls Head in Cosby appears at first to be just another pub in a pleasant English village. But there is much more to the place than first impressions. Yes, it is a friendly, traditional pub where you can enjoy a drink and a bite to eat in convivial surroundings chatting to the locals. It is an Everards pub and the bar stocks their ales, Tiger and Beacon, together with a third guest ale. There are all the other usual offerings together with a selection of house wines on tap. One of the newest additions is the superb decked patio to the rear where there are plenty of tables and chairs for al fresco drinking.

However, it is in the food department that things get a little more interesting. The restaurant was taken over a few years ago by Winleys, a local Chinese takeaway and is now one of the best Chinese eateries in the whole of Leicestershire. The restaurant itself is cosy and comfortable and the staff are friendly and unobtrusive. Open evenings only Monday to Thursdays, and lunchtimes and evenings Friday to Sunday, bookings are advisable at weekends to avoid disappointment. The extensive menu offers a superb selection of Chinese dishes with some English options for those who prefer. There are also buffet options and set meals, with food served until 11pm.

This is a family run pub, under the same management for the past 20 years which has resulted in a relaxed, friendly atmosphere where all are made to feel very welcome.

- 🕐 Mon-Sat 11.00-23.00; Sun 12.00-22.30
- 🍴 Superb Chinese restaurant
- 💷 Visa, Mastercard, Delta, Switch
- 🅿 Patio garden, car park
- 🎵 Darts, skittle alley
- @ email: thebull@surf3.net
  website: www.thebullsheadcosby.co.uk
- ❓ Cosby Golf Club, National Space Science Centre 6 miles, Diving Centre 3 miles, Bosworth Battlefield 12 miles, Tropical Birdland 8 miles

THE CROWN INN

MAIN ROAD, GREAT CASTERTON, NR. STAMFORD, RUTLAND PE9 4AP
TEL: 01780 763362

Directions: Great Casterton lies just off the A1, on the A1081, 2 miles northwest of Stamford

Despite being so close to the A1, **The Crown Inn** has the look of being a remote country inn. At 400 years old it has stood the test of time well and the pretty front garden adds much to the rustic charm. Inside, you will find exposed stone walls, an open fire and striking, red-painted walls which add a stylish touch. Newly refurbished throughout the restaurant is the highlight, and there is nowhere better to enjoy the superb menu.

Both the new owners, Dave and Tessa, are cooks, but it is Dave who rules the roost in the kitchen. With previous experience as a butcher and an army chef, he presents a fine selection of dishes which is far from the traditional pub fayre. You are likely to find such delights as Ostrich Steaks, Game (when in season), freshly caught Rutland Trout and a Whitby Seafood Platter featuring, although as the menu is changed every few weeks there is always sure to be something new to try. The printed menu is also supplemented by daily specials which are presented on a blackboard at the bar. Everything is cooked fresh to order but then you can't expect food this delicious to be ready in an instant.

While you are deliberating the menu, the bar can offer a choice of fine real ales, including Greene King IPA, Abbot, and Adnams Broadside. There is also a surprisingly good wine list offering new and old world wines. Please note that the pub is closed during the day on Mondays.

- ⏰ Mon 18.00-23.00; Tues-Fri 11.00-15.00, 18.00-23.00; Sat 11.00-23.00; Sun 12.00-22.30
- 🍴 Regularly updated a la carte menu
- 💷 Visa, Mastercard, Delta, Switch
- 🅿 Car park, beer garden
- 🎵 Darts
- @ email: daveorms@aol.com website: www.rutlandonline.co.uk
- ❓ Stamford 2 miles, Burghley House 3 miles, Rutland Water 3 miles, Rutland Steam Railway 8 miles, Rockingham Castle 15 miles, Grimsthorpe Castle 9 miles

THE CROWN INN

DEBDALE HILL, OLD DALBY, MELTON MOWBRAY,
LEICESTERSHIRE LE14 3LF
TEL: 01664 823134

> **Directions:** Dalby can be reached from the M1 by taking the exit for
> Loughborough. From here pick up the A60 Nottingham road, and after just a mile
> turn right onto the B676. Continue straight across the A46 and then across the
> A6006. Dalby will then be signposted to the left

In a cul-de-sac in the middle of the charming village of Old Dalby is **The Crown Inn**. Dating back to 1590 the picturesque, ivy-covered building is made up of a number of small, cosy rooms, each with an open fire, and two dining areas. This is a peaceful haven of tranquillity, with no juke-box or electronic games machines, combined with attractive gardens in which to enjoy your drinks al fresco.

The current owner, Alan Hale is also the chef, and has been for over thirty-two years, though he has only owned the pub for the past two and a half years. The quality of the food is absolutely outstanding with the pub having won numerous awards in recent years. The menu is deliciously tempting and offers a wide selection for all tastes and appetites.

Only the best ingredients are used throughout, with the emphasis on mainly locally sourced ingredients for both the bar and restaurant a la carte menus. The Crown enjoys a reputation for serving food of a gourmet standard with people travelling many miles to enjoy Alan Hale's cooking.

Behind the bar a selection of real ales is always available, some direct from the casks. The village's own Belvoir Brewery provides some of the brews, with Old Speckled Hen, Old Peculiar and Bombadier among the other offerings. There is also a good wine list with an extensive range of 30 to suit all pockets.

- 🕐 Mon-Sat 11.00-15.00, 18.00-23.00; Sun 12.00-15.00,19.00-22.30
- 🍴 Award-winning menu
- 💷 Visa, Mastercard, Delta, Switch
- 🅿 Beer garden, car park
- ♫ Lively programme of jazz and folk music and morris dancing through the summer
- @ www.old-dalby.org.uk
- ❓ Belvoir Castle 13 miles, Holme Pierrepoint National Water Sports Centre 12 miles, Nottingham 15 miles, Leicester 14 miles

THE FALCON INN

MAIN STREET, LONG WHATTON, LEICESTERSHIRE LE12 5DG
TEL: 01509 842416 FAX: 01509 646802

Leicestershire & Rutland

Directions: Leaving the M1 at junction 23a heading north or 24 heading south follow signs to East Midlands Airport. After the airport entrance turn left following signs for Diseworth. At the t-junction turn left towards Long Whatton

---

The Falcon Inn is a traditional country pub which dates back to the late-18th century and offers today's visitors the very best in fine ales, good wines and good company. Taken over by business partners Carol and Susan in 2002 the pub has taken on a new lease of life. Refurbishments inside and out have created a welcoming feel with bags of character.

A more major development was the conversion of the former school house and stable block into eleven en-suite bedrooms, each with its own special charm. The rooms are of varying sizes, there is a sumptuous four poster room, and all have a high level of comfort and

facilities. The tariff is reasonable and includes a Continental breakfast.

The Falcon has come to enjoy a far reaching reputation for serving excellent food with the main menu presented on blackboards supplemented by specials and a lunchtime snack menu. The speciality is the home-made beef and ale pie but everything looks pretty tasty. Food is available at every session, except Sunday night, and there are various dining areas, one non-smoking. Such is the popularity though, bookings are advisable at weekends. The bar stocks a couple of real ales from the Everards Brewery, Beacon and Tiger, together with a third guest ale. There is also Stella, Carling, Strongbow and Guinness.

- ⏰ Mon-Sat 12.00-23.00; Sun 12.00-22.30
- 🍴 Delicious home-cooked food
- 💷 Visa, Mastercard, Delta, Switch, Amex
- 🛏 5 double, 5 twin, 1 single, all en-suite; special breaks available
- 🅿 Beer garden, large car park
- @ thefalconinn@freenet.co.uk
- ❓ East Midland Airport 2 miles, Donington Park Motor Racing 5 miles, Grand Prix Collected 4 miles, Calke Abbey 9 miles, Nottingham 13 miles

THE HEATHCOTE ARMS

HILL STREET, CROFT, LEICESTERSHIRE LE9 6EG
TEL: 01455 282439

> **Directions:** Croft lies to the southwest of Leicester between the M69 and M1 motorways. It can be reached by leaving the M1 at junction 21 and following the A563 to the southern side of the town, almost immediately turning right onto the B4114. After just over 3 miles Croft will be signposted on the right.

High on the hill, overlooking Croft and the river bridge, **The Heathcote Arms** is a whitewashed building with an inner courtyard that doubles as a car park. Drivers are advised to keep a keen eye out for the turning though, as it is easily missed. The pub is situated overlooking a former quarry that now serves as a popular inland diving centre while the surrounding area also proves to be popular with ramblers and you will often find them taking a break for some refreshment at the pub.

Originally built as three cottages, the buildings were later used as a butchers and did not become a hostelry until the 17th century. The interior retains a traditional feel though, with beamed ceilings in the main bar at the front and cosy wooden furniture used throughout. The beers on offer are from the Everards range, usually three, plus guest ales from around the country. The locals and younger visitors often congregate in the games room in the evenings, where the spacious room incorporates a pool table, darts and TV. Food is served only at lunchtimes Monday to Friday and the menu includes mainly snacks with a small selection of popular hot dishes. In summer customers can enjoy the split-level beer garden which enjoys great views and there is also a long skittle alley. The place has been run by a mother and daughter team for over a year. Children are allowed in until 9pm.

🕐 Mon-Sat 11.00-23.00; Sun 12.00-22.30

🍽 Served at weekday lunchtimes only

£ Visa, Mastercard, Delta, Switch

Ⓟ Beer garden, children's play area, car park

♫ Skittle alley, darts, pool table

@ www.heathcotearms.co.uk

❓ Burbage Common and Woods 6 miles, Mallory Park Motor Racing 6 miles, Leicester 8 miles, Stanford Hall 15 miles, Jaguar Daimler Museum 17 miles

THE JOINERS ARMS

CHURCH WALK, BRUNTINGTHORPE, NR. LUTTERWORTH,
LEICESTERSHIRE LE17 5QH
TEL/FAX: 0116 247 8258

> **Directions:** From the M1 take the A4304 east from junction 20 towards Market Harborough. After 6 miles head towards Leicester along the A5199. After a further five miles, Bruntingthorpe will be signposted to the left.

The Joiners Arms is a delightful little pub located in one of pretty Leicestershire villages near Market Harborough. The frontage is demure, with white washed walls, small paned windows and only the discreet sign hanging out the front to indicate that this is a pub at all. The inside comes as a real surprise, with the décor being very contemporary. Recent refurbishment has included a new tiled floor, the restoration of the wooden beams to their natural oak, a completely new bar area, and a fresh lick of Chelsea green paint. If you haven't visited for a while when you're in for a pleasant surprise, and if

you're new to the place then we would recommend you drop by.

This is very much a food orientated pub with the superb menus being hard to resist. Every dish is prepared to order by the owner, and chef, Steve Fitzpatrick, and uses only the freshest and best ingredients available. This is not cheap and cheerful pub grub, but ideal for a special occasion or for those that like to enjoy fine dining. There is an excellent wine list of nearly 30 wines from all over the world, and the bar stocks the usual, including a fine Greene King IPA real ale. Although this is primarily a restaurant, there is a bar and you can simply enjoy a beer should you wish. Closed Sunday nights and all day Monday.

- 🕐 Tues-Sat 12.00-14.00, 18.30-23.00; Sun 12.00-14.00
- 🍴 Superb restaurant serving modern cuisine
- £ Visa, Mastercard, Delta, Switch
- Ⓟ Car park
- @ www.joinersarms.co.uk
- ❓ Leicester 11 miles, Stanford Hall 9 miles, Kelmarsh Hall 14 miles, Brocks Hill Country Park 7 miles, Coton Manor Gardens 16 miles, Rockingham Castle 20 miles

MARQUESS OF EXETER

LYDDINGTON, NR. UPPINGHAM, RUTLAND LE15 9LT
TEL: 01572 822477 FAX: 01572 821343

> **Directions:** From the A1 follow the A47 west towards Leicester. At the junction with A6003 turn south. After passing through Uppingham bear left onto an unmarked road following signs for Lyddington

The quiet village of Lyddington is a pretty little place situated in the heart of the beautiful countryside of Rutland. The delightful 16th century former coaching inn, the **Marquess of Exeter**, is now an established family-run hotel offering excellent facilities. It has been extensively refurbished though the bar retains a cosy traditional feel, with exposed wooden beams and open fires, while the walls display the family shields and history of the Exeter family. This is a free house and there are seasonal cask conditioned ales together with a permanent real ale from the local Oakham brewery.

An excellent selection of bar food is served every lunchtime with a more

extensive a la carte menu available in the restaurant each evening catering to all tastes and appetites. The Sunday lunches are also served in the restaurant and these always prove to be popular. Advance bookings for these, and Friday and Saturday evenings, are essential. All dishes are home-cooked and freshly prepared to order using only the freshest of ingredients and great pride is taken in presentation.

The Marquess of Exeter has 16 comfortable rooms, ranging from singles to a four poster room, all named after local historical families. Each is elegantly decorated and furnished and has en-suite facilities and other little extras to make your stay a relaxing experience. The Lord Burghley suite, with a capacity of up to 100 guests, is ideal for corporate and private functions. The hotel is also licensed for civil weddings.

- 🕐 Mon-Sat 12.00-23.00; Sun 12.00-22.30
- 🍴 Charming la carte restaurant and bar meals
- £ Visa, Mastercard, Delta, Switch
- 🛏 16 en-suite rooms
- 🅿 Car park, orchard beer garden, petanque, function room
- ❓ Bede House, Rutland Water 5 miles, Rockingham Raceway 5 miles, East Carlton Country Park 8 miles, Oakham 8 miles, Burghley House 14 miles

THE ODD HOUSE TAVERN

1 STATION ROAD, OAKHAM, RUTLAND LE15 6QT
TEL: 01572 722225 FAX: 01572 722187

> **Directions:** From the M1 take the A46 from junction 21A to the northeast and then onto the A607 all the way to Melton Mowbray. Then head southeast on the A606 which will lead you directly to Oakham.

In Oakham, on a corner site, you'll find **The Odd House**, a substantial stone inn that remains almost unchanged from when it was built many years ago. In fact, the pub claims to be the oldest coaching inn in the whole of Rutland! Richard and Catherine Burley have been in charge for over four years and during that time the hostelry has gained a fine reputation for the quality of its food, drink and hospitality. The place has been immaculately maintained and is beautifully presented with colourful hanging baskets adorning the front, while inside it retains many period features. The glow from open log fires highlights the comfortable, polished

furniture and lends an air of tradition to the place. There are low beamed ceilings, a cosy bar and comfortable lounge, with everything spotlessly clean and welcoming. An adjacent barn is a wonderful venue for darts and pool.

The bar keeps Pedigree and Courage on tap with two other guest ales, plus a range of beers, stout, lager and cider. There's also a comprehensive wine list. The Odd House has a wide range of excellent value meals on its menu with the emphasis on simple dishes that are superbly cooked using fresh produce. If you want a treat, try the big steaks or the mixed grill of steak, kidney, sausage, gammon and lamb and pork chops, and all the trimmings you could wish for. It's a hearty plateful and tastes out of this world!

- Mon-Sat 11.00-23.00; Sun 12.00-22.30
- Excellent home-cooked food
- Visa, Mastercard, Delta, Switch
- Beer garden, petanque court, large car park
- Occasional live music
- Rutland Castle, Rutland Water 2 miles, Burrough Hill Country Park 7 miles, Burghley House 12 miles, Rockingham Castle 13 miles, Deene Park 16 miles, Stamford 11 miles

THE OLD BARN INN AND RESTAURANT

ANDREW LANE, GLOOSTON, NR. MARKET HARBOROUGH,
LEICESTERSHIRE LE16 7SO
TEL: 01858 545215

> **Directions:** From the M1 take the A4304 from junction 20 to Market Harborough. From the centre of the town follow the B6047 north. Two miles beyond its junction with the A6 Glooston will be signposted to the right

Glooston is a picturesque village set amidst lovely countryside and at its heart, at the end of a Roman road, is **The Old Barn Inn**, a former coaching inn dating back to the 16th century. Although at first glance it appears much newer than this, inside it retains many period features, including the many low wooden beams and thick walls that keep the place warm in winter and cool in summer. The owner is Phillip Buswell, also the head chef, and together with his wife Claire and the rest of the staff, ensures that every customer has a

pleasant and enjoyable visit.

The Old Barn is popular with both locals and tourists who come to sample the fine ales and food and, during the time Phillip and Claire have been here, has established itself as one of Leicestershire's premier eating places. The quality of the food is outstanding and the a la carte menu offers an excellent selection of dishes. The house speciality is seafood and there are regular gourmet seafood evenings where there is an even more impressive selection. Such is the popularity of the restaurant that bookings are essential for the gourmet evenings and each weekend. If you want a bottle of something special to go with your meal there's a good choice of fine wines and at least three real ales, with extra guest ales in summer.

🕐 Mon-Sat 12.00-14.30, 18.30-23.00; Sun 12.00-14.30, 19.00-22.30

🍴 Superb a la carte menu specialising in fresh seafood

£ Visa, Mastercard, Delta, Switch

🛏 2 double rooms

🅿 Car park, beer garden

🎵 Regular themed seafood evenings

@ www.theoldbarninn.com

❓ East Carlton Country Park 7 miles, Eyebrook Reservoir 7 miles, Market Harborough 5 miles, Rockingham Speedway Track 13 miles, Rutland Water 14 miles

THE STAFF OF LIFE

MAIN STREET, MOWSLEY, NR. MARKET HARBOROUGH,
LEICESTERSHIRE LE17 6NT
TEL: 0116 240 2359 FAX: 0116 240 4460

Directions: Leaving the M1 at junction 20 head towards Market Harborough along the A4304. After 6 miles head towards Leicester on the A5199 and Mowsley will be found just off to the right after about 3 miles.

The village of Mowsley comes as a pleasant surprise with lots of lovely cottages and is worthy of a brief stroll in exploration. You could use this as your opportunity to work up an appetite for some refreshment at **The Staff of Life** public house. It comes as no surprise to learn that the well proportioned building was once a privately-owned Edwardian house until the local pub was relocated. Set back from the road there is a small patio area at the front and there is further outdoor seating at the back too.

Venturing inside you will find a cosy yet elegant bar with a superb conservatory dining area at the back

which overlooks the rear patio garden. The bar retains some traditional touches, with a flagstone floor and high backed settles and yet if you look up you will see not only a beautiful wood panelled ceiling but also the wine cellar! Here you can enjoy some superb food with a delicious menu of home-made snacks and bar meals available every lunchtime and evening. The more extensive evening menu makes the most of seasonal produce and is changed monthly. To enjoy with your meal there is a good wine list with over 18 different varieties available by the glass. There are also four real ales on tap, including Greene King IPA and Pedigree, and other popular beers and lagers too.

🕐 Mon-Fri 12.00-15.00, 17.30-23.00; Sat 12.00-23.00; Sun 12.00-22.30

🍽 Superb menu with everything being home-made

£ Visa, Mastercard, Delta, Switch

Ⓟ Patio garden, car park

❓ Foxton Locks and Grand Union Canal 5 miles, Market Harborough 7 miles, Stanford Hall 11 miles, Kelmarsh Hall 13 miles, Leicester Racecourse 9 miles, Leicester County Cricket Ground 11 miles

THE WINDMILL INN

BRASCOTE LANE, BRASCOTE, NEWBOLD VERDON,
LEICESTERSHIRE LE9 9LE
TEL: 01455 824433 FAX: 01455 822587

> **Directions:** Brascote is not marked on most maps, however it is adjacent to Newbold Verdon. Coming off the M1 at junction 21A, head towards Leicester then pick up the minor road signposted for Desford and Tropical Birdland. At Desford, turn right onto the B582 and Newbold Verdon is then signposted

The Windmill Inn takes it name from a corn mill which was brought from Syston and erected on this site in 1812. Despite nearly 100 years of work, it became so dilapidated that it eventually had to be dismantled with some of the timbers being taken to Market Bosworth and used in the construction of a hospital. There are records of a brewhouse having been on the site since the 18th century although the present structure is probably not quite that old.

Presenting an attractive, ivy covered frontage to the road there is a ramp up to the front door allowing full wheelchair access. The interior has a cosy, traditional feel with the exposed beams, bare brick walls and antique pine furnishings adding to the appeal. The pub is widely known throughout the area for serving superb food at every session. The menu offers some tasty dishes, classic favourites together with slightly more unusual options, with a fine accompanying wine list. There is plenty of room for diners, although bookings are still advisable for Sunday lunch. Run by Lucy and Steve, together with various family members, The Windmill has been a free house for the past eleven years and the bar stocks a really good range of cask and keg ales.

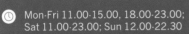

🕐 Mon-Fri 11.00-15.00, 18.00-23.00; Sat 11.00-23.00; Sun 12.00-22.30

🍴 Well known for high quality food

💷 Visa, Mastercard, Delta, Switch

🅿 Large beer garden, car parking

❓ Tropical Birdland 3 miles, Mallory Park Motor Racing 3 miles, Bosworth Battlefield Visitor Centre 6 miles, Twycross Zoo 9 miles, The Battlefield Line 6 miles

THE WOODMANS STROKE

1 CHURCH STREET, ROTHLEY, LEICESTERSHIRE LE7 7PD
TEL: 0116 230 2785 FAX: 0116 292 6433

Leicestershire & Rutland

Directions: Rothley lies just 6 miles north of Leicester. It is most easily reached by leaving the M1 at junction 21A and follow the A46 towards Melton Mowbray. Turn onto the A6 following signs for Loughborough and Rothley is signposted to the left

The village of Rothley is within easy reach of the towns of Loughborough and Leicester, yet it feels as if it is worlds apart. It is noted for having some of the finest timber framed houses in the country and **The Woodmans Stroke**, (a proper pub), fondly known by the locals as Woodies, fits the pastoral scene beautifully. Built in 1714 the thatched property is immaculate and looks at its best during the spring and summer when it is adorned with colourful hanging baskets and overflowing window boxes.

Venturing inside visitors will find a traditional interior of wooden beams, tiled floors and wooden furniture. There

is also a large amount of Rugby memorabilia, with the owners being keen supporters of the Leicester Tigers and sport in general. The pub has been run by the same family for over ten years, with sons Simon (the cricketer) and Jonathan (the golfer and finalist in Golf Pub of the Year 2003) taking on most of the responsibilities these days.

Each lunchtime there is a fine bar menu served, with the offerings ranging from freshly cut sandwiches to heartier dishes, including steaks, home-made steak and kidney pie and the ever popular lasagne. Prices are very reasonable. In warm weather meals can be taken out to the large landscaped beer garden. There is no food served in the evenings, when the pub becomes perhaps even more popular for its liquid refreshments and lively conversation.

- 🕐 Mon-Fri 11.00-15.00, 17.00-23.00; Sat 11.00-23.00; Sun 12.00-15.00, 19.00-22.30
- 🍴 Lunchtime food only (Mon-Fri)
- 💷 Visa, Mastercard, Delta, Switch
- 🅿 Large beer garden, car park
- 🎵 Quiz Tuesday nights, live music Sundays, monthly theme nights, darts, pool, Boule played Weds.
- @ j.warner@totalise.co.uk
- ❓ Rothley Steam Railway, Bradgate Country Park 3 miles, Charnwood Forest 6 miles, Donington Park Motor Racing 14 miles, Calke Abbey 14 miles

YE OLDE BULLS HEAD

MAIN STREET, BROUGHTON ASTLEY, LEICESTERSHIRE LE9 6RD
TEL: 01455 282343

Directions: Leave the M1 at junction 20 and head west towards Lutterworth. Almost immediately head north along the A426 towards Leicester following the line of the M1. After 4 miles, Broughton Astley will be signposted to the left along the B581

Ye Olde Bulls Head stands at the main crossroads in the centre of Broughton Astley and is run by Paul and Jan Harris. The attractive frontage is neatly painted in black and white with bright green signs, making it hard to miss. Dating back to the Victorian period it has recently been totally refurbished by the owners, Everards Brewery. As well as updating all the facilities, there are also new baby changing and disabled facilities, although the highlight is certainly the fully air-conditioned restaurant.

The non-smoking dining area can seat up to 70 diners and looks out over the stream, which runs along the back of the pub. There is an a la carte menu together with specials boards which incorporate the fresh fish that is delivered daily. Everything is freshly prepared and cooked to order and everyone is sure to find something to their liking. Although the prices are very reasonable, there are additional lunchtime offers and meal deals for pensioners. Food is served every lunchtime, with an extended session for Sunday lunch, and Monday to Saturday evenings. The beer on offer includes Everards' own brews, Tiger and Old Original, together with a monthly guest ale. Drinks can be enjoyed in the comfortable lounge bar or, weather permitting, in the beer garden.

- Mon-Sat 11.00-23.00; Sun 12.00-22.30
- New a la carte restaurant seats 70
- Visa, Mastercard, Delta, Switch
- Children's play area, beer garden, car park
- Darts, pool table, skittles
- Burbage Common and Woods 6 miles, Mallory Park Motor Racing 8 miles, Leicester 11 miles, Stanford Hall 12 miles, Tropical Birdland 10 miles, Coventry Airport 18 miles

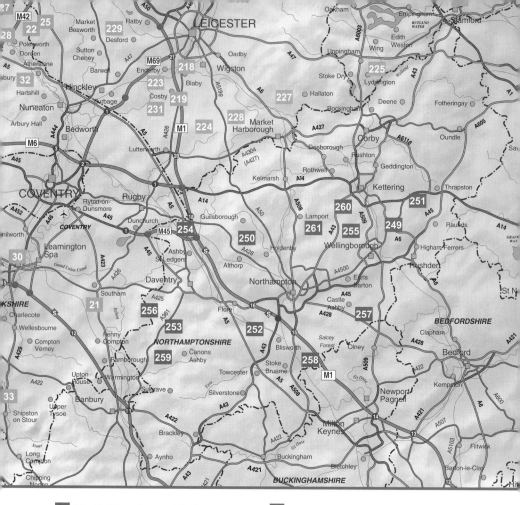

Please note all cross references refer to page numbers

NORTHAMPTONSHIRE

Although it is a relatively small county Northamptonshire has a lot to offer but, as it is crossed by some of the country's major routes, it is also one that is often bypassed. The county town, Northampton, along with other local towns, is famed for its shoe industry although Northamptonshire remains, essentially, a farming county littered with ancient market towns and rural villages. However, it is its long history that is most interesting – the decisive battle of Naseby was fought on its soil and it was at the now ruined Fotheringay Castle that Mary, Queen of Scots was executed.

Northamptonshire is shaped like a laurel leaf, with the River Nene a distinctive feature. Wherever one journeys across the county one is never far from its banks and the reflection of the trees in high summer on its shimmering waters can be quite breathtaking. The alluvial soils and gravel terraces of the Nene Valley have been continuously farmed since Neolithic times and there are remains of many Anglo-Saxon settlements.

A county of great landowners, Northamptonshire also has many royal connections. The original Rockingham Castle was built by William the Conqueror; Richard III was born at Fotheringhay Castle, Mary Queen of Scots was beheaded there; Charles I spent several months in captivity at Holdenby Hall, at that time the largest house in England; and in more recent times, Althorp entered the national consciousness as the childhood home of Diana, Princess of Wales, and as her final resting place.

Another royal death is commemorated by the two elaborate Eleanor Crosses erected by a grieving

Old Stables, Duddington

King Edward I to mark the places where the coffin bearing his wife Eleanor to London from Nottinghamshire rested overnight. One is at Geddington, near Kettering; the second on the outskirts of Northampton; only one other of the original twelve Crosses survives, at Waltham near London.

The county boasts two extraordinary Elizabethan buildings – the Triangular Lodge at Rushton, and Lyveden New Bield near Brigstock, both of them expressing a deeply religious symbolism. The roll-call of outstanding churches in the county includes All Saints at Brixworth, one of the finest Anglo-Saxon churches in England and the only one still in use; the tiny church at Slapton with its glorious medieval wall paintings; and the Church of the Holy Sepulchre in Northampton – the largest and best-preserved Norman round church in the country.

Land-locked though it is, Northamptonshire has an abundance of canals, rivers and lakes. The River Nene is navigable right from the Wash into the heart of Northampton and links

Rockingham Castle, Northampton

up with the Grand Union Canal. The Canal Museum in the popular canalside village of Stoke Bruerne provides an insight into 200 years of history and traditions on the county's waterways.

Sporting enthusiasts will find plenty to interest them, including National Hunt racing at Towcester, football (Northampton Town, Rushden & Diamonds), motor racing at Silverstone which has hosted the Formula 1 Grand Prix for many years, drag racing at Santa Pod.....and the world conker championships at Ashton near Oundle!

ALTHORP

The home of the Spencer family since 1508, Althorp remains exactly that – a

Althorp House

classic family-owned English stately home which the Spencers have stamped with their style ever since John Spencer, a large-scale sheep farmer, acquired the estate. The present house was begun in 1573, and behind the stark tiling of the exterior is a wealth of fine paintings, sculpture, porcelain and furniture. Known widely by connoisseurs for generations, Althorp is now known across the whole world since the tragic death of Diana, Princess of Wales, in 1997. She lies in peace in the beautiful, tranquil setting of the Round Oval, an ornamental lake, surrounded by her family's ancestral heritage.

ASHBY ST LEDGERS

From 1375 to 1605 the manor house at Ashby was the home of the Catesby family, and it was in a room above the gatehouse that Guy Fawkes is said to have met Robert Catesby to hatch the

Gunpowder Plot. On the 5th of November 1605, Catesby rode the 80 miles from London in seven hours with the news that the plot had failed. He fled to Holbeach in Staffordshire, where he was shot dead after refusing to surrender. The **Church of St Mary & St Leodegarious** has much of interest, including Jacobean box pews, an elaborately carved rood screen, a Norman font, Catesby brasses and, most notably, some medieval wall paintings depicting the Passion of Christ.

AYNHO

A peaceful, picturesque limestone village of leafy lanes and lovely old cottages. The former manor house, **Aynho Park**, is a very grand 17th century country house in the care of the Country Houses Association. It was originally the property of the Cartwright family who, it is said, claimed the rents from their tenants in the form of apricots; some apricot trees can still be seen trained into fan shapes and growing on the walls of cottages. The house was burnt down by Royalist troops during the Civil war but was rebuilt by the Cartwrights, who also rebuilt the village church in the same proportions, giving it too the appearance of a country villa.

BLISWORTH

The building of the Grand Union and

Oxford Canals brought trade and prosperity to the area and now provides miles of quiet, picturesque walks or boat trips. On the Grand Union Canal, the **Blisworth Tunnel** between Blisworth and Stoke Bruerne, opened in 1805, is the longest in England, at nearly two miles. The pretty village of Blisworth is a mass of roses in summer, in the cottage gardens, in the Tudor and Jacobean houses and around the 13th century church. The most significant treasure in the church is a high screen of the 15th century complete with doors. Also of interest is a tablet near the altar which tells of the wife of a sergeant-at-arms to Queen Elizabeth I. The tablet records that she lived a maid for 18 years, was a wife for 20 years and a widow for 61, dying in her 99th year.

CANONS ASHBY

This pretty village contains the **Church of St Mary**, once part of the Black Canons' Monastery church and much reduced in size at the time of the Dissolution of the Monasteries. **Canons**

Canons Ashby

Ashby House, built from part of the ecclesiastical building after the Dissolution, is one of the finest of Northamptonshire's great houses. Home of the Dryden family since the 1550s and now in the care of the National Trust, it contains some marvellous Elizabethan wall paintings and sumptuous Jacobean plasterwork. The grounds are equally delightful, with yews, cedars and mulberry trees, terraces and parkland.

CASTLE ASHBY

Two major attractions for the visitor here. Castle Ashby is a fine Elizabethan mansion, home of the Marquess of Northampton, standing in Capability Brown parkland with Victorian gardens and a lake. The building of Castle Ashby was started in 1574 on the site of a 13th century castle that had been demolished. The original plan of the building was in the shape of an 'E' in honour of Queen Elizabeth I, and is typical of many Elizabethan houses. About 60 years later the courtyard was enclosed by a screen designed by Inigo Jones. One of the features of Castle Ashby is the lettering around the house and terraces. The inscriptions, which are in Latin, read when translated *"The Lord guard your coming in"* and *"The Lord guard your going out"*. Inside there is some wonderful restoration furniture and paintings of the English and Renaissance schools.

On a much smaller scale the old **Manor House** makes a

delightful picture by the church; it has a dungeon and there is a 13th century window with exquisite tracery set in the oldest part of the house near a blocked Norman arch. The poet Cowper loved to wander among the trees, and the tree that attracts the most visitors is called Cowper's Oak, the branches of which spread twice as far across as the tree is high. There is a tradition that it will never die because Cowper stood beneath it one day during a heavy thunderstorm and was inspired to write his famous hymn *"God moves in Mysterious Ways"*.

Castle Ashby Craft Centre & Rural Shopping Yard is set in an old farmyard and comprises a farm shop and delicatessen, craft shops, pottery, goldsmith's studio, art gallery and tea room.

DAVENTRY

Old and new blend intriguingly in this historic market town, whose streets are shared by dignified Georgian houses and modern shops. A colourful market is held along the High Street every Tuesday and Friday, and in the Market Place stands the **Moot Hall**, built in 1769 of ironstone. Originally a private house, it became the moot hall, or town hall, in 1806 after the former town hall was demolished. It is now home to the Tourist Information Centre and to **Daventry Museum**, which illustrates the social history of the town and its environs. It also shows regularly changing arts and crafts exhibitions and contains archaeological finds from

Borough Hill and some of the equipment used by the BBC when it had a transmitter station on the hill.

Daventry was once an important stop on the coaching routes, and it is said that King Charles I spent several days at the Wheatsheaf Inn before the Battle of Naseby, where he lost the battle and his kingdom. Shakespeare mentions the town in *King Henry IV (Part 1)*, when Falstaff tells Bardolph the tale of a shirt stolen from a *"red-nose innkeeper"*. **Daventry Country Park** is a beautiful 133-acre site centred on the old Daventry Reservoir. Coarse fishing, a picnic area, adventure playground, nature trails, nature reserve and visitor centre are among the amenities.

DEENE

Surrounded by beautiful gardens and grounds filled with old-fashioned roses and rare trees and shrub stands **Deene Park**. Originally a medieval manor, it was acquired in 1514 by Sir Robert Brudenell and has been occupied by the family ever since. One of the family's most distinguished members was James, 7th Earl of Cadogan, who led the Charge of the Light Brigade at the Battle of Balaclava. Transformed from medieval manor to Tudor and Georgian mansion, Deene Park contains many fine examples of period furniture and some beautiful paintings.

Also near Deene, in the parish of Gretton, is **Kirby Hall**, one of the loveliest Elizabethan ruins in England. Now only partly roofed, the hall dates from 1570 and was given by Elizabeth I to her Lord Chancellor and favourite courtier Sir Christopher Hatton. Alterations attributed to Inigo Jones were made in the 17th century.

EARLS BARTON

A great treasure here is the village **Church of All Saints**, with one of the most impressive Anglo-Saxon towers in the whole country, its surface adorned with purely decorative masonry strips. The tower is 10th century, the south doorway is 12th, the aisles are 13th, the tower arch 14th, the south porch 19th, but they all co-exist in great architectural harmony. Beyond the remarkably well-preserved Norman doorway the most amazing sight is the 15th century chancel screen, ablaze with hundreds of dazzling butterflies on the wing; next to it is a wonderful, heavily carved Jacobean pulpit in black oak.

FLORE

Called *Flora* in the Domesday Book, the village has a wide green that slopes gently down to the River Nene. **Adams Cottage** was the home of the ancestors of John Adams, President of the United States from 1797 to 1801, whose son was also President. In the 13th century church are several memorial windows, one of them dedicated to Bruce Capell, an artillery officer who was awarded the Military Cross at the age of 22 for courage and devotion to his wounded men. A simple wooden cross from

Flanders hangs on the wall, and his window depicts the farewell between David and Jonathan.

FOTHERINGHAY

The first **Fotheringhay Castle** was built around 1100 by the son-in-law of William the Conqueror, the second in the 14th century by Edmund of Langley, a son of Edward III. Richard III was born here; Henry VIII gave the castle to Catherine of Aragon and it later became the prison and place of execution of Mary, Queen of Scots, who was beheaded in the Banqueting Hall in 1587. Sir Christopher Hatton, a favourite of Elizabeth I whom we have met at Holdenby and Kirkby Hall, was one of the judges who sentenced Mary to death. Following her death, it is said that her jewellery was stolen and hidden in the woodlands around Corby. If so, it lies there still. The castle was pulled down in 1627 and 200 years later a gold ring was found with a lovers' knot entwined around the initials M and D - Mary and Darnley? Perhaps the ring fell from the Queen's finger as she was executed. The evocative site of the castles by the River Nene is rich in atmosphere, and visitors to Fotheringhay should not leave the village without seeing the **Church of St Mary and All Saints**, a 15th century former collegiate church in a prominent position overlooking the Nene Valley.

GEDDINGTON

This attractive village, like many in the

Fotheringay

Geddington and Grafton Underwood (where there is a monument to the crews of B17 bombers), stands one of the very finest houses in the country. The origins of **Boughton House**, the Northamptonshire home of the Duke of Buccleuch, go back 500 years to a small monastic building. Extended over the years, it was transformed into "a vision of Louis XIV's Versailles". In addition to the wonderful architecture, Boughton is noted for its French and English furniture, its paintings (El Greco, Murillo, 40 Van Dycks) and its collection of armoury and weaponry.

county, has known royal visitors: monarchs from the time of William the Conqueror used a summer palace as a base for hunting in the Royal Forest of Rockingham. In the centre of the village is an ornately carved stone cross almost 40 feet high. This is the best preserved of the three surviving **Eleanor Crosses** that marked the funeral procession of Queen Eleanor, who had died at Harby in Nottinghamshire in 1290. Her devoted husband, King Edward I, accompanied the body south to London, and wherever the funeral bier rested, he built a cross. Of all the crosses this, at Geddington, is the most complete. Other crosses were raised at Lincoln (where the Queen's heart was buried), Grantham, Stamford, Hardingstone (this still exists), Stony Stratford, Dunstable, St Albans, Waltham (this still exists), Cheapside and Charing Cross.

Off the A43, on a minor road between

Boughton House

The grounds, which include parkland, lakes, picnic areas and woodland play areas, are open May to September, the house in August only.

Large tracts of the ancient woodland of the region have survived, and in the fields by Boughton House are the remains of more recent planting. The

2nd Duke of Montagu, nicknamed **John the Planter**, had the notion of planting an avenue of trees all the way from the house to his London home. The plan hit immediate trouble when his neighbour, the Duke of Bedford, refused to let the trees cross his estate; instead, the Planter set down many avenues on his own estate, amounting to the 70 miles of the distance to London.

GUILSBOROUGH

A handsome, dignified village where Wordsworth came to stay in the vicarage and, it is said, brought with him the yellow Cumberland poppy that is often seen here. The church has lovely windows by William Morris and Burne-Jones, and **Guilsborough Grange** has a wildlife park and areas for walking and picnicking. A short distance south of the village, in the tiny community of Coton, **Coton Manor Garden** is a traditional garden originally laid out in 1925 and embracing several delightful smaller gardens.

HIGHAM FERRERS

Just off the **Market Place** in this delightful old town a narrow lane leads to a unique group of ecclesiastical buildings. These include the 13th century spired Church of St Mary the Virgin, a chantry and bede house, and a 13th century market cross. Also here is **Chichele College**, a college for secular canons founded in 1422, named in honour of a local worthy called Henry

Chichele. Born here in 1362, he progressed from baker's boy to Archbishop of Canterbury, a position he filled for 30 years until his death in 1443.

HOLDENBY

The Royal connections go back more than 400 years at **Holdenby Hall**, which was built by Elizabeth I's Lord Chancellor and favourite Sir Christopher Hatton for the purpose of entertaining the Queen. At the time, it was the largest Elizabethan house in England, and, for the diarist John Evelyn, *"one of the most pleasing sights that ever I saw"*. It was visited but once by Elizabeth; it later became the palace and eventually the prison of Charles I, who was kept under guard here for five months after his defeat in the Civil War. The house stands in magnificent grounds which contain a falconry centre, a smaller scale reconstruction of Hatton's original garden, a fully working armoury and a 17th century farmstead that evokes the sights and smells of life in days gone by. There's a museum, a children's farm and a lakeside train ride together with tea in the Victorian Kitchen.

KELMARSH

Near Junction 2 of the A14, just outside the village of Kelmarsh, **Kelmarsh Hall** is an early 18th century house designed in Palladian style by an outstanding pupil of Sir Christopher Wren, James Gibbs (perhaps best known as the architect of the Church of St Martin in the Fields, London). One of only two surviving houses outside London by Gibbs in this style, it stands in 3,000 acres of farmland, with a lake, beautiful gardens and woodland walks. The Great Hall is the focal point of the house, with many of Gibbs's original features. One of the most attractive rooms is the Chinese Room, where the hand-painted wallpaper, from Kimberley Hall in Norfolk, dates from the 1840s. The church opposite the main entrance to the Hall contains fine marble from Rome, some William Morris furnishings and the vaults of the families who have lived at the Hall – the Hanburys, the Naylors and the Lancasters.

KETTERING

An important town standing above the River Ise, Kettering gained fame as a producer of both clothing and shoes. It was in Kettering that the missionary William Carey and the preacher Andrew Fuller founded the Baptist Missionary Society in 1792, giving a new impetus to the cause of foreign missions all over the world. The parish church of **St Peter and St Paul**, with its elegant crocketed spire, is one of the finest in the country and a landmark for miles around. Much of the old town has been swallowed up in modern development, but there are still a few old houses in the narrow lanes, and the **Heritage Quarter** around the church gives a fascinating, hands-on insight into the town's past.

The **Manor House Museum**, housed in an 18th century manor house, has impressive collections of social and industrial history, archaeology and geology. Individual items range from a mummified cat to an example of the Robinson car built in Kettering in 1907.

In the adjacent **Alfred East Gallery** a constantly changing programme of exhibitions of paintings, crafts, sculpture, photography and children's work ensures that there is always something new to see. The Tourist Information Centre is at the same location.

On the outskirts of town, **Wicksteed Park** is a 148-acre site of leisure and pleasure, with 40 rides and attractions, including roller coaster, pirate ship, train ride, Mississippi river boat and pitch & putt. There are catering outlets, shops, a pottery, a photographic studio and two playground areas.

LAMPORT

Lamport Hall is a fine 16th century house enlarged in the 17th century by John Webb. Home to the Isham family from 1560 to 1976, it features an outstanding collection of furniture, books, paintings and china. It has gardens and parkland, including the first Alpine garden and the first garden gnomes in England, plus a shop and tea room. It is also the home of the **Hannington Vintage Tractor Club**, which houses a wide variety of vintage tractors and other farm machinery.

NORTHAMPTON

Much of its face is modern, but the

capital of the county has a wealth of history for the visitor to discover. At least 6,000 years ago a camp was set up at **Briar Hill**, and more recent traces of early settlements in the area date from between 700BC and 50AD. The Domesday Book of 1086 shows Northampton as a town of 300 houses, comparable in size to Derby or Nottingham. Richard I granted the town its first charter in 1189, and by the 13th century Northampton had become a major market town; its market square, dating from that period, is reputed to be the second largest in the country.

For centuries Northampton has been associated with the shoemaking trade. Tradition has it that in 1213 a pair of boots was made here for King John, and the first large order came in 1642 when 4,000 pairs of shoes and 600 pairs of boots were made for the army. The industry grew rapidly throughout the county and by the end of the 1800s, 40% of the population was involved in the shoe trade. People like Philip Manfield and William Barrett were just two of the major players who started their businesses in Northampton and grew them into extensive chains. William Barrett gave his name to the maternity hospital, and Manfield gave his to another of the town's hospitals. St Crispin, the patron saint of shoemakers, is portrayed in several churches, and Northampton Town Football Club are known as the Cobblers. The **Central Museum and Art Gallery** has the world's largest collection of footwear,

showing shoe fashions down the centuries and the machines that made the shoes. There is also an outstanding collection of British and Oriental ceramics, leathercraft from around the world and some fine paintings including Italian works of the 15th to 18th centuries and British art. The **Abington Museum**, set in a 15th century manor house, has a number of interesting exhibits, including a room with 16th century oak panelling, exhibits detailing the county's military history, a 19th century fashion gallery, and a display titled 'Northampton Life – from the cradle to the grave'.

Northampton has two outstanding churches: All Saints, designed by Henry Bell in the Wren style, with ornate plasterwork by Edward Goudge and two organs by JS Walker; and the wonderful **Church of the Holy Sepulchre,** one of only four remaining round churches in the kingdom. Founded by Simon de Senlis, 1st Earl of Northampton, to commemorate his safe return from the Crusades in 1100, it is often known as the Soldiers Church and carried battle scars from the Wars of the Roses. It is the oldest standing building in Northampton and is almost identical to the original in Jerusalem.

The most prestigious building in town is certainly the **Guildhall**, a gem of Victorian architecture built in 1864 by Edward Godwin and later extended by Matthew Holding and Arnold Jeffrey. **The Royal Theatre** is another Victorian gem, built in 1884 in opulent Italianate style and home to one of the oldest repertory companies in England. The **Welsh House**, one of the few buildings to survive the disastrous fire of 1675, dates from 1595 and recalls the time when Welsh drovers would bring their cattle to the market. Another striking building is 78 Derngate, designed by the Scottish architect Charles Rennie Mackintosh.

In 1290 the funeral procession of Queen Eleanor, wife of Edward I, stopped for the night at Delapre Abbey. To the south of town, at **Hardingstone** on the London Road A508, stands one of the three surviving **Eleanor Crosses** of the twelve originally erected to mark each night of the progress of the mournful cortege to London. (See under Geddington for more about the Eleanor Crosses.)

Northampton boasts over 150 parks and open spaces, most notably **Abington Park** with lakes, aviaries and the museum mentioned above. Northampton's racecourse is the setting for the International Hot Air Balloon Festival, a summer highlight that attracts visitors from far and wide. Other outdoor attractions include **Delapre Park**, where the Cluniac Abbey was built in 1145; and **Hunsbury Hill Country Park**, where the Iron Age hill fort can still be seen – this park is also home to the Northamptonshire Ironstone Railway Trust's museum and railway. Northampton's sports and leisure facilities are abundant: two of the best are **Billing Aquadrome** with extensive fishing and moorings and, opened in 1999, the **Nene White Water Centre** with facilities for canoeing, rafting, rowing and orienteering.

OUNDLE

Oundle is a beguiling little town with some fine stone buildings dating from the 17th and 18th centuries, ancient hostelries and a variety of specialist shops. The town is probably best known for its **Public School**, founded by Sir William Laxton in 1556. An inscription to his memory is written above the 17th century doorway in Greek, Latin and Hebrew. The medieval church, with its magnificent tower and 200ft spire, is an impressive sight, and other notable buildings include three sets of almshouses. The museum paints a picture of local life down the years.

In mid-July, the town hosts the **Oundle International Festival** – ten days devoted to a vibrant mix of classical music, theatre, jazz and film. The festivities include a hugely popular open-air jazz and firework spectacular. On a smaller scale, but generating a wildly competitive spirit, are the **World Conker Championships** held at Ashton, just to the east of the town.

ROCKINGHAM

"450 Years a Royal Castle, 450 years a family home". Nine hundred years of history are contained within the walls of **Rockingham Castle**, built by William the Conqueror on the slopes of

Rockingham

Rockingham Hill, overlooking the Welland Valley and the thatched and slate-roofed cottages of the village. The grand rooms are superbly furnished, and the armour in the Tudor Great Hall recalls the Civil War, when the castle was captured by the Roundheads. Owned and lived in since 1530 by the Watson family, the castle was put to atmospheric use by the BBC in the series *By the Sword Divided*, in which it was known as Arnescote Castle. Charles Dickens wrote much of *Bleak House* at Rockingham.

RUSHTON

One mile west of the village, on an unclassified road, stands **Rushton Triangular Lodge**, described as "the purest folly in the country". It was built by Sir Thomas Tresham in 1597 and symbolises the Holy Trinity, with three walls, each with three windows, three gables and three storeys, topped with a three-sided chimney. Thomas Tresham, known as Thomas the Builder, was brought up a Protestant but courageously returned to the Roman Catholic faith of his ancestors. At Rushton Hall, the Tresham family home since the 14th century, he was caught harbouring the renowned Jesuit Edmund Campion and was sentenced to seven years' imprisonment. Responsible for several intriguing buildings, he died soon after proclaiming the first Stuart king and just before his son Francis was arrested as a protagonist in the Gunpowder Plot.

Neighbouring **Rushton Hall**, also dating back 400 years, is described as a "dazzling example of Tudor and Stuart splendour". Built by Sir John Tresham, enlarged by Sir Thomas and completed by the Cockayne family, it now houses a Royal Institute for the Blind school, but is open to the public by appointment and for special events.

SALCEY FOREST

Reached from the A508 at Roade or the B526 between Horton and Stoke Goldington, the 1,250-acre Salcey Forest has been owned and managed by the Forestry Commission since the 1920s. Part of the chain of ancient Royal Hunting Forests that stretched from Stamford to Oxford, it produces quality timber while providing a home for a wide variety of animal and plant life, and recreational facilities for the public. There are three circular trails at Salcey, named after the three woodpeckers found there: the Lesser Spotted Trail of a leisurely hour; the Great Spotted Trail of about two miles; and the Green Woodpecker Trail of about 2½ hours.

SILVERSTONE

The home of British motor racing, located off the A43 in the village. The **British Grand Prix** is the highlight of the year, but the circuit hosts a large number of other events, including rounds of the Auto Trader touring car championship and the **International Historic Car Festival**. Members of the public can test their skills in a single-seater racer, a Lotus Elise, a rally car or a 4x4 off-road vehicle.

Tucked away on country roads northwest of Silverstone are two of the many interesting churches for which Northamptonshire is famous. The **Church of St Mary** at **Wappenham** has a sculpture by Giles Gilbert Scott from the renowned family of architects, who had local connections; two fonts; a clock from the 17th century; and brass memorials to the Lovett family.

STOKE BRUERNE

A picturesque canalside village at the southern end of the famous Blisworth Tunnel. The canal provides the major attractions, with waterside walks, boat trips to the tunnel and a visit to the fascinating **Canal Museum**. Housed in a converted corn mill, the museum displays 200 years of canal history and

life on the narrow boats (many of which are still in use for pleasure trips). The exhibits include working engines, old photographs, waterway wildlife and the tools used by canal workers and boatmen. The canal has a series of locks at this point, and visitors can stop in the car park at the lower lock on the A508

Canal Museum, Stoke Bruerne

and walk into the village along the towpath, passing seven locks en route. There are shops, pubs and restaurants at this popular place, which is the perfect location for a family day out and an ideal starting point for a canal holiday.

A private drive on the Stoke Bruerne to Shutlanger road leads to **Stoke Park**, a great house standing in a 400-acre estate. Attributed to Inigo Jones, the house was built in Palladian style (the first in this country) around 1630 for Sir Francis Crane, head of the Mortlake Tapestry Works. The main house burnt down in 1886, and only the pavilions and a colonnade remain.

SULGRAVE

The best-known attraction here is **Sulgrave Manor**, a Tudor manor house built by the ancestors of George

Sulgrave

Washington, first President of the United States of America. Lawrence Washington, sometime Mayor of Northampton, bought the manor from Henry VIII in 1539. In 1656, Lawrence Washington's great-great-grandson Colonel John Washington left England to take up land in Virginia, which later became Mount Vernon. This man was the great-grandfather of George. The Washington family arms, which are said to have inspired the stars and stripes on the American flag, are prominent above the front door, and the house is a treasure trove of George Washington memorabilia, including documents, a velvet coat and even a lock of his hair. The lovely gardens include yew hedges, topiary, herbaceous borders and a formal rose garden. There's a gift shop and a buttery serving light refreshments.

THRAPSTON

The **Medieval Bridge** at Thrapston crosses the **River Nene** on one of its loveliest stretches. The town is surrounded by fine pastureland, created when the flood waters and rich mud subsided after the two Ice Ages. The main attraction in the church is a stone tablet carved with stars and stripes. It is thought by some that this motif was the inspiration for the American flag, being the coat of arms of Sir John Washington, who died in 1624. The church and nearby **Montagu House**, home of Sir John, are places of pilgrimage for many American tourists.

TOWCESTER

A busy little place, Towcester is popular with seekers of antiques – there are at least half a dozen different establishments selling antiques.

In Roman times the town was called Lactodorum and it stood on the major highway Watling Street (now the A5). The Romans improved the road and built a fort to guard their troop movements. During the Civil War it was the only Royalist stronghold in the area and in the following centuries it was an important stop on the coaching route between London and Holyhead. By the end of the 18th century there were 20 coaching inns in the town, servicing up to 40 coaches every day. Charles Dickens stayed at the Saracen's Head, then called the Pomfret Hotel, and immortalised it in *The Pickwick Papers*. The parish church of **St Lawrence**, built on the site of a substantial Roman building, is one of the loveliest in the county. The crypt, reached by a doorway from the sanctuary, is 13th century, the arcades 13th and 14th. On the arch of the south chapel is a carved jester's head probably from the 14th century, while the massive tower and the font are from the 1400s. Close to the church is the **Chantry House,** formerly a school, founded by Archdeacon Sponne in 1447.

Towcester Racecourse is set in the beautiful parkland estate of Easton Neston, the family home of Lord Hesketh. The course came into being in 1876, when the Empress of Austria was staying at Easton Neston and attended an Easter steeplechase held in her honour.

WELLINGBOROUGH

This important market and industrial town, known for its iron mills, flour mills and tanneries, sits near the point where the River Ise joins the River Nene. The spire of the medieval All Hallows Church rises among trees in the centre of town, and the other church, whose great tower can be seen on the further bank of the Nene, is the **Church of St Mary.** It was built in the first decades of the 20th century and is regarded as Sir Ninian Comper's masterpiece. He declared St Mary's his favourite church and wished

to be buried here with his wife but his fame demanded interment in Westminster Abbey. Funded by two Anglo-Catholic spinster sisters, St Mary's has been described as "a sort of fantastical King's College, Cambridge", a medley of extravagant Gothic features complete with gilded columns and golden angels.

Wellingborough was granted its market charter in 1201 and markets are still held four days a week. In and around the market square are several interesting old buildings, including the gabled **Hind Hotel**. One room is called the Cromwell Room as it was being built during the Battle of Naseby.

Another fine building is **Croyland Abbey,** now a Heritage Centre with a wealth of local history, and near it is a splendidly restored old tithe barn originally used for storing the manorial tithes. Stone-walled and thatch-roofed, it is 70 feet long and 22 feet wide. It dates from the 1400s and has two great doorways at either side, one of them 13 feet in height. A popular attraction in the centre of town is the Millennium Rose Garden at **Swanspool Gardens.** The Embankment at Wellingborough is a great place for a family outing, where a thriving population of swans lives next to the outdoor paddling pool that dates from the 1930s. South of the town, **Summer Leys Nature Reserve** is a year-round haven for large numbers of birds. Each May, thousands of people attend the **International Waendel Weekend** of walking, cycling and swimming.

THE BELL INN

32 BELL HILL, FINEDON, NR. WELLINGBOROUGH,
NORTHAMPTONSHIRE NN9 5ND
TEL: 01933 680332

> **Directions:** Leave the M1 at junction 16 and follow the A45 around the southern
> outskirts of Northampton and onto Higham Ferrars. Then turn onto the A6
> towards Kettering and you will reach Finedon after just 4 miles

The Bell Inn has a long history which, together with the historic village of Finedon in which it is tucked down an ancient lane, stretches back to the Doomsday book. The present building is of various dates with the impressive ornamental frontage being constructed in 1872. Venturing inside, you can sample the warm and friendly welcome which is extended from both the landlord, Dennis Willmott, and locals, and enjoy some fine refreshment. Dennis has been in charge here for thirty-four years and it is clear that he is popular with the regulars.

The bar stocks a good selection with Bass, Old Speckled Hen and London Pride permanently on tap, together with a guest ale which changes weekly. There is also a full range of other lagers and beers. The wide ranging menu offers an excellent choice of good value meals and snacks ranging from sandwiches and burgers to grills, fish and other popular dishes. Food is served throughout, though the former dairy has been converted into a non-smoking restaurant, at lunchtimes Wednesday to Monday and evenings Wednesday to Saturday. The Sunday lunches are served from midday until 2pm and advance booking is advisable.

Come to The Bell Inn and enjoy a drink and much more besides. On Friday nights for example there is usually live acoustic music and the pub is also used as a regular meeting place for the Kettering Vintage Car Club among others.

🕐 Mon-Fri 12.00-15.00, 17.30-23.00; Sat 12.00-15.00, 18.00-23.00; Sun 12.00-15.00, 19.00-22.30

🍴 Popular menu of tasty meals and snacks

🅿 Car park

🎵 Acoustic music Friday nights, meeting place for many local clubs

❓ Irchester Country Park 4 miles, Kettering 6 miles, Boughton House 8 miles, Santa Pod Motor Raceway 10 miles, Lyveden New Bield 11 miles

THE CHEQUERS

CHEQUERS LANE, RAVENSTHORPE, NORTHAMPTONSHIRE NN6 8ER
TEL: 01604 770379

> **Directions:** From the M1 junction 18, the A428 leads you southeast towards Northampton. After about 8 miles, the village of Ravensthorpe will be signposted to the left

In the pretty village of Ravensthorpe, **The Chequers** is a delightful spot where regulars and first-time visitors can expect an equally warm welcome from owners Gordon and Gill Walker and their family. The Grade II listed building was originally built as a farmhouse but has been operating as a pub since 1900. Stepping over the threshold, you will find beamed ceilings and spacious areas for enjoying a refreshing drink or something tasty to eat. Furnished in a highly traditional style, the walls and ceilings are adorned with collections of banknotes, bottles, jugs and tankards. Gordon is the chef, and visitors to The Chequers can look forward to anything from a hot or cold filled baguette to a full-scale meal. The full dining menu is

available Tuesday to Saturday evening, and lunch and bar menus operate at other times. Steaks are always popular, and other main course choices could include roast pheasant, chicken curry and salmon supreme hollandaise. Tuesday, Wednesday and Thursday are fresh fish nights while vegetarians will always find a good selection of dishes to choose from. The quality of the food, and the reasonable prices, mean that the pub can get busy so bookings are advisable to avoid disappointment. Five hand-pumped real ales are among the liquid assets, and a selection of wines can be ordered by the glass, large glass or bottle.

Close to the village, Ravensthorpe Reservoir is a delightful place for pleasant walks and trout fishing. There are also a number of superb gardens open to visitors, all within a few miles drive.

- 🕐 Mon-Sat 11.00-14.30, 18.00-23.00; Sun 12.00-14.30, 18.00-22.30
- 🍴 Lunch, Dinner and Bar Snacks
- 💷 Visa, Mastercard, Delta, Switch
- Ⓟ Large beer garden, children's play area, car park
- ❓ Coton Manor Gardens 1 mile, Holdenby House Gardens 2 miles, Althorp Park 3 miles, Brixworth Country Park 6 miles, Golf 5 miles, Pitsford Reservoir 7 miles, Cottesbroke Hall 5 miles

THE DUKES ARMS

HIGH STREET, THE GREEN, WOODFORD,
NORTHAMPTONSHIRE NN14 4HE
TEL/FAX: 01832 732224

> **Directions:** From the A1, turn east onto the A14 Kettering road at Huntingdon. After about 17 miles, the village of Woodford will be signposted to the south.

The Dukes Arms located in the lovely village of Woodford, with its many delightful walks around the area, is jointly run by Tony, Simon, Heather and Vanda. Here you will find fine ales and good home-cooked food, combined with a friendly, professional service.

In the spacious saloon bar you can sample the wide selection of beverages. There are five cask ales, including Lancaster Bomber, Greene King IPA and Fuller's London Pride, and other popular beers and lagers. Adjoining the bar is a games room where you can play pool, darts, snakes and ladders and even the traditional game of table skittles. The Lounge Restaurant provides cosy and comfortable surroundings in which to enjoy your drinks and the extensive menu. Food is served each lunchtime and evening. Mainly good wholesome English fayre is prepared using the freshest of ingredients, including many home-grown vegetables. The most popular choices include home-made pies and fish dishes. Tony and the team have between them over 60 years experience in the catering business so you can be sure of a superb meal, especially in The Dukes Restaurant which is open Friday and Saturday evenings and for Sunday lunch. With seating for up to 50 diners, the a la carte menu will not disappoint however advance booking is strongly recommended.

The Dukes Arms has a delightful, large garden which is ideal for families, with its children's play area.

- 🕐 Mon-Sat 11.00-23.00; Sun 12.00-22.30
- 🍴 Extensive lounge bar menu, a la carte restaurant open at weekends
- 💷 Visa, Mastercard, Delta, Switch
- 🅿 Children's play area, beer garden
- 🎵 Monthly folk and country music, pub games
- ❓ Nene Valley RSPB Reserve 3 miles, Hamerton Zoo Park 12 miles, Brigstock Country Park 6 miles, Lyveden New Bield 7 miles, Boughton House 6 miles, Grafham Water 15 miles

THE EASTCOTE ARMS

6 GAYTON ROAD, EASTCOTE, NR.TOWCESTER, NORTHAMPTONSHIRE
NN12 8NG
TEL: 01327 830731

> **Directions:** Leave the M1 at junction 15a and take the A43 towards Towcester. After a little over a mile, turn left for Gayton and follow signs for Eastcote

Located near the centre of the small, peaceful village of Eastcote, **The Eastcote Arms** is a striking little pub at the heart of the local community. It dates from the late-17th century and is full of character and history. This is an inn that was built to last, and it shows! Under the personal supervision of George and Kerrie Scott it has established a reputation in the area as the place to visit for a quiet drink, a bar lunch or an evening meal.

The interior is welcoming and spotlessly clean, with an ambience that is hard to resist. There are two bars with a small restaurant, and in the winter months an open fire adds a welcoming glow. It serves bar and Sunday lunches, as well as full evening meals, and the menus are a mixture of traditional fayre and the more exotic. The bar include such dishes as Lincolnshire sausage, egg and chips, filled baguettes, soup and jacket potatoes. The evening meals are an experience in themselves. Main courses include deep fried Camembert, fillet steaks, poached salmon fillet and beef and Guinness served with green beans and spring onion mashed potato. Sunday lunches include roast beef (of course!) roast pork and a vegetarian dish of the day. All of this can be washed down with a selection of award-winning real ales, as the Eastcote Arms boasts the best beers in the area. There's also a small, intimate wine list.

For nicer weather, there is a relaxing beer garden with a corner set aside for children.

- 🕐 Mon-Thur: 12.00-15.00,18.00-23.00; Fri-Sat: 12.00-23.00; Sun: 12.00-22.30
- 🍴 Bar lunches and evening meals. Served Tues-Sat: 12.00-14.30, Sun: 12.00-15.00; Wed-Sun: 18.30-21.30
- £ Visa, Mastercard, Delta, Switch
- 🅿 Beer garden, car park
- 🎵 Regular theme nights and occasional live music
- ❓ Silverstone Motor Racing Circuit 7 miles, Stoke Park 5 miles, Stowe Gardens 10 miles, Stoke Bruerne Canal Museum 5 miles, Canons Ashby 7 miles

THE FOX AND HOUNDS

BANBURY ROAD, CHARWELTON, NR. DAVENTRY,
NORTHAMPTONSHIRE NN11 3YY
TEL/FAX: 01327 262358

> **Directions:** From the M1, the A45 leads from junction 16 into Daventry. Keeping on the A45, which passes to the south of the town, turn onto the A361 Banbury road. After a little over 3 miles you will reach Charwelton

The small village of Charwelton can be found located directly on the A361 Banbury to Daventry road. In the centre, you cannot fail to miss the **Fox and Hounds** public house. This attractive stone building is over 200 years old and lies directly fronting the road, with a spacious car park behind, making it a convenient place to stop for those travelling by car. Venturing inside you will find a cosy bar area together with a spacious non-smoking restaurant which can seat up to 64. With a superb menu served every lunchtime and evening it is not surprising that the pub has acquired a far reaching reputation as a great place to eat. This is due in no

small part to the owners Stephanie and Leo Stewart, who in their first year here have also completely refurbished and redecorated the pub throughout. The varied selection of dishes caters to every taste and appetite, and ranges from the large mixed grill and 24oz steaks to fresh fish, vegetarian dishes and simple baguettes. There is a children's menu and a special meal deal for OAPs is available weekday lunchtimes. To avoid disappointment it is essential to book at weekends.

To complement your meal, the bar can provide a good selection of liquid refreshments. There are some fine real ales, popular lagers, Guinness, and an excellent wine list. On warm summer days, drinks and meals can be enjoyed out in the beer garden and patio.

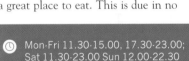

- 🕐 Mon-Fri 11.30-15.00, 17.30-23.00; Sat 11.30-23.00 Sun 12.00-22.30
- 🍽 Wide ranging menu catering to all
- £ Visa, Mastercard, Delta, Switch
- Ⓟ Good wheelchair access, parking
- ♫ Occasional live music
- ❓ Canons Ashby 5 miles, Daventry Country Park 6 miles, Althorp Park 13 miles, Heritage Motor Museum 15 miles, Holdenby House Gardens 15 miles, Upton House 16 miles

THE GEORGE HOTEL

11-13 WATLING STREET, KILSBY, NR. RUGBY,
NORTHAMPTONSHIRE CV23 8YE
TEL: 01788 822229 FAX: 01788 822228

Directions: From junction 18 of the M1, follow signs for Rugby, turning almost immediately left onto the A5. After a little over a mile, before you cross over the M45, Kilsby will be signposted to the left.

The village of Kilsby gives its name to the one and a half mile long Kilsby Tunnel, which was constructed in 1838 by Robert Stephenson for the London-Birmingham railway. **The George Hotel** was burnt down at around the same time that the tunnel was being built, and consequently was reconstructed using the same bricks as the tunnel. The pub remains an impressive structure and presents a fresh cream and green painted exterior to the road. To the rear there is a large beer garden which is a popular

spot in warmer weather.

Inside, the large lounge bar boasts wooden panelled walls and a plush carpet while the adjoining dining area retains much of the period character with a fine wooden floor. Here you can enjoy some tasty home-cooked food, with the grilled steaks being a popular choice, and for which the pub has a far reaching reputation. The well-stocked bar offers all the usual beers and lagers as well as an extensive range of real ales. The pub features in the Good Beer Guide and enjoys a Cask Marque Accreditation.

The owner, Margaret Chandler, has been at the helm for four years and also offers bed and breakfast accommodation comprises six rooms, of varying sizes, with all having colour TV and hot drinks making facilities.

- Mon-Sat 11.30-15.30, 17.30-23.00; Sun 12.00-22.30
- Home-cooked dishes, superb steak dishes
- Visa, Mastercard, Delta, Switch, Amex, Diners
- 1 single, 3 twins, 2 triple beds
- Function/dining room
- Live music twice a month, large screen TV, pool, darts, table football
- george.kilsby@btopenworld.com
- Rugby 6 miles, Daventry Country Park 5 miles, Oxford Canal 2 miles, Coton Manor Gardens 9 miles, Althorp Park 9 miles, Stanford Hall 8 miles, Coventry 18 miles

THE LAMB INN

ORLINGBURY ROAD, LITTLE HARROWDEN, NR. KETTERING,
NORTHAMPTONSHIRE NN9 5BH
TEL: 01933 673300

> **Directions:** From the A1, take the A14 east towards Kettering. As the road skirts
> to the south of the town, turn south onto the A509. After a couple of miles, Little
> Harrowden will be signposted to the right

If you like the idea of a typical whitewashed country inn with small-paned windows, a swinging pub sign and a welcoming atmosphere, then come to **The Lamb Inn** at Little Harrowden. This is a gem of a place, deep in the countryside, which has recently been taken over by Steve and Helen Burgess. One look at the immaculate exterior will tell you that this is a well kept inn which is, not surprisingly, popular with both locals and visitors to the area. The inside is just as clean and spotless and the split level design offers a bar, snug and 30-seat dining area.

- 🕐 Mon-Thur 12.00-14.30, 16.30-23.00, Fri-Sat 11.00-23.00; Sun 12.00-22.30
- 🍴 Wide ranging selection of fine food
- £ Visa, Mastercard, Delta, Switch
- Ⓟ Cash point, beer garden, patio
- 🎵 Live music twice monthly, regular theme nights and other events, skittles, darts
- @ www.the-lamb-at-harrowden.co.uk
- ❓ Sywell Reservoir and Country Park 4 miles, Lamport Hall 7 miles, Boughton House 7 miles, Rockingham Castle 13 miles, Rockingham Motor Speedway Racetrack 15 miles

There is plenty of variety behind the bar, with some fine cask ales including Charles Wells Bombadier and Old Speckled Hen, guest ales and a good selection of new world wines.

A varied menu of sandwiches, baguettes, snacks and three course meals is available each lunchtime and Thursday to Saturday evenings. There is plenty to choose from with mainly traditional English dishes, all freshly prepared to order. There is a good vegetarian selection and all dishes are very sensibly priced. The non-smoking dining room can get busy at weekends, especially for the popular Sunday roast lunch, so advance booking is advisable. There is also a monthly Italian theme night which is worth booking for. Other regular events live music twice a month, special seasonal events, and much more.

THE RED LION

STOCKWELL LANE, HELLIDON, DAVENTRY, NORTHAMPTONSHIRE
NN11 6LG
TEL: 01327 261200 FAX: 01327 264376

Directions: Take the A425 west from Daventry for 3 miles. Just past the roundabout at Staverton turn south onto a minor road. Hellidon is 3 miles.

This is the area to see the soft, rich Northamptonshire countryside at its best. Small fields, woodland, country lanes and streams – it's got the lot. Hellidon itself is a large, handsome conservation village which fits perfectly into the rural scenery, and at its heart is **The Red Lion**. It is a long, two storey pub, and sits complacently on a corner, opposite a patch of green. The walls are of warm locally quarried stone, with lazy, welcoming windows.

The inn is within a sporting area, with golf, tennis and croquet on offer. It's also popular with ramblers, who make good use of the inn. The interior is typically English, with open fires in winter, sporting prints on the bare stone walls and copper topped tables. There's a bar, a lounge bar, function room and dining room, and all are scrupulously clean and comfortable. The Red Lion is one of the few places where you can still play the traditional game of Northamptonshire skittles!

The food is outstanding. Visitors can get everything from a bar meal to a superbly cooked gourmet dinner, and all the food is individually prepared on the premises and beautifully presented. The accommodation too is outstanding. There are eight rooms, and all are en suite, with colour TV and tea and coffee making facilities. The present owners have been running the pub for over fifteen years, and this experience shows through in everything they do.

- 🕐 12.00-15.00 and 18.00-23.00 Monday to Saturday; 12.00-15.00 and 18.00-22.30 on Sunday
- 🍴 Superb food, a wonderful dinner menu and great value pub lunches
- £ Most cards with the exception of American Express and Diners
- 🛏 8 en-suite rooms with TV and tea/coffee making facilities
- Ⓟ Beer garden
- 🎵 Quiz and occasional live music
- @ jdaffurn@aol.com
- ❓ Windmill Vineyard on the outskirts of the village; Hellidon Lakes Golf Course 1 mile; Burton Dassett Country park 8 miles; Daventry Country Park 6 miles; Stanford Hall 14 miles

ROSE AND CROWN

4 NORTHAMPTON ROAD, YARDLEY HASTINGS, NORTHAMPTONSHIRE
NN7 1EX
TEL: 01604 696276

> **Directions:** Yardley Hastings is on the A428, seven miles south east of
> Northampton

Yardley Hastings is one of those idyllic villages that Northamptonshire does so well. It's typically English, with beautiful stone-built cottages, thatched roofs and colourful gardens. The inn itself, which dates from 1748, is totally charming, and built of old, mellow stone that fits perfectly into the serene and beautiful landscape. Inside is equally attractive. Think of a cozy, welcoming English inn, full of history and heritage, and you could be thinking of the **Rose and Crown.** There's a bar, a lounge and a restaurant, all with flagstone floors, oak beams, ornate windows and many original features. No-one could possibly be disappointed here, as it has a warmth and friendliness visitors rarely forget.

But it takes more than just antiques

and old features to turn a pub into a comfortable and relaxing place to have a quiet drink or meal. It has to be worked at, and husband and wife team Tereska and Stephen McAllister have worked hard since they took over in December 2000 to create a place that is a pleasure to visit. The bar is especially attractive, and sells real ales, plus a range of lagers, cider and stout. There's also an excellent wine list, to complements the meals available. There's a wide choice of food on the menu, including meat, chicken and fish, all cooked on the premises.

This is a historic inn. In October 1840, John Dunkley, a gamekeeper, was murdered nearby and an old ballad records the event. The actual planning of the murder took place in the Rose and Crown. No one is suggesting you plan a murder, but you could do worse than have a drink here when you visit the area!

- 🕐 12.00-14.30 and 18.00-23.00 all week
- 🍴 Lunches: 12.00-14.00; evening meal: 19.00-21.00
- 💷 All cards except Diners
- 🅿 Beer garden; landscaped garden
- 🎵 Occasional theme nights, such as blues nights, murder mystery, etc.
- ❓ Santa Pod Raceway (drag racing) 6 miles; Castle Ashby (not open to the public) 2 miles; Burton Dassett Country Park 8 miles; Northampton (historic town) 7 miles

THE ROSE AND CROWN

PARK ROAD, HARTWELL, NR. SALCEY FOREST,
NORTHAMPTONSHIRE NN7 2HP
TEL: 01604 862393

Directions: Leave the M1 at junction 15 and head due south on the A508. After a couple of miles Hartwell will be signposted to the left along a minor road

The Rose and Crown, tucked away in the village of Hartwell, dates back to 1727 and has altered little on the outside. Although the interior has been refurbished it retains an olde worlde atmosphere in which you can enjoy some traditional beers and good food. Very close by is Salcey Forest, an ancient 1250 acre woodland which is a haven for wildlife and offers some delightful walks.

Brian and Josie Reddick have many years experience in the trade and in their four years here have created a popular hostelry that is much loved by the locals

⏰ Mon-Fri 12.00-14.30, 17.00-23.00;
Sat 11.00-23.00; Sun 12.00-22.30

🍴 Extensive selection of home-cooked food

£ Visa, Mastercard, Delta, Switch

Ⓟ Car park, patio and beer garden

🎵 Darts, pool

@ brianreddick77@hotmail.com

❓ Stoke Bruerne Canal Museum 2 miles, Salcey Forest, Stoke Park Gardens 3 miles, Silverstone Racetrack 11 miles, Flamingo Gardens and Zoo 6 miles, Xscape 9 miles

and visitors to the area. It is Brian who does all the cooking, presenting a lunchtime snack menu with a more extensive selection of home-cooked dishes in the evenings. The superb range includes locally sourced steaks, numerous fish and chicken dishes and oriental dishes, all accompanied by beautifully fresh seasonal vegetables and delicious home-made chips. Early evening specials are served and these offer excellent value for money. All in all, the pub proves so popular for food that it is advisable to book at weekends. The selection behind the bar has not been neglected either – here you will find a choice of two real ales, Greene King IPA and Fullers London Pride, together with other popular beers and lagers.

THE ROYAL OAK

LIME AVENUE, EYDON, NORTHAMPTON
TEL: 01327 263167 FAX: 01327 260020

> **Directions:** From junction 11 of the M40, Banbury, follow the A361 towards
> Daventry. At Byfield, after about 9 miles, turn right and Eydon is well signposted

Eydon is as pretty as any village you would find in the Cotswolds but it's not nearly as likely to be crowded during the summer. **The Royal Oak** is a quaint country inn with a long history, a pub having been on the same site since 1692. The name Royal Oak relates to a famous incident during the English Civil War, when Charles II hid in an oak tree to escape his Roundhead pursuers and it became a popular symbol of support for the monarch.

Stepping inside visitors will find a cosy, traditional interior made up of little nooks and crannies in which to enjoy a drink. The bar offers four regular real ales, as well as guest ales. There is also a fine wine list and plenty of lagers, beers and spirits. The food is superb with a carefully selected menu of delicious dishes. The printed menu is supplemented by daily specials at lunchtimes and at the weekends, with everything prepared to order using only the freshest ingredients, including game when in season. Bookings must be made for the busy weekend period.

Nearby Crockwell Farm is under the same ownership, and there you will find bed and breakfast or self-catering accommodation for up to 16 people. There are rooms within the main farmhouse or two charming cottages which have been converted from 18th-century barns. The accommodation is of an exceptionally high standard and has been awarded a 4 diamond grading for the B&B and 4 stars for the self-catering.

- 🕐 Mon-Sat 12.00-14.30, 18.00-23.00; Sun 12.00-14.30, 18.00-22.30
- 🍴 Delicious a la carte menu of carefully selected dishes
- £ Visa, Mastercard, Delta, Switch
- 🛏 Bed and breakfast and self-catering at nearby Crockwell Farm
- Ⓟ Patio garden, skittle table, car parking
- 🎵 Occasional live music
- @ email: info@crockwellfarm.co.uk website: www.crockwellfarm.co.uk
- ❓ SCanons Ashby 2 miles, Sulgrave Manor 4 miles, Towcester Racecourse 11 miles, Silverstone Racetrack 12 miles, Upton House 14 miles, Burton Dassett Country Park 12 miles

THE SUN INN

126 HIGH STREET, BROUGHTON, NR. KETTERING,
NORTHAMPTONSHIRE NN14 1NQ
TEL: 01536 790284

Directions: The town of Kettering lies midway between the M1 and the A1 on the A14, which bypasses the town to the southern side. From junction 8 of the A14 take the A43 southwest and the village of Broughton will be signposted after a mile, to the left

The quiet village of Broughton is tucked away off the A43, and has a long history, extending back to Anglo Saxon times, and as a result, a number of attractive buildings. **The Sun Inn** is a typical village inn and is popular with the locals for its warm, friendly atmosphere. This is down to the owners, Gordon and Carole Jones, who come from the area and have established themselves as popular hosts.

The bar stocks Charles Wells real ales, Eagle IPA and Bombadier, from the cask together with a selection of other popular beers, lagers and ciders. You can enjoy your drinks within the cosy bar area, which opens onto a small dining area, or outside in the adjoining beer garden (weather permitting). There is a fine choice of tasty home-cooked food available at most sessions, except Mondays. The menu ranges from light snacks, such as sandwiches, baguettes and jacket potatoes, to more filling hot dishes. These are usually popular, traditional pub offerings and include such favourites as Yorkshire puddings with Cumberland sausage, and scampi and fries. If you need to while away a wet afternoon, then you could try your hand at the traditional pub games that they have here. There is a skittles table tucked into one corner and an ever popular darts board too.

- 🕐 Mon 5-11pm, Tue-Thurs 12-3pm & 5-11pm, Fri & Sat 12-11pm, Sun 12.00-10.30pm
- 🍴 Home-cooked meals, daily specials and tasty bar snacks
- 🅿 Beer garden
- 🎵 Skittle table, darts
- ❓ Boughton House 6 miles, Pitsford Reservoir and Bird Reserve 6 miles, Lamport Hall 6 miles, Rockingham Castle 10 miles, Coton Manor Gardens 12 miles

THE WHITE HORSE

WALGRAVE ROAD, OLD, NR. NORTHAMPTON NN6 9QX
TEL: 01604 781297

> **Directions:** From the M1 take the A14 towards Kettering. At junction 2, Kelmarsh, turn right onto the A508 following signs to Northampton. Turn left at Lamport Hall and follow signs for Old

The White Horse is housed within what was originally an old mill built during the 17th century. It has however been a country inn for over 200 years with just one or two of the original features having been retained as a reminder of its origins. It lies at the heart of the village of Old and located just across the road from the village green with its Jubilee oak tree. Recently taken over by Richard and Jo Bye, the pub has undergone extensive refurbishment and redecoration throughout. Upstairs there is a 40-seater restaurant, which has the original beamed ceiling and a distinctly

rustic feel, and here you can enjoy the delicious food which is presented on a blackboard menu. All dishes are home-cooked and are prepared using mainly local produce. There is also a snack menu of filled baguettes and salads available at lunchtimes.

Elsewhere, there is a cosy, relaxed lounge complete with comfy sofas, ideal for pre-dinner drinks, and the main bar which has a distinctly traditional feel. There is a beer garden at the back, which looks out towards the village church, and here you will also find a children's play area. This is a Banks' pub and the bar stocks Banks Bitter together with other guest ales. Other draught offerings include Mansfield Smooth and Guinness. There are also a number of good, mainly French, house wines.

- 🕐 Mon-Fri 11.30-15.00, 18.00-23.00; Sat 11.00-23.00; Sun 12.00-22.30 (Closed Monday Lunchtime)
- 🍴 Blackboard menu of traditional dishes
- 💷 Visa, Mastercard, Delta, Switch
- 🅿 Beer garden, children's play area, car park
- 🎵 Table skittles
- ❓ Lamport Hall 2 miles, Cottesbroke Hall 6 miles, Pitsford Reservoir and Brixworth Country Park 4 miles, Coton Manor Gardens 8 miles, Althorp Park 11 miles

ALPHABETICAL LIST
OF PUBS AND INNS

SPECIAL INTEREST LISTS

Accommodation

WARWICKSHIRE

STAFFORDSHIRE

DERBYSHIRE

NOTTINGHAMSHIRE

LINCOLNSHIRE

LEICESTERSHIRE & RUTLAND

NORTHAMPTONSHIRE

SPECIAL INTEREST LISTS

All Day Opening

WARWICKSHIRE

STAFFORDSHIRE

DERBYSHIRE

NOTTINGHAMSHIRE

NOTTINGHAMSHIRE (CONT.)

LINCOLNSHIRE

LEICESTERSHIRE & RUTLAND

NORTHAMPTONSHIRE

SPECIAL INTEREST LISTS
Childrens Facilities

Credit Cards Accepted

Credit Cards Accepted

NORTHAMPTONSHIRE

SPECIAL INTEREST LISTS

Garden, Patio or Terrace

WARWICKSHIRE

STAFFORDSHIRE

DERBYSHIRE

LEICESTERSHIRE & RUTLAND

NORTHAMPTONSHIRE

Live Entertainment

WARWICKSHIRE

STAFFORDSHIRE

DERBYSHIRE

NOTTINGHAMSHIRE

Live Entertainment

Restaurant or Dining Area

PLACES OF INTEREST

Travel Publishing

The Hidden Places

Regional and National guides to the less well-known places of interest and places to eat, stay and drink

Hidden Inns

Regional guides to traditional pubs and inns throughout the United Kingdom

GOLFERS GUIDES

Regional and National guides to 18 hole golf courses and local places to stay, eat and drink

COUNTRY LIVING
MAGAZINE
RURAL GUIDES

Regional and National guides to the traditional countryside of Britain and Ireland with easy to read facts on places to visit, stay, eat, drink and shop

For more information:

Phone: 0118 981 7777
e-mail: adam@travelpublishing.co.uk

Fax: 0118 982 0077
website: www.travelpublishing.co.uk

Easy-to-use, Informative
Travel Guides on the British Isles

Travel Publishing Limited

7a Apollo House • Calleva Park • Aldermaston • Berkshire RG7 8TN

ORDER FORM

To order any of our publications just fill in the payment details below and complete the order form. For orders of less than 4 copies please add £1 per book for postage and packing. Orders over 4 copies are P & P free.

Please Complete Either:

I enclose a cheque for £ [ ] made payable to Travel Publishing Ltd

Or:

Card No: [ ] Expiry Date: [ ]

Signature: [ ]

Name: [ ]

Address: [ ]

Tel no: [ ]

Please either send, telephone, fax or e-mail your order to:

Travel Publishing Ltd, 7a Apollo House, Calleva Park, Aldermaston, Berkshire RG7 8TN   Tel: 0118 981 7777   Fax: 0118 982 0077
e-mail: karen@travelpublishing.co.uk

	Price	Quantity		Price	Quantity
Hidden Places Regional Titles			**Hidden Inns Titles**		
Cambs & Lincolnshire	£7.99	....	East Anglia	£5.99	....
Chilterns	£7.99	....	Heart of England	£7.99	....
Cornwall	£8.99	....	Lancashire & Cheshire	£5.99	....
Derbyshire	£8.99	....	North of England	£5.99	....
Devon	£8.99	....	South	£5.99	....
Dorset, Hants & Isle of Wight	£8.99	....	South East	£7.99	....
East Anglia	£8.99	....	South and Central Scotland	£5.99	....
Gloucs, Wiltshire & Somerset	£8.99	....	Wales	£7.99	....
Heart of England	£7.99	....	Welsh Borders	£5.99	....
Hereford, Worcs & Shropshire	£7.99	....	West Country	£7.99	....
Kent	£8.99	....	Yorkshire	£5.99	....
Lake District & Cumbria	£8.99	....			
Lancashire & Cheshire	£8.99	....	**Country Living Rural Guides**		
Lincolnshire & Notts	£8.99	....	East Anglia	£9.99	....
Northumberland & Durham	£8.99	....	Heart of England	£9.99	....
Sussex	£8.99	....	Ireland	£10.99	....
Yorkshire	£8.99	....	North East of England	£9.99	....
			North West of England	£9.99	....
Hidden Places National Titles			Scotland	£10.99	....
England	£10.99	....	South of England	£9.99	....
Ireland	£10.99	....	South East of England	£9.99	....
Scotland	£10.99	....	Wales	£10.99	....
Wales	£9.99	....	West Country	£9.99	....

Total Quantity [ ]

Post & Packing [ ]

Total Value [ ]

READER REACTION FORM

The *Travel Publishing* research team would like to receive reader's comments on any visitor attractions or places reviewed in the book and also recommendations for suitable entries to be included in the next edition. This will help ensure that the *Hidden Inns Series* continues to provide its readers with useful information on the more interesting, unusual or unique features of each inn or place ensuring that their visit to the local area is an enjoyable and stimulating experience. To provide your comments or recommendations would you please complete the forms below and overleaf as indicated and send to:

The Research Department, Travel Publishing Ltd,
7a Apollo House, Calleva Park, Aldermaston, Reading, RG7 8TN.

Your Name:

Your Address:

Your Telephone Number:

Please tick as appropriate:
Comments ☐   Recommendation ☐

Name of Establishment:

Address:

Telephone Number:

Name of Contact:

READER REACTION FORM

Comment or Reason for Recommendation:

READER REACTION FORM

The *Travel Publishing* research team would like to receive reader's comments on any visitor attractions or places reviewed in the book and also recommendations for suitable entries to be included in the next edition. This will help ensure that the *Hidden Inns Series* continues to provide its readers with useful information on the more interesting, unusual or unique features of each inn or place ensuring that their visit to the local area is an enjoyable and stimulating experience. To provide your comments or recommendations would you please complete the forms below and overleaf as indicated and send to:

**The Research Department, Travel Publishing Ltd,
7a Apollo House, Calleva Park, Aldermaston, Reading, RG7 8TN.**

Your Name:

Your Address:

Your Telephone Number:

Please tick as appropriate:

Comments ☐   Recommendation ☐

Name of Establishment:

Address:

Telephone Number:

Name of Contact:

READER REACTION FORM

Comment or Reason for Recommendation:

READER REACTION FORM

The *Travel Publishing* research team would like to receive reader's comments on any visitor attractions or places reviewed in the book and also recommendations for suitable entries to be included in the next edition. This will help ensure that the *Hidden Inns Series* continues to provide its readers with useful information on the more interesting, unusual or unique features of each inn or place ensuring that their visit to the local area is an enjoyable and stimulating experience. To provide your comments or recommendations would you please complete the forms below and overleaf as indicated and send to:

The Research Department, Travel Publishing Ltd,
7a Apollo House, Calleva Park, Aldermaston, Reading, RG7 8TN.

Your Name:

Your Address:

Your Telephone Number:

Please tick as appropriate:

Comments ☐   Recommendation ☐

Name of Establishment:

Address:

Telephone Number:

Name of Contact:

READER REACTION FORM

Comment or Reason for Recommendation:

The *Travel Publishing* research team would like to receive reader's comments on any visitor attractions or places reviewed in the book and also recommendations for suitable entries to be included in the next edition. This will help ensure that the *Hidden Inns Series* continues to provide its readers with useful information on the more interesting, unusual or unique features of each inn or place ensuring that their visit to the local area is an enjoyable and stimulating experience. To provide your comments or recommendations would you please complete the forms below and overleaf as indicated and send to:

The Research Department, Travel Publishing Ltd,
7a Apollo House, Calleva Park, Aldermaston, Reading, RG7 8TN.

Your Name:

Your Address:

Your Telephone Number:

Please tick as appropriate:

Comments ☐   Recommendation ☐

Name of Establishment:

Address:

Telephone Number:

Name of Contact:

READER REACTION FORM

Comment or Reason for Recommendation: